THE $_{of}$ KEYS
JESHUA

THE KEYS *of* JESHUA

GLENDA GREEN

Spiritis

Back cover painting: *Jeshua,* © Glenda Green, 2005

Cover design by Alecia Jensen

ISBN: 0-9666623-7-7

Second edition, first printing September 2007

Spiritis Publishing
PO Box 239
Sedona, AZ 86339

www.lovewithoutend.com

Acknowledgments

There are not enough words to thank the millions of friends and supporters who took the messages of *Love Without End* to their own hearts and then to the lives and hearts of others. Upon this fertile ground *The Keys of Jeshua* was brought to life.

In my personal life there is no one to whom I am more grateful than my beloved husband, Dr. Larry Jensen. Larry, a renowned psychologist, has for many years been a world leader in the service of personal enlightenment. His love, clarity, wisdom, and endless encouragement have been the wind in my sails. His beautiful daughter, Alecia Jensen has now become the daughter I always desired. And I am blessed by her professional excellence as an art designer. Many thanks go to her for the elegant dust jacket and for the coordinated aesthetic details through this book.

Nancy French has my deepest appreciation for her excellent contribution to this work. Her keen sense of detail and compassionate heart provided just the balance needed to synthesize and integrate such a vast amount of information, while allowing it to remain simple, vital, and fresh. Special thanks go to the staff of Spiritis Publishing, Angie Gerber and Carol Flynn, who kept the wheels turning and the days bright with humor as the book evolved into a reality.

Because one of the goals of this book is to position these new teachings of Jeshua in the context of our rich spiritual heritage, I also want to acknowledge all the known and unknown authors and teachers who have left their legacy for us to learn, enjoy, and pass on. Attributions are given wherever possible, but there are now so many inspirational works appearing in the public domain it is often difficult to determine original authorship of some ideas. In addition to that, so many thoughts once regarded as unique are now revealed to be one of many similar ideas that have traveled on the rivers of our history. Yet, it is with a heart of gratitude that I praise every contribution that has moved us closer to our higher state of love and consciousness.

To the One who saw our goodness
… unconditionally.

To all humanity,
…   for whom these messages were given.

Table of Contents

Preface

The brilliance was intense. It filled the room so completely that all shadows departed. Glancing upward, I observed the chandelier was off. This was not surprising because I sensed that there was nothing artificial about the soft white radiance engulfing everything like a cloud descended from Heaven. The whole house possessed the wonder and silence of newly fallen snow.

Silvery threads of light streamed through the quiet, reverent space. The air pulsed with energetic ripples, as if a flame was propelling them. The ripples, which flowed in all directions, took their source from a spot of hyper-luminescence that was almost blinding. This resplendence was like a sun, though not fiery. More than likely, it was a concentration of the same quality of light filling the room. Its special glory was in its dazzling brightness and the patterns of silver and gold, which were laced with opalescent white and sparkles of lavender, blue, and rose.

I could look toward the center for only a second before the light caused my eyes to fill with tears. Stunned, I had to look away, and at that moment I heard sounds forming into the pattern and cadence of language, although it was no language I had heard before. As the "words" formed a meaning in my mind, the message was "Greetings Glenda."

In this Presence, there was unspeakable Holiness. If light could sing, it would have been chanting celestial sounds. If light were fragrant, it would have exuded the innocence of high, mountain air. I turned to look again, but the radiance was simply overwhelming. Closing my eyes, I protected them from the glow and wept at the same time. No sooner had I escaped within myself than The Presence shot a beam of energy from itself to a point between my eyebrows. There was a sensation of pressure, which caused me to open my eyes and verify. What I saw was a stream of energy pouring in. Returning to the comfort of my inner vision, I

i

watched as a picture was being etched into my mind. It took about five seconds for the rendering to be completed. The vision was implanted in my optic nerve – immutable – and available for me to view whenever I chose.

Mesmerized by its beauty, I gazed in rapture upon the vision of Jesus Christ, which was complete, three-dimensional, and holographic. Majestically, he stood on a hilltop overlooking a green river valley, towering above grazing sheep, while a billowing cloud on the horizon was forming the shape of a lion.

I clutched my chest and took a deep breath. Was I still in the realm of ordinary life? If so, was I in my own home or transported to another time and place?

When my awareness finally externalized, I found that the radiant Presence had gone and objective reality conformed to normal expectations. Nevertheless, I knew that something about me would never be the same again. That intuition proved to be true, for everything in my life would change after that Holy Moment.

The splendid light would be forever etched on my soul or perhaps united with my heart in a single, enduring beat. Within me now, a spark of light had been awakened which would become the doorway to greatly expanded awareness and life. I could not imagine how far it would reach, but one thing was certain. I would be painting the portrait that had been foretold in dreams and visions.

Although I was a professional artist and usually welcomed the spirit of creative challenge, the many months of being called to paint a portrait of Jesus had filled me with great reservation rather than excitement. Now, all my objections were laid to rest, for I had seen his face.

Forty days would pass before I would be secure enough about the meaning of this miracle to actually begin painting. Each morning I eagerly rekindled the vision through reverent acknowledgment and meditation. I would study its every nuance, and inhale it into my being like the breath of life. As the days passed, the vision became more complete and the presence of Jesus grew more alive. This alone distinguished it from my experience with visual inspiration and dreams, which usually diminished through repeated recollection.

At first, the sensation was like that of peering through a clear window and greeting a friend looking back from the outside. The beautiful eyes engaging my devotion would eventually dissolve the "glass" boundary between us and magnetically draw me into his world. As that happened, his presence was correspondingly more compelling and dynamic. I perceived that I had entered a world of sensory richness as vivid and complete as an epic dream, but the "dream" was in a state more wakeful than any I had ever known. Suddenly I had taken a quantum leap into a realm of cosmic and infinite possibility!

The days between November 23, 1991 and January 1, 1992 were fertile days of creative preparation, explorations of personal reality, and intellectual contemplation.

I recalled my years of being on university faculties. As a scholar of Medieval Christian art, I was familiar with many recorded, and often illustrated, paranormal visions of Jesus or Mary. Considering the monastic life of extended hardship and duress that usually accompanied those sacred visitations, I felt some concern at first about my own well being. However, my glowing health and confirmation of sanity from others soon dispelled those fears.

Considering the approach of Christmas and holiday activities, I decided that it would be better to start the painting early in January. Besides, this would give me time to make some preliminary decisions and prepare the canvas. The first thing I needed to establish was the scale. So I cast my attention on the vision and asked for guidance from Jesus. This was the first time it ever occurred to me to regard the vision as a means through which to dialogue. The answer was clearly given to me in a telepathic mode, though no words were spoken. The canvas was to be forty-eight inches square.

Reassuring myself frequently with inward glances, the vision remained crystal clear and intimated that a whole new world was being born. It was clearly living, and I beheld it in awe. It was presenting and magnifying so much of his Life Force that what started out as only a visual image gave witness to a feeling that "He was there!"

The days grew long and tense, although the sense of communion between us was bursting with excitement, and the silence that filled the spaces of my anticipation was rich with words yet spoken.

On January 2nd I entered my studio with a peace that made for uneasiness ... a peace that my body could only recognize as the bristling and imminent presence of destiny. Although the room smelled of linseed oil and turpentine – not holy incense – it possessed the subtle ambiance of a temple. Perhaps my own feelings were displaying the nature of my expectations. Or perhaps there was a holiness of spirit, which preceded my arrival on that day and had prepared a place for the "opening lines" of the creation to come. Either way, my senses were clear and clean, as if I had been newly born to this world. Everything – from the dust on the windowsill, to my slightly askew arrangement of brushes, to the towering easel in front of me – adorned the moment with details I will never forget. The room was filled with natural sunlight, although it conveyed the sense of another sacred light I had experienced earlier. As I passed through its rays, my body's motion slowed down to time frames that were seconds long and moving toward stillness. I was overcome by the serene inevitability of the moment—as if everything was suspended in time and space. It felt as though a thousand eyes were upon me, and I searched the space within and without to discover my "watcher."

The silence was broken only by a chant of "meows" outside the studio door. Gunner, my beautiful Himalayan cat, wanted to join whatever was happening in the studio. I moved with some reservation toward the door, and hesitantly opened it. Somehow, I expected to see more than Gunner, but was quite relieved to see that it was only a pair of little blue eyes twinkling up at me. He darted in quickly, as if to suggest that timing and opportunity were essential to the moment; something was about to happen which was not to be missed. Then he scurried over to one of the two white pillows I used for meditation and prayer.

I turned to face the large pristine canvas mounted on my easel, but I did not yet have the right feeling to begin. So I joined Gunner on the other pillow and began my daily practice of focusing on the spot of light within my mind's eye until the vision emerged. Today, especially, I wanted to study its details as closely as possible, because once I switched my focus outwardly toward the canvas, my whole attention would be cast into the creative process. Suddenly, another "meow" from Gunner disrupted the intensity of my meditation as a gentle wind swept through the room, brushing my face. The light "within," which had been illuminating the picture in my mind was now shining through my eyelids from without! With a certainty unparalleled in my life, I opened my eyes to behold Jesus standing in front of me, towering above my seated position at his feet!

With slow and careful reverence, I arose, took my place in the painting chair, and began the preliminary drawing. The problem of how I could behold the vision and paint at the same time had been solved, although by what power of majesty or mystery, I could not say.

No words were spoken that day, but I could not stop smiling as I began to transcribe his aspect onto the pure white surface. Whenever I worked on the painting, Jesus would appear as a presence of three-dimensional reality before me. Day by day, it became more than a vision. He was there, and we were united in our task of creating a painting. As the years have revealed, there was a greater purpose to his visit than I could imagine. Nevertheless, in keeping with his pragmatic spirituality, he first called me to service in the area of my greatest strength.

By profession, I am an artist and educator, having exhibited in many of the nation's finest museums and taught at two major universities. I was professionally readied for the project at hand, but nothing could have prepared me for the life transformation that was about to occur. This event would change my life forever. While it was seemingly directed toward a more specific purpose of painting his portrait, there was much more occurring than I could ever have known. Not only was there a sacred presence before me, visible to my eyes, but also there was a beautiful voice, and I engaged it in conversation. For sixty days we spoke, all but for Sundays when we both rested. This was a deeply personal experience, yet it was also external to me.

The conversations we shared were not the result of telepathy, automatic writing, or trance channeling. Channeling is a way of directing communication from other realms into this one, and is a very ancient practice currently revived in its popularity. I neither commend nor disparage that practice, but merely distinguish it from my experience – since we are all channels for God. The voice of Jesus was audible, and I responded in full consciousness as a second person in dialogue. As we spoke, I listened and took extensive notes. More importantly, I experienced a transformation of awareness that would manifest more deeply with the passing of time.

The painting, entitled "The Lamb and The Lion", was completed on March 12, 1992, and the purpose for his original visitation was fulfilled. At that moment, the energy that had created his appearance began to dissolve into pure light. A new vision was ready to be shared with the world, and I immersed my whole life in it. The original painting was exhibited throughout many states for two years, and prints were carried to every country. I did not give a hint to anyone for four years that there had been conversations. Then in the spring of 1996, Jesus appeared again and asked me to give his messages to the world. That began with public lectures over the next six months, which were recorded as audio-tapes (Conversations with Jesus), and eventually became my internationally best selling book, Love Without End...Jesus Speaks. The ripples of this new wave, and the voice of his calling, have reached every corner of the planet. In the winter of 1992, when Jesus first spoke the words, "Love is who you are", I had never before heard or read such a statement, although many of the great and universal teachings would certainly support it. Today that concept—if not those very words—is central to our spiritual awakening.

The impact of this work was growing exponentially, and my own experience would continue expanding into other dimensions of life, transfiguring them with its grace and power. When we first began our relationship, I was timid, formal, and properly restrained toward him, as my religious upbringing had conditioned me to be. As familiarity increased, my formality and timidity slipped away. For the first time, I knew what it was like to be spiritually intimate with one who knew my every thought and anticipated my questions before I asked them. By the time the painting was finished, I had been transformed by the experience in more ways than I could count. Not only was my heart changed, and my consciousness expanded, but also my relationship with Jesus was significantly different from what my religious pre-conditioning had prepared me. I no longer saw him as a distant Lord, but a transcendent Being of unconditional love and infinite grace who was not only approachable, but also intimately accessible from within my own being. Our relationship grew in depth and richness as the days passed, and I came to know him as a personal friend and Divine Light that shone on me from every direction.

This change of relationship actually began much earlier when I was still working on the painting. One day as I painted, I noticed myself relaxed in a rare and peaceful way. Something within me had changed and dispelled my nervousness, allowing me to know him better and with more ease. Suddenly, I wanted to hear him say his name the way it was spoken in his lifetime. I asked, and he granted me that wish. For the first time, I heard the beautiful baritone voice say, "Jeshua". Phonetically, it sounded more like "Ye shu ha", [ye·shu·ha \ye-'shь-a\] with the first syllable being soft, the middle syllable being the strongest, and the secondary emphasis on the last syllable. Instantly, it struck a cord in my heart and consciousness, like two prongs of a tuning fork in resonant harmony.

I knew about his Hebrew name from books, but I was shocked at that moment to realize that I had never before heard it spoken. Jesus is the name used in our English translations of the Bible, and I had never questioned the value of reading or hearing it another way. I had blithely assumed that "a rose by any other name would be the same." Now, I was emotionally jolted to "feel" the name by which his friends, family, and disciples knew him. No one in his lifetime had ever heard or spoken the name "Jesus".

He noticed my realization and eased me through it with more understanding. The name he was given by his parents was Yehoshua ben Joseph. That would be the closest translation possible, considering there were no vowels in the Hebrew language. There are also Hebrew variations of that name such as Jehoshua, Jeshua, and Joshua. Another important factor he explained is that the Hebrew language in his lifetime was greatly modified by Aramaic, the more common language of the people. In Aramaic, his chosen language for reaching and teaching people, the formal name of Yehoshua would have been shortened to Yeshua or more likely, Jeshua. Today the initial "Y" is preferred by a majority of people in Messianic Israel who feel it is important to stay close to the formal Hebrew name, but actually the use of "J" is more characteristic of the Aramaic language. According to his expressions to me, he has, to this day, a great fondness for Aramaic, the language through which his truth was first spoken. Nevertheless, either spelling would be accurate enough and would mean the same. The sound is what is important.

Today, virtually every Christian scholar agrees that he did not go by the name of Jesus. There is a growing movement to restore his true name, along with typical human disagreements about how to spell it. With so many archeological discoveries available to balance theology, the truth is being revealed. Some things are already known. Jeshua was brought over into Greek as

Iesous (IhsouЯ); Iesous became Iesus in Latin, and then Iesus in English. In the 16th century, Iesus became Jesus because of a linguistic change in the alphabet. "I" and "J" had been interchangeable in Old and Middle English, but in the sixteenth century, the harder sound of "J" was officially classified as being different from "I". For some reason, those who were empowered to decide upon his name preferred the harder sound of "J", and so Jesus replaced Iesus in the modern English language. Up until that time, the name Jesus was never heard. After that time, Jeshua, the beloved name called upon by his first believers and followers, was virtually forgotten in the modern world.

The restoration of his name in my own consciousness had a more profound change than I could have imagined. Not only did it foster a closer, more authentic relationship with him; it also caused his words to elicit knowledge already within me that I did not know existed.

At first, I felt uncomfortable about referring to him in public as Jeshua. Somehow, that name was too precious to become the object of disagreement or even common debates that I did not feel qualified to enter. The English translations of the Bible called him Jesus, and who was I to change that? Agreement is an awesome force, and the printed word has had an incalculable impact on common agreements about what his name really was. I made hundreds of presentations of the painting in churches, and always felt that I needed to respect tradition as well as the truth. For that same reason, I continued to call him Jesus when I spoke in public, as well as in the recorded lecture series, and the book that followed. To do so was true enough, because I, too, had known and loved him by the name of Jesus, and through that name I had engaged in many conversations with him. Therefore, I could relate to those who held him in their hearts as Jesus and hesitated to disturb their dedication of faith with an unfamiliar name. More could be lost than gained, especially considering that his ultimate true name is Love.

Experience has revealed that my early inhibitions on this

matter, while driven by thoughtful intent were unnecessary. In the few instances when I ventured to use his true historical name, it had the same impact on others that it did on me. It brought more warmth, clarity, and connection with a sense of Inner Light and greater faith. Under the guise of propriety, I had vainly deferred to tradition against my greater knowing. Then one day I opened my Bible to Matthew 26:34, where Jesus (Jeshua) said to Peter, "Verily I say unto you, that this night, before the cock crows, you shall deny me three times. Then Peter declared, 'if I have to die with you, I will never disown you.' And all the other disciples said the same." Later that evening, Peter fulfilled the promise, by telling ordinary people in the courtyard, "I don't know the man." I wept as Peter did, to think that I had held back a witness about Jeshua that could have nurtured the hearts of others. It was time for the discrepancy to work its way out, because in my heart, Jesus was really Jeshua.

In the days and years after our first visitation, I would think about him and say his name. Whatever understanding I needed would come forth into consciousness. I would start my days with "Good Morning, Jeshua", and he would be there. We would share thoughts and experiences, and he would continue his teachings. When the day was over, I would say "Thank you and Good Night, Jeshua", and he would often visit me in my dreams. In the years succeeding the original visitation, his appearances have been spontaneous and frequent. Sometimes visual and audio perceptions were available and sometimes not. Often Gunner would see him. They are great friends. Regardless of what my senses revealed, there was always a definite presence unmistakable to my heart and the core of my being. Whenever I pronounced his name, my heart would be filled with his love and wisdom.

Life is more fluid than our perceptions normally suggest. Space adapts to the requirements of a given purpose, and time is simply a loom that weaves the threads of destiny, causing the events of our life to approach and disappear. Daily I was seeing evidence of the promise he made long ago that, "I am with you always." In addition to our direct visitations and dialogue, I would see him in my prayers and meditations. He would speak through scriptures and other words of wisdom. I would find him teaching me through practical applications of life and truth, and always there would be an expanded message that would unfold through other sources or through my personal readiness to discover examples of his truth.

Soon I began to notice a predominate quality about his teaching: it was holistic, appealing to all my senses and contexts of life. At times, he would be explicit and direct. At other times, he would lead me intuitively into realizations of the heart or perhaps discoveries in nature. This broader scope allowed the information and ideas in Love Without End…Jesus Speaks to be topically explored and more completely developed. Each subject could be approached, examined and expanded through many faculties for learning such as: objective, subjective, contemplative, exploratory, experiential, and pragmatic.

The first words of this current manuscript were written in the winter of 2000. Initially my motive was to summarize and relay to others the continuing lessons in life that I was receiving from Jeshua. In the beginning, I surmised that the purpose of this new manuscript was to elevate and complete the contents of my first conversations with him. Therefore, I released it to many of my students, chapter by chapter, as "A Course in Life." As the messages came forth they possessed a power and momentum that went beyond my original expectations. This work was standing on its own merit, and it became obvious that, through me, he was writing a new book! Not only did it reach greater heights of inspiration, but it also expanded into topics not touched upon in our earlier conversations … topics that extended well beyond my personal mastery. My predictions of what would come next were always being revised and magnified by further revelations.

In the spring of this year, a new element began to appear recurrently in each chapter. As I brought each chapter to summation, and sought to highlight its central theme, it became apparent that embedded in each one was a "Key to Life." As the book moved into the "home stretch", these keys began to surface with greater clarity. The final organization and presentation of a new book was at hand. Each chapter would contain a message from Jeshua, which would then be developed into an explanation of the "Key to Life" within it. There would be applications to life, correlations with the Bible and other words of wisdom. Last, but not least, for subjective realization of the message, there would be a meditation and prayer for each chapter. It is recommended that you enjoy this book with all your faculties of understanding, from objective to subjective, and allow a holistic perception of these revelations to develop in your heart.

To assist your study, I have presented Jeshua's words in italics. That way, they may be isolated from the larger context and savored independently. At the same time, I have made every effort to remember and to reconstruct the anecdotal aspects of our conversations, revealing the queries, motives, and emotions that I brought to the situation. The book you are about to read is the result of 12 years of journaling his revelations. The only hindrance in relaying them to you is the inadequacy of language to transmit a living experience, rare and unusual, through the windows of existing and familiar reality. Therefore, I would be very happy (and you would be well served) if you suspended all belief and simply entertained the thought that I happened to stumble onto a heightened wave of consciousness, which—like a grand 'Rosetta Stone'—revealed truths both common and elevating to the human spirit.

As for existential explanations of it all, my perspective is not yet grand enough to encompass the many possibilities. What happened on November 23, 1991 and continues into the present is nothing short of miraculous. It is not necessary that it be explained to the satisfaction of logic, or regarded in any particular way. The purpose of this book is not to solicit, reinforce, or change existing beliefs. I hope that you, the reader, will receive the teachings about to be revealed as a gift to your heart.

Those who struggle over how to mentally explain Jeshua's

appearances to me will be restrained from the full enjoyment and inspiration of these teachings. In this regard, it would be wise to consider two important facts about the nature of spirituality and belief. Truth always transcends any context that presents it—be it real or fiction. Actually, many of the greatest truths and philosophical premises of all time have been advanced into consciousness through fictional or imaginative presentation. Because of this, you need not feel compelled to believe in the events of this, or any, story in order to discover the truths within it. Secondly, the power of personal and subjective belief is far greater than any formal or external belief system. You will form your own beliefs, and they will be according to your individual nature—as they should be.

Mysteries are all around us, and the greatest, most fascinating mysteries of life are to be savored and not resolved. Perhaps the most amazing and humbling discovery of modern science is the fact that ninety-nine per cent of all existence is not only invisible to our senses and instruments, but also without mass or structure. Even the one per cent that comprises our physical universe is solid only because of relatively stable configurations of energy. Among the greatest scientists—including Niels Bohr, Max Planck and Werner Heisenberg—it has been conceded that there is room in a rational universe for incomprehensible wonders.

Most of the time our perceptions are focused upon the one per cent of existence that we can see, hear, and touch. But, what about the remaining 99 percent? How do we engage with that? More than likely that occurs through senses not yet identified or even developed in most individuals. Yet, we all participate of the endless universe in ways that we take for granted. Whenever we disengage the great filter called "self" and lose ourselves in play, service, conversation, sharing, imagination, meditation, prayer, study, or sleep, we shift our focus from survival pursuits into larger patterns of connection with unlimited possibility. Most often, our experience of the infinite is not a mystical ascension into some distant paradise, but a quiet and personal epiphany at moments when we realize that the miraculous and the mundane are one and the same. At such moments, we see clearly that everything is already before our eyes awaiting only a shift of perception. Marcel Proust said that, "The real act of discovery consists not in finding new lands but in seeing with new eyes."

There is no question that the exploration of human consciousness is the last great frontier. Well in advance of our understanding, Jeshua stimulated an expansion of awareness two thousand years ago that will see no end. In many ways, he ignited this through demonstrations of what seemed like paranormal mastery of life. Yet, the power behind his miracles and the reason for them was his instruction that they were not paranormal for him, and actually NORMAL for his level of love, perception, and power. Indeed, he promised that through spiritual attainment, love of God and man, and the elevation of consciousness, 'All these things and more YOU shall also do.' If Jeshua had been merely dazzling his audiences with mystical abilities to impress them, his miracles would have had no lasting benefit. By that same standard, if you struggle over why this author was chosen for such extraordinary experiences—by what virtues of goodness or strangeness she has been set apart from others—you will miss the value of this book. My value lies in what I share with you, not in what separates us. The principles, clarifications, inspirations, and truths within this book are their own witness to a power existing within the human soul accessible to all.

Regardless of whether you call him Jeshua or Jesus, Friend, Teacher, Master, Lord or God Incarnate, it still remains an historical fact that no single individual has had more influence upon the course of human events in the last two thousand years. Regardless of one's beliefs, or even disbelief, the impact of his life is a legacy to us all. Well beyond the countless numbers who center their religious convictions on him, there are millions who behold his influence, wisdom, love, and virtue despite their disinterest in the religions built in his name. This reality exceeds all varieties of private or collective faith.

Albert Einstein said: "The most beautiful emotion we can experience is the mystical. It is the power of true art and science. He to whom this emotion is a stranger, who can no longer wonder and stand rapt in awe, is as good as dead. To know that what is impenetrable to us really exists, manifesting itself as the highest wisdom and the most radiant beauty, which our dull faculties can comprehend only in their most primitive forms—this knowledge, this feeling, is at the center of true religiousness."

Glenda Green, September 2003

Jeshua

LOVE IS WHO YOU ARE

The Message

The beautiful words streamed forth from Jeshua: *"The waters of life give no more power to the mighty surf than to a mountain brook. It is the joy of water to be itself, and to provide its substance for the nourishment of life. And a soul alone is great who inhales the breath of life, and with exhalation gives it forth in joy and complete release, knowing between breaths, there is nothing but the self and God."*

"Is this what you mean when you say, *'Love is who we are?'"*

"You cannot see yourself as love any more than a light can see itself shining. This is why you have focused your perceptions of love on external deeds. However, to be yourself in the fullness of God's creation is none other than love being itself. By honoring this truth, you serve God and others. Most of all, understand the power that love has to transmit itself from one soul to another; to bestow the many gifts of life, wisdom, experience and sustenance that abound and exist for all to share. Love is the great medium of exchange, which can penetrate any barrier. Love informs and unites souls in their common destiny, so that the assembly of a few may equal the power of many. When you know this you are beginning to know compassion. And when you know compassion, you may enter all dimensions and know all realities, including death, without fear or judgment. As you surrender to the pathways of love, you will arise to know yourself as the love that you are.

As you move on the pathways of love you will also begin to see the presence of Divine Love leading you to people, places, and situations where your love may be fulfilled. The Ultimate union of your life is between the love oat you are and the love of God. This is your true actualization."

Correlations

1 Corinthians 13:7-13 "Love bears all things, believes all things, hopes all things, endures all things. Love never ends; as for prophecies, they will pass away; as for tongues, they will cease; as for knowledge, it will pass away. So faith, hope, love abide, these three; but the greatest of these is love."

1 John 4:16 "God is love; and he that abides in love abides in God, and God in him."

Romans 13:10 "Love does no wrong to his neighbor: therefore love is the fulfilling of the law."

Galations 5:14 "For all the law is fulfilled in one word, even in this, you shall love your neighbor as yourself."

The Key

Love is who we are, and what one soul feels for another. "Liking" is what we feel for objects, places, events, actions and circumstances. Liking is always conditional no matter how intense, because it is an expression of preferences and evaluations. LOVE IS SIMPLY UNCONDITIONAL! It fits anywhere and supersedes everything. There is no force more powerful than love! Therefore, it has no cause or parallel in the physical realm. It is unattached to circumstances. Love is the divine, mystical, and holy power that creates and sustains life for the simple joy of doing so. In its purest form, love is where creation creates itself. **The key to love rests in knowing our own connection to that power.**

Love is a force. It is also the pure essence of being. If love has any complementary nature, parallel, or other symmetry, that would be simply the dialogue between love's own active and passive aspects—doing and being. As Jeshua said to me, *"Love has no necessary complements, attachments, or obligations in the world of materiality."* His own life most certainly proved that it is possible to be **in** the world and not be **of** it.

Though it is not of the world, Love IS a "world of power" among souls. Not only does love refine and clarify the innate potential of each soul, but also it is the medium of exchange that allows one soul to support and enrich another! Although we would all agree that good deeds most certainly add to the quality of life, we would be underestimating the power of love if we regarded it only as an enhancement to living. Jeshua was very clear with me that the love exchanged between souls resulted in a great deal more good than simply to support external affairs. On one occasion he delved into the subject further saying, *"Love is trans-dimensional, knowing no boundaries, not even the boundaries of 'nothing' or the more obvious boundaries of hatred, fear and opposition. All manner of consciousness, experience, and knowledge may be transposed from one soul to another through the mastery of love. This is the omnipotence of compassion. Whatever is transmitted from one soul to another by the power of love is forever."*

Love has one relentless challenge in this universe. By its very nature, love is inclusive. On the contrary, physical particles and configurations of energy perpetuate their existence through intervals of space, patterns, and boundaries that separate them. Energy is created by the act of propulsion through space against resistance! Therefore, from the beginning and for all time there are two powers generating creation in this universe: the power of love, which is inclusive, and the power of physical existence, which persists through exclusion and separation. The soul has a fascinating challenge of witnessing both powers, while selecting, integrating, and balancing these options for building a life. Whatever a soul chooses will have a profound effect on its priorities, how it sees itself, and how it relates to others.

When a soul's sense of self is rooted in love, there is harmony within the self, and that improves the whole of life, allowing purposes to be fulfilled. When the soul is not in harmony with itself, then it seeks for balance within the material realm. This could be creative or destructive. Imbalance is necessary for growth, yet it is imperative that balance be restored in order for cycles of creation to continue. For example, if you did not lose your balance, you could not walk. If you did not restore your balance, you could not stand. Balance and imbalance are both necessary to life. When we do not understand the appropriate place for each function, we may allow material existence to bring imbalance to us, and fail to bring balance to it. Often this requires a skillful exchange of potential.

Fortunately, love is of God! Therefore, it cannot be conquered and knows no boundaries. Regardless of what choices have been made and what conflicts and barriers have accumulated, the greater power of love permeates, resolves, and unites as it moves ever on its way toward the fulfillment of life. It matters not whether we start with being love or doing love, as long as we appreciate the inevitable balance between these two aspects of its power. As we are, so shall we do. As we do, so shall we become. As we are to one another, the circle expands.

Grand as these ideas may sound, they are also the heart and soul of how life revolves even around simple daily problems. An interesting and amusing challenge presented itself to me years ago when I was on the Art School faculty of the University of Oklahoma. At that time, OU was best known for its national championship football team. In the fall of 1975, I had the mixed blessing of seeing the starting line up on the front row of my art appreciation class! Healthy, robust, and immensely bored with this required course, the players knew the cobwebs on the ceiling better than Mona Lisa. However, my problem was that their passing grades were more important to the coaches than the Sistine Chapel. If my integrity as a teacher were to remain intact, I would have to come up with a solution very quickly. With a spirit of ingenuity, colored by frustration, creation, and hope, I dismissed the class and requested that we meet next time on the quadrangle. Privately I asked the team players to bring their footballs. They looked confused, but anything was better than rote memorization of art and artists.

I knew that if I were to reach these boys and the rest of the class, I would have to translate my subject into their language. As it turned out, the next class day was beautiful and the refreshing fall air seemed to lift all our spirits and foster esprit de corps. I directed my first words to one of the players, and asked him to teach me how to throw a pass. As he fumbled on his words, and demonstrated with actions, I refined his instruction until the subject of "quality", "precise intention", and the idea of "art" began to apply to something he understood. The enlightenment that gradually occurred was visible in the eyes of every student.

Until then, there had been a chasm between us due to perceived and believed differences of being—I was a sissy art instructor and they were jocks! My sudden shift of classroom environment and teaching techniques put a new twist on that fixed idea. Now all that remained was for me to take their familiar realities and expose the common threads shared with art and principles of quality. Once a transmission of consciousness took place, the rest was easy. In one playful session, I had created a basis for learning from which everyone benefited. The players finished my class with passing grades earned honorably, and I received complimentary tickets to the remaining games. I have to admit that I enjoyed the games with a new pleasure as well.

There is another instance—a very moving and historically true story—where the love transmitted between four souls changed the history of our world. It started with a poor Scottish farmer named Fleming. One day, while trying to make a living for his family, he heard a cry for help coming from a nearby bog. He dropped his tools and ran to the bog. There, mired to his waist in black muck, was a terrified boy, screaming and struggling to free himself.

Farmer Fleming saved the lad from what could have been a slow and terrifying death. The next day, a fancy carriage pulled up to the Scotsman's sparse surroundings. An elegantly dressed nobleman stepped out and introduced himself as the father of the boy Fleming had saved. The nobleman was expecting to repay the farmer for saving his son's life.

"No, I can't accept payment for what I did," the Scottish farmer replied, dismissing the offer. At that moment, the farmer's own son came to the door of the family hovel.

"Is that your son?" the nobleman asked.

"Yes," the farmer replied proudly.

"I'll make you a deal. Let me provide him with the level of education my son will enjoy. If the lad is anything like his father, he'll no doubt grow to be a man we both will be proud of."

And that he did.

Farmer Fleming's son attended the very best schools, and eventually graduated from St. Mary's Hospital Medical School in London. He went on to become known throughout the world as the noted Sir Alexander Fleming, the discoverer of Penicillin.

Years afterward, the same nobleman's son who was saved from the bog was stricken with pneumonia. What saved his life this time was Penicillin. The name of the nobleman was Lord Randolph Churchill. His son's name – Sir Winston Churchill.

Inspirations

Kahlil Gibran (b.1883 – d.1931) Persia:
The Prophet: "Love gives naught but itself and takes naught but from itself. Love possesses not, nor would it be possessed: for love is sufficient unto love. When you love

you should not say, 'God is in my heart', but rather, 'I am in the heart of God.' And think not you can direct the course of love, for love, if it finds you worthy, directs your course. Love has no other desire but to fulfill itself."

Applications

Remember three times in your life when just being WHO you are made a difference for others.

Remember three times in your life when WHO someone else was made a difference for you.

The old adage that "it matters not what you know but who you know", has been applied toward such exploitative ends, that sincere people often cringe just to hear such a suggestion. What a pity that such a jewel of truth has been so corrupted that its savor has been lost. For purposes of learning, however, let's just suspend all judgment and selfish applications of that concept, and consider that the "who of a person" is truly important.

Recently, some old friends of mine moved a long distance away. We had not shared life actively for quite some time, and in their absence there is now an unmistakable vacuum. I miss them! In my youth, I grew up knowing a boy who was a lot of trouble to his parents. They tried different approaches to education and discipline, including military school. As a young man in his early 20's, he was killed in Vietnam. Only then did his grieving parents shift from issues with his behavior to acceptance of his being. Most often we focus on the value of behavior, or its lack of value, and forget the "who" that is behind the behavior! No wonder our relationship struggles are so tenacious.

As you do this, you are simply to look – without judgment, projection, or expectation – at who is in your life and who you are to them.

We will never know where we belong in the lives of others or where they belong in ours until we focus beyond the imperfect behavioral issues and expectations. All of the humor, wit, graciousness, and facility that we see in ideal relationships is there because a greater perspective has been discovered, which honors something more important than behavior—the power of being. If you would lift your relationships above the level of issues, simply acknowledge the greater value of "who", until love "as being" transcends the need for judgment and control. If you would end conflicting situations with others, or resolve actions that are inappropriate or challenging, simply suspend the issues for a moment and consider *who* is engaging your attention. You may be surprised to find clarity and resolution on both sides that lie behind the question of "who?". Often this is the truth that will set you free. No doubt, we would all be shocked to learn how many people have never been respected by considerations or even questions of who they are.

As you proceed to ask "Who?" of yourself and others, be careful to look beyond labels and job descriptions. Too often in advanced industrial nations, we seek first a plan of doing that which will define the self in a desirable way. The most commonly asked question after being introduced to someone is, "What do you do?" Our work identity has replaced our personal identity for the sake of insuring survival of our employment. Lifting the "who" above such capturing fences can bring miracles to life, but more importantly, gaining the ability to know yourself by your love will result in miracles instead of just survival.

What activities in your life truly define and support the love that you are?

How would having similar information about others improve your relationships with them?

Meditation

Jeshua said, *"The Kingdom of Heaven is within you."* Dense though our bodies may seem, they are actually mostly space, and the few densities that comprise them are condensations of light. The only other reality or context that defines our physical existence is that our bodies are also part of the genetic-biological cycle of life, with its desires, needs, perils, and pleasures. This extends into the various contexts of social living. For most of our lives, we are focused on these more complex challenges of physical life. Just imagine what might happen if we shifted our emphasis to the first aspect of space and light, which is equally physical from another perspective.

The Divine forces, which have produced your higher immortal body, are literally waiting within each cell to be released. Through deep meditation, you have an opportunity to meet the living Christ existing within and around you. He will accompany you on this journey homeward.

Now, let's discuss the pathway. From the crown of your head to the end of your spine, there are at least eight cerebrospinal centers. These are the nexus points where organic substance, energy, emotion, thought, consciousness, and spirit are joined. Where they are, what they are called, and their possible functions are probably less important than a simple awareness that they exist. Though their differences may be subtle, the elements joined at these points form the bridge between Heaven and Earth. Their union also results in certain vibrational qualities, which may be opened through visualization, activated through energy, and explored through consciousness. The master vibration is love, and the most basic perceptions are of light, color, and subtle movement.

To begin, find a comfortable chair or mat where your spine may be straight. Steady your gaze as you allow your eyes to gently close. Observe your breath and begin to softly inhale through the nostrils, relaxing the abdomen outward. This permits the diaphragm to move downward and the lungs to expand into the lower chest cavity. Hold a deep, full, inhalation for a moment and then slowly exhale through the nostrils. Repeat this until a calm state of mind and an ample supply of oxygen fill your being.

Now visualize your spinal column as being a hollow pipe. Begin using it as a breathing instrument by mentally transferring the sensation of inhaling and exhaling to it. Perceive that your breath is moving inter-dimensionally through your spine— upwardly as you inhale and downwardly as you exhale. As you inhale from the earth, imagine this gift of energy and love to be the presence of our beloved Mother God, and as you exhale, experience the cleansing release of all things temporal as you are received into the embrace of our Almighty Father God. Allow this process to continue until complete surrender has induced a rhythmic and harmonious flow of energy on all levels of consciousness. After this happens, focus your attention on the area of the heart and visualize a spark of light. See this light grow through the nurturing of God's love and your acceptance of it until it becomes a womb-like aura containing the presence of a child. Look into the eyes of this child and form a steady gaze until there is a transmission of love, recognition, and wisdom. This child is not the youngster of your human history—but the eternal soul that you are, ever young, tender, and innocent, though compassionate and wise. This is the divine child that is YOU, as seen through the eyes of God. This is the divine child who lives in the Kingdom of Heaven.

In the presence of this child, allow yourself to be accepted for all that you have been and all that you have experienced. On the flow of your soft and rhythmic breath enjoy the sweet and eternal dialogue between your original self, created in the image of God, and yourself that embarked on an adventure. LOVE as pure being is now engaged with love that is having an experience. Enjoy the pleasure of knowing thyself. Remain in the Kingdom as long as it beckons to you.

Prayer

Singing glory and praise to my Creator,
I see my spirit as one with eternity
And my life as an endless sea.
I pray that my love may be extended to all
As Your love has been given to me.

In our joy we give thanks for Your blessing.
Let us love like we've never known hurt.
Let us live in the spirit of caring.
Let us act like it's Heaven on Earth.

Amen

2

RECOVERING THE AUTHENTIC SELF

The Message

A simple and unassuming question on my part initiated a profound response from Jeshua. One day, as I painted, I wondered how, "in the beginning of all existence, something could be created from nothing." As usual, His answer was very much to the point:

*"Things were not created from nothing. **Everything was created from `Being'.** The ultimate state of pure being is the totality of energy and potential, resting in stillness and peace with itself. In such a state all ideas for creation are formed, and these ideas are merely extensions of the self. Creation is the consequence of I AM moving into action, or life, through multiplying ITSELF. There was no instrument of creation outside of Divine Being. I AM THAT I AM is God. So too with yourself, the truth of who you are will not be found in actions or personal history, but in the simplicity of who you are within the stillness and peace of your inner being. In this universe and for all time, Being is Supreme. All that you do and have is an extension of your being and an outward gesture of the way you consider yourself to be.*

"When I walked on the earth, my mission was accomplished not by deeds, miracles or stories, but by one central teaching which I presented in countless ways and my life embodied: In the beginning and forever 'I Am is the way; I Am is the word.' I lived the principle and instructed all who would listen to the power of that truth. It is the secret to reconciling compassion, reality, and integrity, and for surmounting the perils of illusion, judgment, and separation. There was only one ritual commonly shared by all congregations of the early

church. That was the bonding I shared with my apostles on the eve of my surrender. Unfortunately, much of the original meaning has been lost. I was not warning them of impending bloodshed and martyrdom. I was giving them one last, and meaningful, opportunity to master the central teaching of my life and to seal it in the drama of things to come. I was to conquer death, not by miraculous powers or even by prayer, but by the body and blood of MY BEING. Except that I am one with you and you are one with me, we can do nothing for one another. The same is true for all mankind. Through the joining of love, which is compassion, and the unity of spirit, which is peace, light is brought to the world and all is accomplished."

Correlations

Exodus 3:14 "And God said unto Moses, I AM THAT I AM, and thus shall you say unto the children of Israel I AM has sent me."

John 8:58 "I tell you the truth, Jesus answered, before Abraham was born, I AM."

John 1:1 "In the beginning was the word and the word was with God and the Word was God."

The Key

After two decades of building a career, working in museums, teaching at universities, and successfully building name recognition for my art, I had every expectation that success would come only as a result of these efforts. I believed that success was the end-point of applying oneself to desired objectives in life whether it might be careers, relationships, service, or pleasures. Therefore, when the spiritual prompting to paint a portrait of Jesus Christ began to direct my life, there was seemingly no place in my agenda for it. I regarded the idea more as a inspired diversion rather than a meaningful culmination of anything I had intended to do. Little did I know that I was about to be given a new definition of personal success, which is the ability to be truly who I am in the midst of any experience, and surmount the temptation to identify with it or limit myself by it.

The story of my surrender has already been told in *Love Without End...Jesus Speaks.* What I am about to share with you is the intrinsic meaning of that experience. On November 23rd 1991, I was first greeted by the light of Christ—a presence created only BY ITSELF! External forces, such as electricity, did not generate this light, nor was it reflected from any surface. I was in the presence of I AM that existed only TO BE ITSELF.

The consequences of that day are now history. But the memory of that first encounter did not diminish. Though years passed, the original moment of inspiration remained vivid. Despite the many blessings and great honor of bringing forth a physical portrait of Jeshua, my heart longed to share a vision of the Living Christ as true light—a spiritual presence that would transcend space, time, race, and gender. I frequently considered the possibility of attempting such a painting, but always abandoned the idea as impossible. After all, how could the reflective surface of a painting portray pure light?

In the spring of 1998, as I was writing *Love Without End...Jesus Speaks,* I gained an extra measure of confidence and decided once and for all either to make every effort to accomplish that desire or finally abandon it. Earnestly and carefully, I analyzed all the problems and obstacles, addressing them one at a time. Since every layer of paint would measurable darken the surface, I needed to begin with the brightest painting ground possible. Then my first attempt at manifesting the vision must employ only the lightest tints of color. My first day's work yielded a lovely and fragile painting that might appropriately be entitled "Impressionist Snow Storm." Little was accomplished, although I still had a measure of hope. The next day I began to develop the artistic composition and intensified the colors to gain more projection. At the end of day two, I had achieved an interesting abstract painting, but no one would guess that it was supposed to represent Christ. Frustration was beginning to challenge my dream, but I vowed to continue.

I began day three with a meditation, which lucidly brought back into focus the original experience and all of its details. One important element I had missed in the painting were the waves of radiant energy accompanying the light. So I introduced many white undulating paint strokes radiating from a common center. I was sure that I had accomplished something this time. But when I stepped back to view my day's work, I felt embarrassed. The progress of the previous two days was now buried beneath a cartoon-like illuminated octopus with many tendrils. My eyes began to fill with tears as my heart sank into a sense of dismal failure.

Since I was scheduled to speak at a conference over the weekend, it seemed as though the most logical and therapeutic solution to my issues would be to set the project aside and take a rest from the struggle. If I found any fresh perspectives or new creative possibilities, then I would pursue them at a later time. On my way back from the conference I recalled that I knew how to apply gold leaf. Recently, when I had been in a local art supply store, I had also seen silver leaf and other colored foils that might be quite effective for infusing more brilliance into the painting. On Tuesday morning I returned to work, with hope in my heart and gold leaf in my hands. The metallic "tiles" were dazzling and bright, and I lost myself creating seamless patterns of them across the surface. As I neared completion I began to observe the "patchwork" effect that was emerging. Doubtless, I would have objected to the inappropriateness of such a structural design, but before I could address my feelings, I heard a familiar voice and the touch of a comforting hand on my shoulder.

Jeshua was there, and in a gentle happy tone, he simply asked, *"Would you like some help?"* Of course I would, and my heart jumped with joy and relief! Then to my surprise, he directed my attention to a roll of packing tape lying on the daybed in my studio. I was instructed to tear off a dozen or more strips of tape and hang them from the edge of the worktable. This was a bit perplexing, but I was curious. Were we going to pack the painting and ship it to Heaven? The answer soon came when he told me to wrap my hands in the tape, sticky-side out. As soon as I did, my hands were moved by his love, and we began removing foil and other layers of paint from the surface. After two hours and many strips of tape, a masterpiece was created. I could hardly believe my eyes, for it had all been accomplished through a subtractive process. By cutting through layers of paint, allowing one to show through the next, the surface was now resplendant with color, texture, and richness.

Jeshua, Master of Parables, had created another one. By redeeming a project that was hopelessly inadequate to its goal, he had turned it into a metaphor of life. The painting before me even possessed some of the quality of my original experience, for it now expressed the nature of a higher truth.

Unknowingly, at every step of creation, my frustrated labor had provided all the necessary ingredients. I had developed each layer of creation through my willingness to search, experience, and apply my best effort. Even though the direction was often unclear (the results often seemingly pointless, and the goal out of reach), I continued by faith alone. All that was necessary to reveal the imbedded light, was a simple change of direction and a return to simplicity. By just taking away the expressions that did not belong, or no longer served a purpose, an indwelling beauty and meaning were exposed.

My attempt to portray Holy Essence would have failed except that Jeshua transformed the process into a mirror for reflecting our human relationship to the Divine. In life, we each move from chapter to chapter, often through overgrown paths in very dense forests. Joys are mingled with disappointment, and most often we tell ourselves that true success will come with the next development, until at last we realize that each new layer of experience simply dims the light a little more.

Now, through layers of experience that have each contributed to the richness, depth, and uniqueness of our character, we may again uncover the light and allow it to shine brightly as the simplicity of Authentic Self.

BEING is fundamental. That is the **second key.** It is described by nothing but itself. The light of our being is original. Therefore, it is something to be recovered, not created.

In life, as with the painting of *"First Light"*, our realization of true being comes always as liberation from attachment. The revelation of light and the return to innocence is a subtractive process, not an additive one! The I Am that we are has BEEN from the beginning. It has always been the power underwriting our varied experiences. To judge or to celebrate any isolated experience, as if it were the reason for one's existence, is to miss the point of who one really is.

Inspirations

Lao Tzu (6th century B.C.) China:
   Tao Te Ching: "The Way is eternally nameless."

William Shakespeare (b.1564-d.1616) England:
   Hamlet: "This above all: to thine own self be true, and it must follow, as the night the day, thou canst not then be false to any man."

Applications

In the years that I have had to study and apply his teachings, I have observed the power of a quiet and peaceful heart and a spirit of simplicity for revealing right actions...even if the answer does not come all at once. Perhaps this observation also casts some light on the depth and importance of observing a day of rest in honor of one's sacred source. The I Am of our earthly personae is never more in harmony with the Divine I Am than when we are in a condition of peace and stillness. In the words of David, Psalm 46:10, "Be still and know that I Am God."

For every life it seems there is a basic program, and according to Jeshua those programs are written by the nature of each person's love. Through the energy of that one Universal Power, the apparent paradox of God's will and personal free will are reconciled. At point of perfect synchronicity between the love that you are, and God's will that it be that way, there are endless opportunities for rewriting, refining or enhancing the life you are experiencing.

This concept may be easier to grasp than to implement because of the challenge in returning to our essential pure self. Finding the original self involves a process of surrendering the defenses we have installed against accidental or untimely intrusions of it into our lives, thereby disrupting the stories in which we are but players. It is part of the experience of life to create other identities which are designed to provide a learning experience and an interface with the reality of others. Only our true self survives the games of life. In the meantime, however, there is a tug of war, since the temporal identities need to occlude the soul in order to make their own survival possible. This is a kind of soul-level autoimmune struggle. Perhaps we have in that a mirror of this problem in the many tragic autoimmune disorders that are plaguing humankind at this time in history. Even cancer, our number one killer, displays an irrational reprogramming of the bodily systems to support that which is killing it. In more commonplace ways, we may find ourselves working so hard to support the externals of life that we have no sense of living it. In many of our relationships we are struggling to find harmony so intensely that the mere joy of being together is lost.

Is there a single and simple message here that we need to heed? Perhaps we are being challenged to understand again the ancient teachings of Jeshua that we must first slay the illusions of self in order to reveal that which has been true from the beginning. There is both divine and practical logic in that, which is crucial to the fulfillment of life. The many identities of one's life may exist for a number of reasons, ranging from conditioning and practical necessity to the adventure of having selective and different experiences. Whatever our reasons, all identities are variations from the truth, and have no life of their own. To become solidly locked into any one of them is to be positioned with death. To defend any of them above one's true being is to reverse the direction of Divine Supply and empty the storehouse of life and well being. The truth of one's being requires no defense, except for an occasional restating of the primary logic of Power—that it Originates in God, descends into the original self, and then manifests as the identities and creations of one's life. I have found that the simple reinstating of this logic in life is a most effective way of managing the identities created only for experience or practical function.

Throughout the many centuries of sacred teaching, most likely there was more verbal conveyance of this pivotal truth than has survived in literature. With the many political agendas that sought to undermine personal sovereignty, this idea was repeatedly the target of despots and tyrannical governments (both secular and religious). When I spoke with Jeshua, he remarked that the few mentions of 'I Am' in the New Testament were scarce evidence of the central place they held in the body of his teaching. Moses also gives us two crucial clues to the prominence it may have held in early Hebraic teaching. In Exodus 6:3 it is written, "And God said unto Moses, 'I AM THAT I AM', and thus shall you say unto the children of Israel I AM has sent me." In conjunction with this, let us then consider that the second commandment of Moses admonishes us not to take the name of God in vain. By his own definition, he was specifically referring to the words I AM. Our modern misconception of that teaching is attached to the assumption that the word "God" is a name, and therefore never to be used irreverently. While I agree that any reference to the sacred is best presented with reverence, that aspect of conduct is probably not to what Moses was referring. More than likely he was instructing his people in the power of I AM and how anything attached to it contains the pivotal power of the Name. Whatever is named becomes manifest. Therefore it is perilous to use the words I AM carelessly or attach them to anything negative. For example, a commonplace misuse of the power would be to say, "I am unhappy." Such a statement invariably calls forth more unhappiness. It would be far better to acknowledge the unhappy situation and then follow up with "I am going to do something about it."

Your first and continuing application is to observe your language and thought patterns around the words "I am." Bring your habits of speech fully into consciousness so that you may have intentional respect for the higher power of I AM which guides your life.

Your second and continuing application is to study the nature of your character and being in its peaceful, contemplative state. For some of you this may mean first setting aside moments in your day when you may have such an experience. Then as you achieve greater clarity and certainty on this core aspect of your nature, begin to infuse it into the rest of your life and activities. In this way, you will gain a greater understanding of what and who you wish "I am" to be.

Your third application is one that will phenomenally improve all your relationships and at the same time do more than anything else to restore your own personal sovereignty. When Jeshua told us to "love our neighbor as ourselves", it was not just an instruction on how to have a better community. More importantly, it is the key to restoring one's own true being through honoring others. One of the greatest mistakes we make in trying to see our own uniqueness is by contrasting ourselves **from** others. Often this is through judgment, which creates walls of separation. For a change of direction, do this process that he recommended to me. It involves asking yourself the following two questions about each person in your life.

1. What part of me are you?   2. What part of you am I?

This exercise may bring up aspects of yourself that have been neglected and long forgotten, or even dark, occluded areas that you need to view. Whatever you experience, after sincere and repeated application you may find, as I have, that true acknowledgment of others brings greater clarity to the self, and true acknowledgment of self brings greater clarity about others. In this way there is unity with honor, and discernment without separation. In the words of the Master, *"I AM is the way."*

Meditation

The meditation for this chapter will be a silent one. You may prepare for it by reading the following affirmation written for you as I dwelled in the Sacred Heart with Jeshua and beheld the wonder of who you are:

I behold you in your peace and in your love. I behold the light of your being, the love that you are. I behold the beauty of your soul. I behold your presence and indwelling peace.

Be filled with the love and the wonder of the cosmos. Be filled with the wonder of all existence. Be filled with the Holy Spirit, and the love and wonder of God. Be filled with the majesty of your own being and the love that you are.

And the voice of Jeshua speaks from within your heart: "I give you peace that in its presence you may know your own being. Come to me in your peace and I will give abundantly to you. Come to me in your joy and I will rejoice with you. Come to me with your illusions, and I will give you truth. Come to me with your pain and I will give you healing. Come to me with your fears, and I will give you hope. Come to me with all that you say you are and I will give you who you really are. I Am is the light and the truth, I Am is the power, I Am is the way. In this sacred place, know yourself. I call you by your name and simply say, Behold!

"You are beautiful, you are glorious, and you are the majesty of creation. And none of this is by your doing, but by your being. In the image of God you were created. As you consider yourself to be, so too will your life unfold. Know yourself within the peace of God. The peace of God is beyond all illusion, and it knows no limitation, no death, and no end. This is your home. I welcome you with love."

Prayer

Father Mother Source,
I pray for the simplicity of being which honors all of life,
That in honoring you and all others,
I am honored as well.

I was given everything and did not know how to receive.
I did not know how to honor the blessing of life.

I asked for my needs to be met,
When my only need was
To honor the power of Love.
Now, in knowing this, I rest in Your peace,
Create with Your infinite supply,
And exist forever in Your truth.

Amen

3

COURAGE TO BE CONSCIOUS

The Message

One of the recurring themes of my conversations with Jeshua was that faith and consciousness were both essential to human fulfillment. Interestingly, each of these attributes requires courage and together they are guardians of our wholeness.

During my original conversations with Jeshua I asked about the woman who had touched his robe and was healed. He replied, *"She touched my love and was made whole."* I was still curious. "What caused the wholeness?"

"In the presence of love, the power of God can work miracles. Considering that God is the source of all love, how could it be otherwise? Therefore, when one soul truly honors the presence of God in another, wholeness and holiness are welcomed. Whenever love is transmitted from soul to soul, wholeness is embraced by more than one, and greater consciousness is brought to light. This is the power of the Holy Spirit.

"Such transmission does not have to be conspicuous or dramatic. Every day there are miracles of healing and creation that you do not see. You often regard positive occurrences in life as inevitable without ever considering that it could have been otherwise. When you consider the random possibilities contained in every situation, you will see that life's positive momentum could only be directed by consciousness and led by faith. In hindsight, you call it logic! Yet, faith is not blind, and beliefs are not addressed only to the unknown. On the contrary, true faith brings vision, and true belief serves to reveal that which is knowable. As a matter of fact,

transmuting the unknown into the known is the ultimate use of logic and the ultimate achievement of faith. Without that foundation of understanding, you cannot appreciate how intrinsic is the connection between faith and consciousness.

"Consciousness is considerably more than wakeful perception or inherent awareness. Consciousness is the integration of perception, experience, knowledge, and aspiration to create a parable or analogy of life. These models of awareness support further thought to formulate intentional experience. Regardless of whether the object of consciousness is personal happiness or scientific precision, the process is the same. A meaningful story is a parable, and so is algebra! Both are models of awareness and refinements of belief, reconciled with truth and practical evidence. Without faith, however, such reconciliation could only occur through hindsight, and all advancement would be stifled.

"Courage is the heartbeat of consciousness and fear its mortal enemy. What you will not face will elude you, or else it will erode or corrupt some part of your life in unsuspecting ways. Consciousness is the light of the soul. Therefore, darkness will avoid it or dwell in the shadow of some external light. It takes great courage to be a light in the world and great faith to know that one ray of light may turn a darkened room into one that is safe to enter. I came to the world to empower faith and unleash a new dimension of consciousness not seen before.

"Never would I lead you blindly into the unknown, guided only by mysterious belief. I came to give you answers to life and keys to your unfoldment. As humankind aspires to greater faith and consciousness, fear will be conquered. Fear is the foundation of all mis-belief. It is tragic that many who stake their lives and prayers on blind faith, also underminine their own faith with fear. On the other hand, when faith is an affirmation of one's certainty in life and a progression toward greater consciousness, fear subsides and the Holy Spirit may enter and perform miracles."

His answer prompted a heartfelt, though hesitant, request from me. "If faith, love, and consciousness can make one whole, then why do good and faithful people continue to suffer and die, even in the face of their prayers? Did you not say that faith is enough?"

*"The problem here is not in the quantities of faith, for only a grain is necessary. The problem lies in knowing what faith is! Faith is not blind hope. **Faith is the cessation of fear.** In the absence of fear, there is genuine surrender to all positive possibilities. This permits an expansion of consciousness. It adds conviction to belief. This is how faith and consciousness work together, one increasing the other.*

*"Belief is a confirmation of faith. **It is the certainty you have in what you know or consider to be true. This in turn affects your state of consciousness.** Unfortunately, not all beliefs are positive, and many have been adopted without sufficient examination of what is true. Faith and belief are very misunderstood in the modern world. They are often considered to be nanve and irrational. Often this is true. Even so, beliefs are powerful. This is why they must be balanced with consciousness in order to be truly effective.*

"For many people belief has no foundation in logic. Today so much of our logic is based on scientific, mathematical, and mechanical premises, that faith and belief are discounted as intuitive, emotional, and unexamined ideals formulated to make the mysteries of life bearable. If one considers faith to be an alternative to logic there will not be enough conviction or belief to generate miracles. Indeed, such ignorance about faith has often fostered great exploitation of people in their most vulnerable moments.

"In the world of 2,000 years ago, faith was not a tranquilizer that masked one's fear of the unknown, and belief was not an alternative to logic and reason. To ancient man, belief was his assurance that the sun would rise tomorrow. Faith was the 'North Star' by which he navigated without doubts or reservation. This is what I meant when I said, 'All things are possible to him that believes.'"

Correlations

John 8:12 "Then Jesus spoke again to them saying, 'I am the light of the world: he that follows me will not walk in darkness, but shall have the light of life.'"

John 14:26 "But the Comforter, which is the Holy Ghost, whom the Father will send in my name, will teach you all things, and bring all things to your remembrance, whatsoever I have said to you."

Proverbs 4:7 "Wisdom is the principal thing; therefore get wisdom: and with all your getting get understanding."

The Key

The key to consciousness lies in acceptance of it as the light of our souls. It is not an external dimension to which we aspire, but rather a way of knowing about life from a higher perspective. Faith is the candle, and courage is the force. They carry the light into dark passages as we gain insight into that which was previously unseen.

Consciousness resides with being. It originates in the innocent, sacred, and compassionate center of your soul where, in peace and serenity, you are capable of perceiving all things without prejudice. In all its forms, consciousness takes courage, because it requires acceptance of oneself...and others. Unlike knowledge, (which is derived from patterns and comparisons of experience and the integration of data), consciousness begins with the simple awareness of oneself existing within an environment. Its full realization comes when you can accept yourself for all the ways you are "in the world" and yet not be defined "by the world". There is much talk of consciousness today. Some believe we are about to enter the "Age of Consciousness". If so, what would that look like? Certainly, we are on the cusp of some great leap forward. And assuredly, our progress will involve technological advancements and even greater accumulations of knowledge. As we look for the answer to that question, it might help to consider first the possibility that technological advancements could occur without sufficient progress in consciousness to make life worth living. This would be the gloomy state of existence portrayed by science fiction writers when they saw their worst fears manifest in future civilizations. Such dreary conditions were the result of accelerated competition for survival, where the ultimate weapon was knowledge. That could be the end-point for a journey that humankind embarked upon several thousand years ago. Or there could be another choice.

Contained in ancient literature from every culture, there are similar stories about a time when man chose to leave the experience of innocence and seek for knowledge. Typically, these stories trace back about five to seven thousand years, to a time when the earliest roots of urbanization were taking hold. What allowed people to live together in large numbers with increasing diversity and conflict was the ability to "objectify" knowledge and compare experience. Agreements were obtained as people conformed to ideas, economic exchange, and common threats. In this challenging atmosphere the first philosophies, schools of thought, and religions were formulated as a means of coordinating larger groups of people into communities with shared efforts and beliefs. This was a crucial step in man's development, but there was also an immense sacrifice, which all of the ancient stories carefully point out.

That sacrifice becomes evident when we study the differences between consciousness and knowledge. Consciousness begins with self-awareness seeking to unfold and express itself in a larger context of existence. Knowledge begins with observations seeking to isolate, examine, and detach experience from subjective interference. In the story of Eden, it is very significant that after their choice of knowledge over innocence, Adam and Eve put on clothes (which hid the self) and gained vision in order to see that which was outside themselves. Now after thousands of years of accumulating knowledge it is equally significant that we have finally developed such refined and sensitive instruments of research that the observations are no longer distinguishable from the impact of examination. In other words, the observer and "the observed" are undeniably intertwined again. At last, we have come to a point where once more we may choose on the issue of knowledge versus consciousness.

There is also a third option. We may retain the value of knowledge while appreciating the greater power of consciousness!

In his life on earth, Jeshua prepared a way of understanding that would enlighten us concerning the choices we are about to make and impel us to seek higher ground. That new way of understanding is the way of compassion. Although ancient man was closer to God in his way of subjective perception, that approach to life was not providing him with a solution for coexisting with other humans in an increasingly diverse and challenging population. Therefore objective perception, or knowledge, became the basis for agreements, beliefs, and rules of conduct. Through knowledge, a level playing field could be established…at times. History is filled with turbulent contests over who would control the playing fields and the players. It is obvious in the history of man that neither subjective perceptions nor objective conclusions have been adequate for our complete fulfillment.

The third option is open … to enter an accelerated state of consciousness, which integrates subjective and objective reality into a continuous framework of shared experience. This involves the ability to see others as an extension of oneself and oneself as a microcosm of all that is. In his two final commandments, Jeshua provided us with the flight plan to this higher plane. *"Love the Lord your God with all your heart, and with all your soul and with all your mind. This is the first and greatest commandment. And the second is like unto it: Love your neighbor as yourself.*" (Matthew 22: 37-39) If we were to express the feeling of this in one word, it would be **compassion**.

It is truly unfortunate that we tend to limit the meaning of compassion to acts of sympathy and charity, when its greater meaning suggests an encompassing connection with all of life and existence. If compassion is actually a key to higher consciousness, it has to be relevant to all areas of life and significant to solving problems in all venues. For example, is this broader definition of compassion equally valid in the sciences? Indeed, we see a pivotal change in the life and consciousness of Albert Einstein as he confronted the limitations of objective measurement in his study of light, and transcended the limitations of deductive reasoning by "joining with light" and imagining himself to be riding on a light beam. Even earlier, Copernicus drew from his "imagination" a model of the cosmos quite different from conventional geocentric beliefs. Then he proceeded to integrate his theory with observable phenomena until he brought forth a new vision of our solar system. Is it possible that all of the extensions of life may be regarded and enjoyed as an experience of compassion?

Years ago, when I was a college art student, I had an opportunity to have dinner with the Director of the New York Art Students League. This was a highly respected man with much experience in all of the arts. Therefore, I decided to explore his wisdom. I was confounded and reduced to silence by his answer to my first and only question about art. I asked, "What do you think is the most important character trait of a great artist?" His answer was simply, "Compassion." I did not yet have the wisdom to understand this profound reply, but I knew anything else I might ask would be trivial by comparison. Later that year I would receive further instruction about this truth from another professor. The second lesson was close enough to my personal issues that I began to comprehend.

Art school in the 1960's was a rather uncomfortable place for any student with a preference for realistic art. That was the heyday of abstract expressionism. The fact that I was an honors student only pronounced my problem, since I was clearly not displaying my marks of achievement in a fashionable way. The tension I felt was undermining my progress as a student and artist. Finally, in the beginning of my senior year, exasperation gave way to the necessity of learning. I initiated a confrontation with my painting instructor; wherein I expressed my disappointment with not being taught realistic technique. I queried the reason for expressing oneself in paint only for its own sake. I soon found out that my professor had become as frustrated with me as I was with him. In an impatient gesture, he slapped a book of Leonardo Da Vinci's work on the table in front of me and asked in an irritated tone if I would like to paint like that. "Yes, that's what I'm talking about," I replied snappily. He opened the book to *"Mona Lisa"* and presented the following challenge. "If I teach you precisely how to recreate this painting, I want you to commit yourself totally to doing it. Or else you will abandon the project and explain all of your reasons in an essay." I accepted his dare but had no idea that my greater lesson would come from failure. The project began with excitement and optimism, but soon it turned into a sluggish exercise of detail and technical imitation. By the end of two weeks, I began to feel distress and then an ominous realization that I would never create a new *"Mona Lisa"*. With a sense of embarrassment, I resigned myself to write the essay. The words came slowly as I searched for reasons. Suddenly, the ground of my being shifted as a light turned on. From "nowhere", a new understanding allowed me to see that art is **a footprint of consciousness**. Of course, I could not paint *"Mona Lisa"*, and no amount of technical study would change that. Only Leonardo had the appropriate consciousness to bring forth that masterpiece! His art was an expression of his **very being**, and an **extension of the compassion** he had for his life and times. In that moment, I also saw the incredible value of art and artifacts left behind from those who came before. At last, I understood the critical value of compassion to creating great art. My professor returned my essay marked with an "A" and a final comment: "Well done, and remember to master your art through first mastering yourself. The techniques of your craft are only secondary instruments of creation."

There is an inseparable connection between consciousness and BEING. The future has not yet happened, and therefore cannot be fully known. The past is falling into place as memory. Therefore, the only perspective that can provide a full and living panorama of all possibilities is at the center of one's own being. It is up to each individual to decide what proportion of his consciousness is held subjectively and what proportion is developed into objective reality. Certain factors seem to be constant: consciousness is either expanded or limited by one's beliefs, experiences, connections, and attachments in life. All of this is summarized by one's **relationship** to life.

Jeshua said that many of the problems we focus on are not directly solvable, because they are not our personal problems at all, but simply "furniture" belonging to the level of consciousness in which we dwell. He instructed that we must release attachments and beliefs inherent to our **level of distress** if we would rise to a higher level of existence. There is a particularly revealing incident told in the Book of Matthew where a woman poured a jar of expensive perfume on Jeshua's head. The disciples rebuked her for wastefulness, when this could have been sold and given to the poor. Jeshua responded by saying, *"Why are you bothering this woman? She has done a beautiful thing to me. The poor you will always have with you, but you will not always have me."* In this instance and many other times, he pointed out the tenacious persistence of such conditions as poverty that we do not have to banish in order to transcend.

As he would say to me, *"Always look for higher ground. Such lower conditions were not created by conscious individuals, but by large masses clinging together in fear and unconsciousness for the safety of numbers. Individuals in their love of God and others will always find greater possibilities open to them, either through simple or magnanimous gestures.* **You are not the condition in which you find yourself.** *Knowing the difference will make all the difference."* He was adamant that serving a condition without examining one's relationship to it would create persistence for unwanted elements. The solution to any problem will not be found at the level of its creation, but on a higher level of consciousness where it simply dissolves in the light of greater truth.

Through honoring God and the presence of God in others and oneself, the source of all consciousness is revealed. As we become immersed in the conditions of life, that truth becomes hidden. This is where courage enters the formula for consciousness, as well as the need for faith. The ultimate goal is to rediscover the truth of who we are; yet in the process of doing so, much is unclear and lost in forgetfulness.

Faith is greatly misunderstood, and all too often, it is considered the opposite of consciousness. This is because faith is most often associated with blind obedience to unseen forces. If that were true, then to live a life of faith could mean living a precarious existence, moved along by irrationality. I have not found that to be the case. Jeshua said to me, *"Faith is the cessation of fear."* Irrationality subsides as fears depart. Prior experience may then be applied more intelligently, and beliefs may be upheld with more conviction! Since the first rays of inspiration fell upon me in the fall of 1991, Jeshua has directed me to act with faith in small measures, continuously! In his usual deliberate and courteous way, he has led me into a practical and realistic understanding of faith as a means of expanding consciousness. As I followed his lead, I gradually penetrated the unknown and developed a more comfortable understanding. For example, when he asked me to begin speaking his message in 1996, I resisted in my typical fashion. He responded by suggesting that I speak first at a gathering in my own gallery, and then to see how I felt about his request. In other words, I learned to strengthen my faith through experience, self-realization, and the enjoyment of service to others. His subtle guidance has allowed me to grasp the essential power of faith in **all that I do,** and to realize the critical role it plays in our attainment of consciousness.

It takes great courage for anyone to engage in conscious living, especially against a backdrop of fear about past accountability and consequences of less than responsible actions. But there is no greater solution for past regrets, than to rise to a level where the fostering conditions no longer exist. This is true forgiveness…and healing…which is universal and enduring.

Inspirations

William Wordsworth (b.1770–d.1850) England: *The Excursion:*
"And when the stream
Which overflowed the soul was passed away,
A consciousness remained that it had left
Deposited upon the silent shore
Of memory images and precious thoughts
That shall not die, and cannot be destroyed."

Saint Augustine (b.354 - d.430) North Africa:
The Confessions of St. Augustine:
"Not with doubting, but with assured consciousness, do I love Thee, Lord. Thou hast stricken my heart with thy word, and I loved thee. Yea also heaven and earth, and all that therein is, behold on every side they bid me love Thee."

Simon Newcomb (b.1835 - d.1909) America:
The Extent of the Universe:
"When attention is concentrated on the scene, the thousands of stars on each side of the Milky Way will fill the mind with the consciousness of a stupendous and all-embracing frame, beside which all human affairs sink into insignificance."

Applications

Like the air we breathe, and the space in which we live, consciousness is such a foundation to waking life that most of our involvement with it goes unnoticed. Unlike knowledge, there are no precise ways of measuring consciousness. When we want to gain knowledge, we study or obtain personal instruction. When some error or mistaken knowledge is exposed, we proceed to correct it. We can test for knowledge, supplement knowledge, or apply one area of knowledge to another. But what is the medium through which all knowledge flows, by which we are able to **know** that we know or that we **do not** know? What is the extra dimension that connects our lives and experiences, individualizes knowledge, and utilizes it for surviving, thriving, creating, and interacting with one another? It's consciousness! It is an indelible part of our being, so close as to be virtually invisible to us. In a paradoxical way, consciousness is the seat of our integrity, and yet it is conditioned by our experiences, connections, attachments, and beliefs. It may be limited through neglect and denial, or it may be expanded through attention and appreciation.

The four applications below can help anyone increase or enhance the quality of consciousness, and give rise to expanded or higher consciousness. Each of these will contribute to a richer state of conscious living.

1. The first is "consciousness housekeeping". In this application, you will uncover forgotten attachments, neglected friends or family, tucked away projects and old dreams that make up the "dusty attic" of your consciousness.

To bring up these memories, you may need to rummage through boxes, old address books, closets, briefcases, and recipe books to name only a few of the repositories where attachments could "go to sleep". The purpose of this is not to make things tidy, but to discover and bring to light **attachments, which are still defining your life and consciousness,** even though your life has moved on to other pursuits. Take notice of how your consciousness responds to each area you uncover. In some cases, you may find that what you once considered important is now only clutter. In that very recognition, you will have liberated some degree of consciousness. In other cases, you may find attachments that you still cherish and want to recultivate. In doing this, you are integrating an element of your past with your present and bringing more fullness to your life. There may be a few attachments that have been put in a box due to unpleasantness. Especially look at these. As long as your consciousness is invested in them, they are defining your life. Any decision is better than avoidance, because it will be from the perspective of your current place in life.

Notice the items, areas, and people who capture your attention the most, and learn from this application how your consciousness has no limits with regard to the past or future. Consciousness is a tenacious servant that will not leave an area of attachment until it is released with intention or actual completion. Its loyalty may serve you well or perhaps sabotage your life. Unattended negative attachments could be instructing the rest of your consciousness on how to perform. Therefore, as you rummage through the past, make note of old issues that are now complete. There will be other things that you have now replaced with better options, and perhaps a few things can be quickly finished. As for the rest, establish new priorities from your current way of viewing life.

2. Look at your life today and make a list of the major decisions facing you. If there is nothing major, then any decision will do. This is not only a learning exercise, but also one that will result in immediate improvement. Observe and write down whatever is restraining your decision. These factors could range from lack of information, time, support, and funds to fear or counter-influences from others.

Notice that your reason, whatever it is, has absorbed at least as much of your consciousness as the goal itself. Your unresolved decision has momentarily absorbed as much consciousness as the subject under consideration. If this is not what you want, then there is a simple remedy available through practical faith. **Implement progress toward your goal anyway.** By gaining whatever information, time, agreements, and/or funds are presently available, you are clearing the way for greater action when it is possible, and giving yourself the best chance of making a wise decision. The secret is to direct your consciousness *intentionally* **beyond the decision** with a practical faith that you are capable of implementing the greatest good. Actually you will have made a "greater decision", which encompasses the lesser one. The power of faith and consciousness are always available for you to employ.

3. The third application is directed to the way in which you address problems. Select a problem and focus on it until you can see and feel the whole situation surrounding it as well as the level of consciousness to which it belongs.

Ask yourself honestly how you feel about the entire situation containing your problem. This will help you identify whether you have a momentary challenge within a positive area, or whether an elevation of consciousness is the real answer. This is important to discern, because problems within a positive or desirable context may be addressed directly and usually find answers rather quickly. In positive environments, consciousness is naturally expanding. In either case, the answer will always be found at a level **above the cause**, because answers are delivered **by expanding consciousness.** A swelling river of consciousness eventually spills over the dam. Therefore, in many instances a little patience and a short wait is all that is necessary. That illustration also serves to expose why a declining situation generates problems with no easy solution. Consciousness is not progressing in these areas. In such areas, what you are calling a problem may only be a snag within a larger area of distress, and the real problem is more likely stemming from beliefs and attachments restricting your life. Once you know **what** to correct or enhance, your consciousness has a marvelous way of healing itself.

4.   The fourth application will cause the greatest expansion of consciousness, and possibly the most profound change in your life. This is the deliberate exercise of compassion, **beginning with YOU.** Sit before a mirror and take an honest and unreserved look at yourself. Consider your health, happiness, appearance, relationships, finances, mental clarity, enthusiasm, and spiritual beliefs.

Now this is the hardest part: ACCEPT WHATEVER YOU SEE. Acknowledge your efforts, successes, and difficulties. Acknowledge aspects of yourself that have survived periods of hardship and lack. Acknowledge other aspects that have responded to abundance. Acknowledge your modesty as an aspect of moderation. Acknowledge your humor, and all your emotions. Find acceptance (not justification) for every part of your being, until you have acquired a serene compassion, free of all expectation, disappointment, or prejudice. This is not the time for recrimination, amendments of behavior, or even self-forgiveness if it is prefaced by guilt. This is your opportunity to experience automatic forgiveness by the higher grace of compassion.

Be patient. Your first attempt may only bring up judgments that you and others have placed upon you. Compassion is your truest prayer, and so let this be a prayerful state in which you pierce all illusions of judgment and end separation from your highest self. You will know when you have accomplished this by the greater feeling you have about simply BEING CONSCIOUS, rather than fitting your consciousness to the size and shape of your beliefs, attachments, or judgments. As Jeshua said to me, *"There is little difference between compassion and the highest consciousness."* You may find that unfiltered consciousness is like a pane of clear glass through which you may peer in one direction to perceive true love, and in the other direction to perceive true life.

Once you know the exquisite feeling for yourself, apply this to everyone in your life.

Meditation

As I close my eyes and surrender to the inner peace of my own sanctuary, I let my consciousness float like a feather on the breeze, freely moving on the currents of spirit within. This gentle movement of consciousness draws like a moth to a tiny spark of light. Small though it is, this glimmer of light is firm and true like the North Star. It matters not where I find it, because everything else is illusion. This is the center of my being, which I approach with reverence. As I draw near, I feel the warmth of a welcoming hearth, and my consciousness slips into the light the way a hand fits perfectly in a glove.

In this state of blessed reunion, I am in the home of my being. What was once only a spark, when I was separate from it, now surrounds my whole being and baths me in a luminous glow. I am nourished and blessed with the presence of God in this inner sanctum. I look into and through the light, where I begin to find wondrous possibilities. What I hold to be most true is coming to life in this place, and what I most believe is taking shape before my very eyes. I behold the truth of Jeshua when he said, *"All things are possible to him that believes."* All of my fears have fallen away, for in the light of my true being there are no shadows of doubt and no hiding places for harm or evil to dwell.

I see now the great revelation that everything good was supplied before time. It was only I who needed to seek through faith and awaken through consciousness to the miracle of creation. I receive and take unto myself the wealth of God, knowing that whatsoever I believe, in completeness of faith and absence of fear, shall be done by the grace of God. I simply dwell in the glow of this Inner Light for the nourishment and strength it gives. And slowly, gently, I begin to realize that the light has now become one with my life and I awaken to a new birth.

Prayer

Holy Creator and Source of all supply,
I pray above all else that my separation from You be ended.
In serenity and humility, I ask to be rejoined with You
That I may know the enlightenment of compassion
Where all is made whole and all possibilities are revealed.

In the spirit of Compassion
I pray for the poor that they may be fed.
I pray for the rich that they may show others how to prosper.
I pray for the sick that they may be healed.
I pray for the well that they may be strong for us all.
I pray for the grieving that they may be comforted.
I pray for the happy that their joyous hearts may be
A beacon of love.
I pray for those in prison that they may find freedom
In other ways.
I pray for those who have freedom
That it be guarded with honor.
I pray for mankind that we would look for the
Good in all things
And honor Your Holy Presence in one another.

Amen

4

RIVER OF LIFE

The Message

While discussing adamantine particles, I inquired about their place in the order of things. How was it that mass as we know it suddenly appeared in primordial space, seemingly as a mutation within the grand unmarked expanse of infinite potential.

"The answer lies in a realm of awareness beyond human consciousness. I can only instruct you with metaphors. Human consciousness itself is a grand metaphor of existence.

"In the beginning there was Love, and Love existed in alternating rhythms of release and self knowing. In knowing Itself, Love created a viewpoint, and from that viewpoint It created points to view. These points were all good and existed only because Love said that it was so. In the relationship between Love, It's viewpoint, and Its points to view, there came to be space and unity. Love knew this as Spirit. In that same relationship, there also came to be rhythm, energy, and differences of potential. Love knew this as Life. All of this existed only because intention and thought propelled Love into the prospect of 'having an experience'. Initially, every potential, thought, and action occurred in perfect synchronicity; therefore its reality existed at the speed of light. As Love desired to have an experience, a new pattern of relationships was necessary; one that included points of random change and finite passages of what is now called 'time'. To accomplish this, Love entered a dialogue with Spirit, and so life acquired a new tendency toward novel response. After all, what is a dialogue if the response is pre-determined? Through this dialogue, the foundation

was created for free will and choice. Thus, for the first time it was necessary for Love to 'mark the spots' where life and spirit had emerged into manifestation. Wherever change occurred in a field of equilibrium there would be mass. Love was adamant about this! Nothing must ever be lost from spirit, regardless of the changes, distresses, or configurations that may unfold in the course of existence having an experience. Consequently, you may call this emerging presence 'adamantine'. Only a whisper, a trace, at first, and yet it was the first manifestation of substance, and the beginning of the universe as you know it. From this, all matter was created. But to understand this, you must respect the essence of Spirit, the Love from which it sprang, and the river of life in which it flows."

When he said this, I knew that Life as he perceived it was not bound by the fragile and limited perimeters of organic substances we normally call "life". It was a sacred emission from God, much more powerful than any form or structure could ever fully embody. I was yearning to know more...

"All knowledge begins by observing relationships and patterns. Subatomic particles have no meaning as isolated entities. They can be understood only as interconnections that result in observable events. In this universe, patterns represent the probabilities of interconnection, not the probabilities of things. Life is not a collection of isolated objects, but a network of phenomenon that are fundamentally interconnected and interdependent. The spirit of the earth may be fully known only through ecological understanding. To understand anything in life, whether it be life on earth or life eternal, one must appreciate and respect relationships.

*"It has been the tradition of classical science to believe that in any complex system, the behavior of the whole may be analyzed by examining the properties of its separate parts. This is the process of analytical and deductive reasoning that has created the picture of a linear universe comprised of rigid, inert structures and dwindling quantities of energy. As it will eventually be learned, there are no parts at all—merely more intricate refinements of pattern within a great system of life. Every living being has **intrinsic value** to the whole*

rather than mechanistic function within limited structures."

"Then is everything living? And what about the second law of thermodynamics which states that loss or dissipation of energy is inevitable in the universe?"

*"There are both open and closed systems in the universe. Open systems supply new life and closed systems maintain order but eventually lead to death. Therefore, a balance is necessary. Most inorganic matter functions within closed systems that have stabilized around symmetrical actions and reactions. A closed system may only experience change through tendencies toward disorder and loss of energy. However, alongside the closed system is a living universe of open systems ever moving from disorder to order, thus **increasing** in energy.*

"Only as you shift your thinking from objects to relationships will you conquer separation, and harvest the power of life. To know this power is to know the experience of caring. Just as you care for yourself, without reservation or enforcement to do so, when you extend that sense of caring to include all others, you will know the full measure of being alive. Human suffering is greatly accelerated by attachment to fixed ideas, isolating boundaries, and structures that either separate or deteriorate. Out of ignorance, man divides the perceived world into separate objects and categories of existence that he sees as fixed, but which are really ever adjusting aspects of life's fluid nature. Since organic life first appeared on earth, over 99 percent of all species have served their purpose and been absorbed into other or higher life forms. The river of life ever widens its possibilities and increases the complexity of its manifestations. At the foundation is simplicity.

*"It may shock you to know that all the world's bacteria have access to a single gene pool, which has provided an immense resource for adaptation, manifesting an array of breathtaking combinations and re-combinations for three billion years! Any bacterium—at any time—has the ability to use accessory genes, provided by other strains, which permits it to function in ways its own DNA may not cover. The global **trading of genes** through DNA re-combinations provides for*

*almost endless adaptation possibilities. Therefore, what has been done to one has been done to all. Widespread use of antibacterial agents is both futile and disastrous. Future life sciences and medicine will comprehend the more effective use of agents to stimulate positive adaptation of bacteria resulting in chains of supportive symbiosis. In the presence of love, these positive adaptations naturally occur. In the presence of hatred and fear, negative and resistant strains of bacteria are more likely. Life forms are ever changing, and yet the basic chemistry of life remains the same. Do not cling to forms that are passing, but seek for an understanding of life that embraces and includes all possibilities. This is accomplished through integrating and expanding patterns and relationships. In this way, you will see God as the creative power of life. When I asked that you love one another, I was not just giving you a recipe for human fellowship. This is **the** doorway to life eternal."*

Awestruck as I was, he must have caught my other thought, for I was also wondering, "Are we then just noodles floating in cosmic soup?"

"Unity and connection do not imply the loss of individuality and personal authority, nor do they sanction careless or indiscriminate agreements which could lower the quality of life. To the contrary, unity provides a fertile context in which rare and unique creations may flower."

Correlations

Luke 12:22-25 "And Jesus said to his disciples: 'That is why I say to you, Do not be anxious about the life here--what you can get to eat; nor yet about your body--what you can get to wear. For life is more than food, and the body than its clothes. But which of you, by being anxious, can prolong his life a moment?'"

John 4:14 "But whoever once drinks of the water that I will give him shall never thirst any more; but the water that I will

give him shall become a spring welling up within him--a
source of Immortal Life."
John 6:63 "It is the Spirit that gives Life; mere flesh is of no avail.
In the teaching that I have been giving you there is Spirit
and there is Life."

The Key

To even know our wholeness, much less accept it, we must
look far beyond our current focus, beyond our tolerances, and
beyond our momentary preferences. It is natural to enjoy one
favorite emphasis in life that provides gratification. The same is
true about the different "parts" of our own being. The challenge is
to know the wholeness that includes and utilizes our every
connection without partitioning, limiting or separating. The
greater power of life is that which coordinates, integrates, and
synthesizes all its parts into seamless harmony. From the viewpoint
of the whole, all parts are intrinsic and necessary. For example, is
your sleep less necessary than your waking life? Are your
unconscious responses less meaningful than your cognitive
awareness? Have your struggles, failures, regrets, and
embarrassments not shaped your character as surely as your joys
and accomplishments? Those who only chase after the light, who
only pursue rainbows, and who only surround themselves with
artificial comforts are set apart from themselves as surely as those
who only know darkness, and only view life as an invitation to
misery. An earnest search for wholeness may begin with
forgiveness, or it may begin with planting one's feet on "terra
firma". In whatever way it begins, an earnest examination of one's
own wholeness within an extended community and larger
environment will surely result in greater compassion and depth of
concern for all of life.

Mankind lives an eternal paradox. We have been given the blessing of knowing that "we are", and also the challenge of knowing we are "part of ". We were created as love, in the image of God, and yet we were given to know goodness as the caring and supportive interconnections we have with one another and with nature. Thus the greatest good we will ever experience will be found in the dawn and the twilight which knit together the night and the day of our experiences. Only at such moments are we able to see the whole of our own being in silhouette against the grandeur of the universe. The Holy Spirit is our counselor and teacher to help us find strength and wisdom in the power of these extensions and transitions embracing us.

It took years of experience and simplification for me to comprehend the meaning behind a dialogue I had with Jeshua concerning two scriptures from the New Testament. I wanted to know how, in one place, he could have said, "Be ye perfect, even as your Father in heaven is perfect"… and then in another circumstance could have said, "None among you is without sin." I had heard explanations before, but what I wanted was the truth! He replied, *"You were created as love in the image of God. As you draw into that truth, and enjoy the blessings of God, you will receive the strength and wisdom to be **in** the world but **not of it**. And yet it is not the glory or privilege of mankind to stand apart from life and creation, never to stand in the rain or feel hunger or loss. To know that you are in the world for service, fellowship, and experience is to cultivate a broader comprehension of your connections with all of life. In this way you will know the wholeness of yourself, your history, your community, and the earth. You cannot know such completeness without looking into the shadows as well as the light. For many, the shadow is all that has ever been real, and for them it is important to seek and accept forgiveness that they may stride confidently into the light. Then there are others, who judge so greatly against the shadows that they are prisoners of what little light they know. "*

"You are the wholeness of your love and all your experiences. The misguided idea that your life, and the lives of others, may be

*'edited' until the whole epitomizes the sum of your **favorite parts**, is sheer foolishness. Any connection that you sever with the river of life reduces your potential and weakens your capacity for giving or receiving compassion."*

All of life is a flow, and that flow may be viewed even more simply as the syntax of connections that allow for experiences and the sharing of them in a field of consciousness. Not only do we "swim" in this flow, but we are also creating it as we go and connecting with it as an immense extended environment. When I began speaking about my conversations with Jeshua a few years ago, I would often greet my eager and spiritually aware audiences with a trick question. I would ask, "How many of you believe you have a soul?" Almost unanimously hands would rise to the affirmative. Suddenly faces would sink, as I coolly said, "No...you don't." After a moment's pause, I would redeem their confidence by proclaiming, "You ARE a soul!" Using that as a prelude, I would now like to suggest that you respect the experiences of your life as something you **are** rather than something you **have**! In light of this, please do not confuse your **feelings about** your experiences with the experience itself. This is not a suggestion that you should BE your regrets, your disappointments, or even your satisfactions. Suspend for a moment the conclusions you drew **about** your experiences. Be with your feelings as they are now, and yet ponder this: How could love be in a world that challenges its very presence? Could it be that love has dared to deepen its experience and extend its connections into those realms most in need of change and growth?

Compassion is the answer to the paradox of mankind. This is a word that literally means, "feel with". **Compassion is the key to life!** The beauty of compassion is that we may find the perfection of God intrinsically present in any situation, while at the same time there is allowance for learning, choice, and even mistakes. Life is a network of connections and opportunities for expansion, whether it is on the subatomic scale or in the more complex environments.

49

In the words of the Apostle John, "In the beginning was the word, and the word was with God and the word was God." Could the word have been anything else but "Love?" Then love set out to know itself in all forms. How much could love BE love, against how much challenge, against what odds? Thus the world of experience has ever widened and moved into complexity. As we seek meaning in these vast and endless connections, we move from the innocent "first word" to phrases with syntax and whole sentences of life. But the simplicity of it all is that Love – which is fundamental — is teaching us compassion through experience.

Inspirations

Chief Seattle (b.1786-d.1866) Native America:
>"How can you buy or sell the sky, the warmth of the land? …If we do not own the freshness of the air and the sparkle of the water, how can you buy them? Every part of this earth is sacred to my people. Every shining pine needle, every sandy shore, every mist in the dark woods, every clearing, and every humming insect is holy in the memory and experience of my people…. This we know: All things are connected. Whatever befalls the earth befalls the sons of earth. Man did not weave the web of life; he is merely a strand in it. Whatever he does to the web, he does to himself."

Heraclitus (lived c. 500 BCE) Greece:
>"Everything flows."

Marcus Aurelius (b.121-d.180) Rome:
>"Observe always that everything is the result of a change, and get used to thinking that there is nothing Nature loves so well as to change existing forms and to make new ones like them."

Applications

In these exercises, you will be creating what is essentially a portrait of your own life. You will accomplish this through examining the lines of flow, the patterns, and the relationships that connect you with your environment. Life always has patterns, and it flows most agreeably when these patterns are consciously chosen, or at least harmoniously accepted. Too often we feel there is nothing we can do about the patterns of our lives. Some patterns may seem to be fixed due to inheritance or tendencies of the physical universe. Those with whom we share life often respond to change very slowly because they are deeply embedded in social traditions. All that being true, life is still remarkably flexible, adaptable, and responsive to the choices and revisions we make. Were that not true on every level of existence from sub-atomic to human environments, the very concept of free will and the power of choice would be a mockery.

A. Examine your relationships in every major area or element in life. This is not an exercise of psychological introspection regarding your feelings **about** these relationships or your compatibility or agreements with them. There are no right or wrong answers. You have successfully completed this exercise when you are clearly and consciously aware of the flows, interconnections, and rhythms that are really happening in your life. Be the fisherman on the banks of your river watching the fish swim. Notice how they flow in patterns, how some get separated into shallow pools, and how they get out, how boulders block or accelerate the flow of water, and how logs on the riverbank give shelter, etc…

Here are some key focal points and questions to ask yourself:

1. FAMILY

Do you have meals together? Do you share activities and recreation? How do you communicate? Is individual privacy respected? How do you make your agreements? How do you settle your differences? What brings pleasure to each person?

2. FRIENDS

Do you have a small circle of close friends, or a large circle of social friends? In what circumstances do you most easily make friends? How do you show friendship to others? What do you most value in a friend? Are your friends an extension of your family? Do you mostly make friends at work or school? Are you drawn to people who are very different from you, or very much like you?

3. NATURE

What place does nature have in your life? How far is your home from the nearest park or open land? Do you have a pet? Do you have plants in your home? Do you ever walk, bicycle, or relax in a garden? Do you make a point of opening the windows to let in fresh air? How have you adjusted to the climate where you live? Do you watch the sunset or sunrise? Do you play?

4. HEALTH AND DIET

How is your sleeping and resting cycle? Do you eat on a programmed schedule or when you are hungry? Do you know when you are hungry? How is your breathing? How much water do you drink? Do you pursue any kind of regular exercise? How do you determine what you eat?

5. WORK

How many hours of a day does work consume? How does your work build or diminish relationships with your family, friends, and self? Is your work fulfilling? Does your work apply your abilities? Does it pay for your needs? How do you advance yourself at work? How do you respond to instructions? How do you supervise others?

6. SPIRITUALITY

How do you connect with God? Is spirituality part of your pattern of life? Are there special times you set aside for prayer, meditation or inspirational reading? Where do you find meaning in life?

Now you may choose additional areas where patterning is important in your life. Examples: creativity, study, recreation, etc. As you gain an overview of your life patterns, you will invariably discover that life functions best in those areas where patterns allow energy to flow freely yet agreeably with your nature.

B. Examine your boundaries in life. Boundaries are best dealt with when you consciously know what they are, where they are, and why they are. There are few things more disturbing than sleepwalking into a wall you saw in your dreams as a pathway! There are many boundaries that can be re-negotiated or removed, but few that can be ignored.

What are the boundaries in your life? Did you choose them? Did others place them there? Are they due to lack of resources or ability? Did you just fall into them by habit or through fear? Do they serve you?

Consider the nature of constructive, dynamic boundaries, which are like the riverbanks that contain and direct the flow of life without stopping it. Are there static, and limiting boundaries in your life that may be turned into dynamic ones?

C. In what area of life are you most free?

Meditation

This meditation is performed with your eyes wide open, in a listening and receiving mode … and most especially listening and receiving responses from within yourself. Choose a place away from your normal programmed behavior, preferably a place in nature. Sit with a straight back, poised, at ease, and attentive.

Begin to breathe deeply until your breathing patterns are smooth and regular. As you come into full harmony with this quiet state, ask this question on an out-breath: "What is this?"

This is not a chant or a statement with intellectual or symbolic meanings. Voice the words with innocent sincerity to bring on a state of unconditional "beholding". Do not keep this question in your head, but with the whole of your being ask, "What is this?" "What is this?"

The answer is not found in a thing, or in any physical place, on your breath, or even in empty space. You are asking, "What is this?" because you humbly surrender to what you **do not know**, and lay aside all your pre-conceptions about what answers may be revealed.

Ask this question on your breath until all other thoughts and distractions have ceased and you are in a state of innocent beholding. Once you are centered in this state, begin to notice what answers come in reply to your question. You may notice your head being turned, or your whole body may be drawn in a certain direction. Birds, animals, or falling leaves may appear with an answer. More than likely, thoughts, sensations, and emotions from within you will begin to appear. This is not the same as mental chatter, but fresh unexpected flashes of insight that would have been snuffed out by the "noise" and "filters" of your daily experience.

The question, "What is this?" is actually an antidote to distracting thought, for it will turn upon the thought itself to expose its true source or motive.

By truly and deeply asking this question without any limits to its application, you are opening yourself to the whole of experience, to the profound wonderment and awe of life.

When your meditation is over, move all body parts and "shake out" until your body is supple and awake. Move out of this experience into the world, but take your fresh and quiet awareness with you.

Prayer

Father Mother Source,
I humbly seek to be filled with Your love. May I be filled with the
Holy Spirit, and see the wonder of the cosmos.
May I see the immensity of all existence and discover
In my own being the power of love.
In respect and homage of the earth,
I would venerate her, and say:
You are beautiful; you are wondrous; you are
The majesty of creation.
From the Heart of God you were created.
From your womb all life has sprung.
All creatures of the air, land,
And water know you as Mother.
In the glory of God I behold you.
May the peace of God reign upon you.

And the Earth replies:

"I return this honor to you, that you may know your own creation.
Come to me in your peace and I will give abundantly to you.
Come to me in your joy and I will rejoice with you.
Come to me with your illusions, and I will give you truth.
Come to me with your pain and I will give you healing.
Come to me with your fears, and I will give you hope.
Come to me with all that you say you are and
I will give you who you really are.
My heart transcends illusion, and it knows
No limitation, no fear, and no end.
I give my body to be your home, and I receive you
Always with love."

Amen

5

Desires of the Heart

The Message

"The desires of the heart are not directed toward seeking that which you do not have or toward attaining that which is inappropriate for your life. Your heart sees beyond the illusions of insufficiency, for it knows the greater truth that everything you ever will have has already been given. The sacred heart of your being knows no sense of lack except to fulfill its relationship with God. The desire of your heart is to discover the hiding places of your wealth, and to make you joyful enough to receive it. Equal to that is its expression of gratitude for what you already have, including that which has not yet been attained or received. It is the pleasure of the heart to make you ready for your treasure.

"Do not be fooled by illusions of neediness which only make you more thirsty. Instead, strengthen your love by giving thanks for that which is yet unborn, and by singing praise even if the pain of life would make you cry.

"The game of life is to pierce the illusion of need. There is a special reality within every soul that contains a seed for growth and eventual harvest. As you cultivate this gift with love and faith, your heart will discern your bounty and unfold it in your life.

"You could not even conceive of that which has not already been planted in your soul as an eventual reality. So when you pray, do so in joy for that which has been promised and pray for guidance that your mind may work in harmony with your heart, to direct your life toward its fulfillment. Whenever you do this, you strengthen both *your faith and your integrity to know and attune your life to that which is truly yours. When you seek and pursue that which is not truly yours, you will develop a kind of hunger that cannot be appeased, and a deep sense of 'neediness', which distorts your life and creates dis-ease.*

"The root meaning of desire is 'of God'. And indeed, without the passion of desire, nothing is ever attained. However, this power has often been misunderstood. Desire is commonly associated with wanting and a longing for attachment and things of the world. This lower meaning is what all the teachers and spiritual masters of the ages have warned against. The wrongfulness of desire is not in the power itself, but in the way you direct it. When the heart is in its true desire, it has no need at all, only immense gratitude for what has already been given and a boundless desire to give in return. This is what I meant when I said, 'Seek first the Kingdom of God, and His righteousness, and all these things shall be added to you.' Only your heart knows your true desire. Only your heart can recognize your treasure when it appears. Only the heart knows that all of life is sacred and to enter the sacred is to pray. It matters not what you say, or how you arrive at the altar of sacred experience, or what beliefs you have. What is common to all sacred moments is surrender of the human condition to possibilities beyond estimation and comprehension. Through such faith and receptiveness, awesome wonders may be revealed and seemingly impossible deeds may be accomplished."

Correlations

Mark 11:23 "I tell you the truth; if anyone says to this mountain, 'Go throw yourself into the sea' and does not doubt in his heart, but believes that that what he says will happen; it will be done for him. Therefore I tell you, whatever you ask for in prayer, believe that you receive it, and it will be yours."

Luke 6:45 "A good man out of the good treasure of his heart brings forth that which is good."

The Key

The most common mistake we all make with regard to desire is defining or expressing our desires as emotional attachments or requirements. Every emotion is an indicator of our well-being on some scale of survival. While innocent direct emotions are as refreshing as a child, many emotions are conditioned, compulsive, and reactive. All emotions develop from some orientation toward need—or satisfaction thereof, and that brings us to the second most common mistake we make about desire. We justify our desires by attaching them to needs.

If desire is "of God", then in its truest meaning, it would have nothing to do with neediness, survival, or competitive achievements. The best way I can summarize Jeshua's teaching is that desire is the passion we feel for finding our place within the wholeness of a complete universe—a universe that has no insufficiency and nurtures its every part as if it were the whole. Desire would be the passion we direct toward receiving abundance and blessings that already have been set in motion through Divine provision. According to Jeshua, true desire actually begins with faith and expands through gratitude. As desire progresses in its cycle of fulfillment, it dissolves fear, lack, and need, and ignites the miraculous nature of a soul to transcend illusions of time, space and limitation.

Many of our great teachers and spiritual leaders have admonished against the perils of desire. And in fact, such warnings would be appropriate if desire were no more than the common "wanting" we feel for things of the world. The problem with wanting, needing, craving, longing for, and lusting is that all of these dispositions and intentions have their foundation in a belief that, without the sought for satisfaction, one is incomplete, insufficient, or bereft of fulfillment. The plight of "neediness" is that it not only perpetuates itself, but also amplifies itself, because any belief that one acts upon will multiply.

In saying this, there is no denial or disrespect of true and great need which many souls are suffering, and which compassion directs us to relieve. For indeed, once need has become a physical reality, we are called to join in a common and practical remedy. However, it behooves us to take a higher perspective and study the source of how needs evolve and grow into desperate conditions. Only as we have that greater understanding may we become the embodiment of a solution and not an additional participant in the problem.

Whenever Jeshua spoke of desire, he did so in a context of appreciating universal abundance and infinite potential. It seems that desire was a navigational tool that allowed him to direct the passions of his heart into their full realization. **The key to this is faith and understanding of universal wholeness and connection of all parts within the whole.** Desire activates potential that is already present though yet unknown or undiscovered. The most wasteful actions we will ever make in the pursuit of our desires are the efforts we make toward fulfilling our desire with acts of separation. Separation limits potential. Many people strive and work most of their days to establish a lifestyle that is set apart from what they do **not** want. The result of such activity is considered to be "desirable". However, this would be exactly opposite to what Jeshua meant when he spoke of the heart's desire.

Some desires of the heart may seem quite impossible if they are estimated only by existing external conditions. But once a desire is committed to faith, and strengthened by action, an immediate shift in external conditions begins to occur. This shift may be so subtle at first, and so indirect, that without faith one's desire might be abandoned. I am very fond of the following true story because it illustrates the often indirect but absolute fulfillment of desire.

This story is a legend of love, and there are many fictionalized adaptations, but apparently this is what really happened: Dr. Howard Kelly was a distinguished physician who, in 1895, founded the Johns Hopkins Division of Gynecologic Oncology at Johns Hopkins University. According to Dr. Kelly's biographer, Audrey Davis, the doctor was on a walking trip through Northern Pennsylvania one spring day when he stopped by a farmhouse for a drink of water. A little girl answered his knock at the door and instead of water, brought him a glass of fresh milk. He visited with her briefly, then went his way. Sometime after that, the little girl came to him as a patient and needed surgery. After the surgery, her bill was delivered and on it were the words, "Paid in full with one glass of milk."

Every good deed of our life is a resource payable toward the fulfillment of some future desire ... and this is well in addition to the immeasurable resources of the Creator. The key to that bank account is our feeling and expression of gratitude for what already exists, because in that ground of being we celebrate the wealth and fullness of existence rather than a dread of lack or fear of insufficiency.

Many times when we pray, or when we express our needs and wants in other ways, these requests are far removed from the foundational desires of our heart. In my conversations with Jeshua concerning the differences between illusion and sustainable reality, he made the comment that many prayers are pleas to *"save the sand-castle from encroaching tides"*. Such prayers cannot be answered directly or in the way that is asked, because the heart has no true desire to perpetuate failing illusions. When one knows this, and prays in true knowledge of what the heart desires, the love that has been heaped into collapsing sand-castles can be redirected into other more fulfilling venues. If our prayers are to be answered, it is imperative that we know our own hearts, for it is only through the heart that communion with God takes place.

Through contemplation of unity, love, life, respect, honesty, justice, and kindness (the dimensions of higher consciousness within the heart), we may clarify and refine our understanding of all existence—most especially our own. And yet it is not enough to gain understanding and be detached from it. To truly activate the powers of the heart, we must be willing to enter the place within us where the Highest dwells, and the sources of all nature are within the grasp of our consciousness. Within the heart, our Essential Being knows no distance between itself and the infinite heavens. There is no boundary in the soul where we (the effect) cease and God (the cause) begins. The immortal words of Ralph Waldo Emerson's great poem, *"Within Us,"* capture the essence of this truth:

> "Within us is the soul of the whole; the wise silence,
> The universal beauty, to which every part and particle
> Is equally related; the eternal One.
> When it breaks through our intellect, it is Genius;
> When it breathes through our will, it is Virtue;
> When it flows through our affections, it is Love."

To experience this place is a passion like no other. So intense is this passion that it can weave a dream into reality, bring Heaven to Earth, liberate the slave, heal the sick, and bring forth wonders never before dreamed. How do we enter this most precious and powerful of places? In responding to similar questions from his disciples, Jeshua told them the secret 2,000 years ago. His words were very simple and pure, but unfortunately, they have become so heavily encumbered with religious attachments and definitions that the graceful, transcendent emotion they convey has been virtually lost. The disciples were seeking attainment and gratification for their hopes and dreams, when Jeshua instructed: *"Seek you first the Kingdom of God, and all these things shall be given to you."* (Matthew 6:33) To paraphrase in modern words: "Seek the Kingdom of God—feel it, embrace it, express it, gratify it, and celebrate it with all your heart, and whatsoever desire that passion holds shall be given to you." This is **the key** to desire's fulfillment.

Inspirations

Kahlil Gibran (b.1883 - d.1931) Persia: *The Prophet:*
"For what is prayer but the expansion of yourself into the living ether? And if it is for your comfort to pour darkness into space, it is also for your delight to pour forth the dawning of your heart. And if you cannot but weep when your soul summons you to prayer, she should spur you again and yet again, through weeping, until you shall come forth laughing. When you pray, you rise to meet in the air those who are praying at that very hour, and whom save in prayer you may not meet. Therefore, let your visit to that temple invisible be for naught but ecstasy and sweet communion. For if you should enter the temple for no other purpose than asking, you shall not receive: And if you should enter into it to humble yourself, you shall not be lifted: Or even if you should enter into it to beg for the good of others, you shall not be heard. It is enough that you enter the temple invisible. I cannot teach you how to pray in words. God listens not to your words save when He Himself utters them through your lips. And I cannot teach you the prayer of the seas and the forests and the mountains. But you who are born of the mountains and the forests and the seas can find their prayers in your heart. And if you but listen in the stillness of the night you shall hear them saying in silence "Our God, who art our winged self, it is thy will in us that willeth, It is thy desire in us that desireth. It is thy urge in us that would turn our nights, which are thine, into days which are thine also. We cannot ask thee for aught, for thou knowest our needs before they

63

are born in us: Thou art our need; and in giving us more of thyself thou givest us all."

Applications

About fifteen or twenty years ago a movement began, which is now generally referred to as "Positive psychology." It was made credible and brought to public attention by Dr. Martin Seligman, a former President of the American Psychological Association. Today, many writers and counselors are focused on the subject of how to achieve happiness. The most powerful conclusions I have ever found are the ones that coincide with this Key of Jeshua, most especially the idea that happiness is a choice.

From the time we are children, we are conditioned to believe that happiness is the result of other choices or behavior patterns. Extensive research now reveals that other choices are actually the result of whether or not we first choose happiness. It has been proven through the ages that those who truly choose happiness can deal productively and creatively with just about anything in life ... good or bad.

1. As a Child of God you have been given the power of choice: Examine what you have actually chosen for your life. This is your compass, guiding all your decisions and actions.

2. Choose to create the life you really want: Assume responsibility for your actions, thoughts and feelings. Refuse to blame others for your unhappiness. Blame is just a way to avoid responsibility. Happy people don't see themselves as victims— regardless of their circumstances. They focus on finding solutions to their problems and ways to make their lives better.

3. Choose to look deep into yourself continuously: Assess what makes you uniquely happy, rather than accepting what others say should make you happy. It is an act of supreme kindness to yourself to look into your soul, identify your needs, aspirations, and passions, and decide, "Is this what I really want?"

4. Make creating of happiness important: Adjust your priorities to match your dreams. Do something every day that makes you happy. Don't automatically expect this from others. The only thing you should assume in life is responsibility for making your own life work.

5. Dare to admit your true desires to God: Then begin to find others with whom you can share your dreams.

6. Express gratitude for what you already have: Make a list of all the blessings in your life for which you have never expressed thanks—not only to God, but also to others and to yourself.

7. Ask to be the answer to someone else's prayer: When you contemplate this sincerely, others can be great teachers to you about desire.

8. Think about how another may be the answer to your own prayers: This will help you include others in what you desire.

9. Pray for another: This is not to impose your will on the lives of others, even for benevolent reasons, but to celebrate the reverence and joy that can be felt for the oneness of all souls in the presence of God.

10. The surest way to enter the Sacred Heart is to give thanks earnestly for prayers that have already been answered. You have many. Take stock. If you must revise your expectations of life in order to see them, then do it. This same process will expose your true desires, for God only answers the prayer of your true desires. Examine the nature of your answered prayers. This will allow you to better understand the nature of prayer.

Meditation

Be seated in a sustainable pose that permits deep and easy breathing. Relax your body and quiet your mind. Ask the innermost presence of love and spirit to fill every part of your being and prepare to receive the blessings of God. Inhale deeply and release completely. Repeat three times. Allow your fourth in-breath to expand into the energy field surrounding your body. As you release this energy breath, see it compress to a single point of Inner Light. With every in-breath, see the lungs expand. As this happens, notice that your entire energy field expands. As you draw in energy from the universe, every dimension of your body, being and energy increases in dimension. As you release and give back to the universe, your energy field compresses and moves into a different phase of power. In the next few breaths, observe the way your energy is expanded as you receive, and compressed as you release. Know that nothing is ever lost.

With every in-breath, expand the energy field around your body further and further. With every out-breath, experience the release of all effort to create or enhance anything that is not naturally present. Accept the blessings of this peace, and give thanks for the nourishment it brings.

As you completely accept the peace that is being received and relinquish all other needs, you will begin to perceive some filaments of inner light, a gentle glow, or even a spark of twinkling light at the center of your being. Focus upon this quality of light and allow your breath to include the light in its rhythms of inhaling and exhaling. Expand the light through your entire energy field when you inhale, and concentrate the light to a brilliant sparkle as you release on the out-breath. Continue this rhythm until it is natural and vivid. Then add one more ingredient—the expansion and release of the love that you are.

This is the eternal breath of your soul in which you need nothing except to know your oneness with God. There is no time and space. The breath of life, energy, and love is in perfect rhythm with the breath of light, which knows no time and space. Past, present, and future are one. In this breath of life, you may change your personal history by accepting and forgiving. You may choose your future by accepting and praising. Whatever your desire, it may be addressed in this free zone of time and space, free from attachments and need. Bring your true desire into the spark of light as you fully release, and see it expand into reality as you freely receive.

Prayer

I praise You, O Infinite God of all life,
All existence, and all goodness.
I thank You for sharing your life, and goodness,
So freely with me and making me one with You.
Help me to discover and nurture the treasure
You have already given, that I may find my place
Within Your rich abundance.
Teach me to respect the evolving nature of all creation,
That I may see every day as the answer to a prayer
And every prayer as the faith I pledge
For the coming of a new day.

Amen

6

INNOCENT PERCEPTION

The Message

"*When you can live each day as if it were your first and only day, you will enjoy innocent perception. On the other hand, if you decide about life before you look at it, or filter your expectations only through past experience, you cannot have a direct unbiased perception of what is before you.*"

"If true perception begins and ends with simple impressions, how can we establish credibility within complex ideas or constructs such as language...theories...formulas?"

"*Your question is directed to a real problem for mankind. The manifestations of reality around us are marvelous, but they are the final stages of creation ...not the means of it. If you study only the cycles of manifestation and consider them the result of prior manifestations, you will never find your way out of the labyrinth of illusion. Just because an object or function in life appears to be complex does not mean that your understanding of it must be. The secret is to look deeper, to a level of greater simplicity. When you observe manifestation as it is...neither adding to it nor subtracting from it...you may see the true order of creation and be freed from the perils of material existence.*

"*There are, indeed, cycles of duration and dissolution within physical forces, forms, and things. It seems as though physical reality has its own unbroken lineage from which forms emerge and then adapt to the next requirement for survival. What you see, however, depends on your perspective. For example, rocks are formed from molten earth and shaped by other natural forces. Our consciousness of them and their purpose in the order of things does not come from the consent of those prior forces. Their value exists in a dimension of consciousness that considers them TO BE. Had consciousness not perceived the value of rocks and connected them with other forms of BEING in a useful way, molten earth would have become something else. When you say that YOU ARE, then you BECOME...not the other way around!*

"All of man's illumined realizations began as innocent perception. One's learning progresses by way of simple verifiable perceptions. If complex concepts are to be taught, they must be reduced to simple images that are universal in meaning. For that reason, I often speak in parables—they contain a spark of timeless truth that adapts to the moment, place, and person.

"Imagine a vertical shaft of love, will, and light passing through all stages of creation, providing an axle around which manifestation expands horizontally. This power turns the wheel of life. Now imagine a hub embracing the axle, extending spokes of light in all directions horizontally. These are the developing realities of life. As these spokes extend out from the hub, reality becomes more complex. At the rim of the wheel, cause and effect grind upon the pavement of physical existence. When you study only the rim and the complexities of physical substance, you become trapped in the horizontal extensions and have no way of gaining altitude or higher perspective. Innocent perception allows you to penetrate the veil of these manifestations and experience creation as if it were all happening NOW."

"It has been said that our consciousness is shaped by our beliefs. Is this true?"

"There is actually a recurring cycle from perception, to consciousness, to belief, which in turn affects perception and consciousness. You are always experiencing something—new or old. All of reality has been given to you. Your willingness to receive determines what you experience. What you perceive is the gateway to experience and the catalyst for belief. You were created to be aware

and self-aware. You were also given free choice so there would be nothing slavish about your love of God or your perceptions of life.

"Although it is important to know and affirm your beliefs, I encourage you to develop faith beyond any limiting beliefs. When your beliefs are restricted by fear or founded on opinions and judgments, you will perceive little that is new. This causes a dwindling spiral of faith and consciousness. Fortunately, there is an alternative. Innocent perception becomes a way of life to those who seek in good faith to know life as it really is. Innocent perception is the heartbeat of freedom and the heart of a child."

Correlations

Matthew 5:8 "Blessed are the pure in heart: for they shall see God."
Matthew 19:14 "Jesus said: 'Let the little children come to me, and do not hinder them, for it is to the childlike that the Kingdom of Heaven belongs.'"
1 Peter 1:22 "Now that you have purified yourselves by obeying the truth, so that you have sincere love of your brothers, see that you love one another with a pure heart."

The Key

We as human beings are admittedly part of the realm of manifestation and yet we are redeemed by Spirit to have a higher and broader perspective whenever we choose. Often we simply forget to choose—indeed we even disclaim that the choice is ours. We take for granted the mechanical nature of our human perceptions and assume they are flawless—give or take the margins of age and health. The truth is, our perceptual machinery can give us a very distorted picture of reality. Without the guidance of consciousness, higher thought, and an abiding intention to pierce the veil of illusion, we can settle for convenient limitations and the prisons they bring. The "Flat Earth" belief is a classic example of that phenomenon.

A clinical illustration of our optical functions will confirm this in another way. It can be demonstrated that a small object will disappear at a certain distance from your eyes. This happens because the object has fallen between the two fields of foci sending data from your two eyes to your brain. Large objects and continuous fields with repeating patterns are "cloned" in the brain to create a seamless image. Instinctively we move our heads or approach our environments from different angles to compensate for this problem. How many times have you "lost" your keys only to find them moments later on the counter where you left them? When that happens, your brain has recorded the blind spot and "filled in" the continuous texture of the counter surface. You will not be able to see the keys until you return freshly with renewed vision. We must also be alert to the "blind spots" of our belief systems. All too often we exalt the light and fear the darkness of earth's shadow. Were it not for the evening sky, the noblest part of creation would remain unseen, and the stars in heaven invisible.

How then do we discover our blind spots and agendas of limiting belief? The answer is simple: With the heart of a child, the sacred child within. The great cellist Pablo Casals had a great passion for both children and music, appreciating the way both surrender their complexity to exquisite harmony in the presence of love. He once said: "Beauty is all about us, but how many are blind to it? They take a look at the wonder of this earth—and seem to see nothing. Each second, we live in a new and unique moment of the universe, a moment that never was before and will never be again. And what do we teach our children in school? We teach them that two and two makes four, and that Paris is the capital of France. When will we also teach them what they are? We should say to each of them: Do you know what you are? You are a marvel! You are unique! In the entire world, there is no other child exactly like you! In the millions of years that have passed, there has never been another child like you. And look at your body—what a wonder it is! Your legs, your arms, your cunning fingers, and the way you move! You may become a Shakespeare, a Michelangelo, or a Beethoven. You have the capacity for anything. Yes, you are a marvel! And when you grow up, can you then harm another who is, like you, a marvel? You must cherish one another. You must work—we all must work—to make this world worthy of its children."

The key to innocent perception lies in the spirit of discovery when we release our fixations and judgments about life and begin to explore it again with the freshness and wonder of a child.

Inspirations

The Buddha (c.563-483 BCE) India:
> "There is only one moment in time when it is essential to awaken. That moment is now."

Basho (b.1644-d.1694) Japan:
> "How I long to see among dawn flowers the face of God."

Rumi (b.1207-d.1273) Persia:
> "Let the beauty we love be what we do. There are a hundred ways to kneel and kiss the ground."

Ralph Waldo Emerson (b.1803-d.1832) England:
> "Will you not open your heart to know what rainbows teach, and sunsets show?"

Thomas Traherne (b.1637-d.1674) England:
> "Your enjoyment of the world is never right until every morning you awake in heaven, see yourself in God's palace, and look upon the skies and the Earth and the air as celestial joys, having such a loving regard of all these as if you were among the angels."

Applications

Innocent perception is the most natural and least complicated practice in life. And yet, in a complicated and unnatural world, it may require the most deliberate intention and focus to experience. In cultivating your practice of innocent perception, remember that it occurs primarily in a receiving mode with a neutral attitude. Begin by allowing yourself to receive. This includes everything from gifts, to nourishment, learning, feelings, sensations, ideas, help and love. For many of you, receiving may be more difficult than you thought it would be. In some cases, you may find that prayers you felt were not answered, **could not be answered,** because you would not receive.

We have been told there are angels among us, but we see them not. The first step to innocent perception is teaching yourself that ALL perception occurs through receiving. Were it not for input through the sense channels, the heart, the mind, and the body, there would be no perception at all. Do not take my word for this. Teach this to yourself beyond all doubt! Notice how your world brightens up when you allow yourself to receive anything, whether it is information, recognition, help, or love. In the receiving mode your perceptions are keener. There is a corollary that also needs to be observed: When you open your senses and BEHOLD, your receiving of everything else increases as well!

If you ever thought that receiving was selfish or self-serving, then I suggest that you reconsider that notion. Receiving allows you to give, and to better understand that which you would serve. The stream could not flow to the ocean except that it was first given water by the upland springs.

Once you have convinced yourself of the fundamental correlation between perceptions and receiving, then you may progress toward the next step of innocent perception. That is to receive without expectation. This is easy for children, but inherently difficult for anyone who has experienced life for very long. Not only have we developed habits, patterns, and attitudes, we also have filters through which we color our lives. We have scheduled needs and requirements to which we must shape our lives. We have limits of tolerance and risk, and most challenging of all, we have painful memories we hope to not repeat. It is asking a lot to receive without expectation, and it would be improbable for most people to move to this point immediately. Your safety in doing so, and the rationality of positive results, must first be established. To do this you will first need to recover, discover, or polish your ability to say "NO"—consciously, intentionally, and firmly to that which does not support your life. Once you are assured of your ability to refuse undesirable experiences, then it is safe to approach life with a primary attitude of "YES." It is an attribute of wisdom to use past experience and observations for making constructive decisions about the future. Unfortunately, most people say "No" to **prevent** an experience or perception, instead of saying "No" from WITHIN an experience once they have determined it is not desirable. For example, if a salesman comes to your door, the typical response is not to answer the door, instead of making a decision AFTER you know what he is selling. This is because you have not fully examined the common assumption that if you enter an experience, you are saying "Yes" to the entirety of it. Nothing could be further from the truth. You were created with free will and the ability to be conscious in all things at all times. Once you know that you can say "No" at any point **within an experience**, it will become easier for you to say "Yes" to more opportunities and open your self to the rich banquet of life. Only then can you begin to receive without expectation.

As you develop more understanding of this, you will find greater trust for yourself, for God, and the basic goodness of life. Without the willingness to receive, your perceptions will be limited to the narrow range of what you already have. Without trust, your perceptions will not be innocent. Develop the two fundamental behavior practices of receiving and trusting with discernment.

Then express and enjoy these abilities through such activities as the following:

1. While waiting in a public line, talk to someone around you and experience a new acquaintance.
2. Write a thank-you letter to someone.
3. Notice somebody's work or service and give a heartfelt acknowledgment of how this makes a difference for you.
4. Talk to a child and relate to his or her perceptions of life.
5. Let an animal tell you what it wants.
6. Recall your dreams and let them speak to you.
7. Write down a goal or dream that you have considered improbable, and for a moment accept it as possible. Write a script for it as if it were really happening. Play it out and then re-examine your feelings about it.
8. At work, let "what you are doing" really talk to you. It has a message. Listen.
9. Respond to some request instead of dismissing it with non-attention.
10. Act on something about which you have been procrastinating.
11. At home, consider the value of your relationships—not just the actions and words. There is a message.
12. In your prayers, ask for the will of God to be revealed in life and promise to listen.
13. In nature, ask for restoration and peace.

Expand this list with fresh ideas relevant to your own life.

Meditation

In a state of talking, we are expressing ourselves. In a state of listening, we are free to simply **be** ourselves. Both aspects are important and essential to a healthy state of awareness.

Communication itself is essential for conveying motion from one to another. However, listening is the more powerful part of communication, which balances and stabilizes the dynamic ever-fluctuating motion of the universe and life around us. It allows us to be ourselves in the midst of change. Listening allows us to **be** without having to become. Only by listening, can we see the motion around us without having to move into it. Only by listening, can we allow others to be exactly as they are without joining them in actions or expressions that are inappropriate for us. Only by listening can we intercept and redirect reactive cycles of action. Only by listening, can we see things as they really are. Not only do we need to listen to others and the world around us, but we also need to listen to our bodies, our daily habits, and ourselves. What are they saying to us? Most of all we need to listen to the voice of God.

The reason we do not listen because we are afraid to be moved—moved by emotion, moved by inspiration, or moved from our fixed positions. Often there is a history of upsetting, damaging, or unpleasant communication. Disturbing opinions have been forced upon us…not to mention deceptions. The damage, however, occurred not by listening to such things, but by not listening carefully enough to catch ALL that was being said! The moment we catch a disagreeable word, we tend to draw the curtains on hearing anything more and pass through the remaining passage of communication with our defenses up. In this state of defensiveness, we are operating with reduced consciousness and miss much vital information that lies behind the words. We become the unwitting victims of another's limited perspective on reality. Communication often reveals the impending presence of change or invites a possibility for it. When our intolerance for change is high, we often draw back from communication or attempt to steer it by talking. This is one of the most self-defeating habits many people have, because the fact is nothing increases one's prospect for directing change toward a beneficial result more than listening…not only with one's ears, but also with one's heart and total awareness.

Ordinary conversation can be meditation if you give it your complete attention and focus on the dialogue as if it were your breath of life. Be completely present in your conversation and observe each of the following instructions:

> Be attentive. Do not make mental lists of what you would like to say after your friend is finished speaking.
> Allow yourself to be moved.
> Be tolerant, and try not to react to the words or events that are being discussed.
> Be safe to talk to, and appreciative for an opportunity to listen.
> Be aware of how you were participating as a listener.
> When you respond, let your sense of courtesy and compassion lead the way.
> Notice your words. Are they fluid and natural or fixed and positioned?
> Notice your response. Is it rehearsed or spontaneous, appropriate or inappropriate for the moment?
> Are you speaking honestly but with kindness and respect?
> Can you disagree without disallowing? ○
> Is your response contributing to greater understanding?
> Is the dialogue moving toward mutual realization?
> When spaces occur in the dialog, and there is silence, is it comfortable? Can you relax into it as a different kind of communion?

As you progress in this meditation, allow yourself also to develop a conversational relationship with friends no longer with you. Then include your non-human friends, animals, plants, and vital activities. Most importantly, converse with God. Learn to develop your relationships as if they were each vital conversations. In fact they are just that! Allow your friends to become your teachers in the art of listening. As you become a master of listening, this skill will apply to everything in your life from cooking to prayer. When you are preparing a meal, you will listen to the ingredients, instead to telling them how to perform. You will listen to your family's needs instead of telling them what to want. You will listen to your own body and give it true nourishment. In prayer, you will listen to God, but not in passive submission. You will listen with a vital desire to understand, and respond with greater joy and consciousness, moving into the prosperity of life. Only by engaging in constructive conversations with patient diligence can we uncover what we most need to know.

Prayer

O Lord,
Take us to the place within
Where your wisdom is revealed.
Take us to the state of beholding
Where your wonders are made known.
Take us to where your light gathers
Upon the hills with the rising and setting sun.
Open our ears to your voice in the wind.
Open our eyes to the specter of eagles.
Open our minds to the healing of truth.
Brighten our nights with heavenly glow.
Brighten our hearts with moments of laughter.
Brighten our lives with Your love.

.

Amen

7

THE POWER OF PEACE

The Message

Two thousand years ago Jeshua came into a world much like our own. It was a world dominated by a large prosperous nation, resented by other smaller nations that were disadvantaged in one way or another. It was a world on the brink of change forever. In the face of many challenging decisions, it is imperative that all people have a better grasp of the universe in which they live. We are in such need today. Perhaps more critically than ever.

In the Book of Matthew, Jeshua is quoted as saying, *"Do not think that I came to bring peace on earth. I did not come to bring peace, but a sword."* This seemed so inconsistent with his character that I wanted to know if he really said it, or if perhaps there was a change of context, which significantly altered the original meaning. *"There was perhaps more lost in this translation than in most things I said. My true instruction was, 'I did not come to bring order and harmony to the outer world, but to bring peace to the heart of man.'*

"Your inner peace is the knowledge of who you really are. That is the power that cuts through the illusion of false reality and the conflicts contained within it. Using this power does not always result in immediate harmony or increased orderliness in the world, but it does result in the least harm to all and the most lasting state of peace for all to share. It is YOU that can know peace...not the world!

"*To prepare you for greater understanding, let me first remind you that your soul took its birth in a dimension of unlimited existence and potential, where joy, peace, and love were unending. If the whole of existence could be discussed in percentages, this original state of existence in which you were born would comprise about 99% of all that is. For the sake of simplicity, you may refer to this as the essence of Pure Spirit.   This is stated as a generality. Actually physical substance comprises less than 1% of existence. It is basically composed of stable configurations of energy emerging from chaos. Despite the orderliness that it presents to you, the physical universe actually has chaos — not harmony — for its foundation. If you do not understand this, then you will not know the correct (or respectively different) applications of science and spirituality.   And you will not know where to find true peace or even what peace is. In the dimension of chaos, which is the physical universe, order is brought out of chaos through structural integrations and harmonious alignments. This leads to predictability and growth.*

"*The discovery, development and management of these tendencies is the role of science, whether it is the science of physics, engineering, agriculture, politics, health, or government. Through the application of constructive effort, order can be brought to chaos and this is good.*

"*But this is not peace. Like vines in a rain forest, chaos always engulfs order in the physical realm, because chaos requires less energy to produce than order. Nature follows the path of least resistance and moves toward the greatest conservation of energy. Chaos is native to the 1% physical universe. That is the foundational power behind the second law of thermodynamics, which states that every process in the physical universe involving the transfer of energy is moving toward an increase in entropy.*

"*If you would have peace, you must invoke the power of Spirit where peace is native and sustainable. Only peace can remove you from chaos. Each soul is connected to the essence of peace, for that is where all souls took their birth. Peace is your connection with the 99% endless place of pure being. The doorway is your heart, and what is revealed there is the truest portrait you will ever see of yourself."*

Correlations

Job 33:33 "Hold your peace, and I will teach you wisdom."
I Corinthians 14:33 "For God is not the author of confusion but of
      peace."
Matthew 5:9 "Blessed are the peacemakers: for they shall be called
      the children of God."
John 14:27 "Peace I leave with you, My peace I give to you; not as
      the world gives do I give to you. Let not your heart be
      troubled, neither let it be afraid."
Ephesians 4:3 "Make every effort to keep the unity of the Spirit
      through the bond of peace. There is one body and one spirit
      … one God and Father of all who is over all and through all
      and in all."

The Key

The key to peace rests in understanding that it cannot be found in the world, but resides within oneself. Have you ever noticed that within your consciousness are many chambers, like rooms within a mansion? Each chamber is furnished and decorated according to the nature of thoughts, purposes, and activities generated by these areas of your being.

Peace is also a quality of space, and it is important to visualize it that way, for in fact peace infuses your being with the most unlimited space you will ever know. Like the hub of a wheel, the peaceful center of your being connects, balances, supports and integrates every other part of the wheel extending to the rim. Also like the hub of a wheel, peace is that which engages with the axle of power. Another way of understanding peace is to see it as the quality of infinity emanating from the Sacred Heart. Whatever image works for you is fine as long as you see that peace begins first within your being and only then extends outwardly to the environment.

The issues and evolutionary challenges of life invariably bring dramas to our doorstep. These dramas may be on the scale of international conflict or threatening environmental factors, but most typically our dramas come in the form of such things as flat tires and misunderstandings in the workplace. The scale of chaos matters not. Whenever it erupts, we are challenged to decide on our response.

Jeshua was diligent in teaching me about the power of peace as the only solution to chaos. He was also careful in teaching me about the difference between order and peace. The natural tendency of all physical substance is toward chaos—not order. Therefore, no matter how much order or structure we impose on the tendencies of physical nature, without constant support and correction, it will reverse to chaos. If order were our only tool for handling chaos, the battle would be endless and hopeless, **because order requires more energy than chaos.** A simple exercise in mathematics would confirm the gloomy prospects of such a process. No matter how much order we create, chaos continues to erupt through every crack that went unnoticed. Our experience with this phenomenon is what many have come to call "evil". To detest this condition is a justifiable emotional response, but not one that contains a potent solution, for in fact hatred and fear generate reactive and negative attitudes about life—not solutions to it.

† If we are to be **in** the world, but not **of** the world, we must learn the skill central to that ability. That is the power of peace. Except for peace, which comes from the Spirit, there would be no

end to chaos. Peace begins with a rediscovery of our own true self and a return to our home in the 99% existence of Pure Spirit. This 99% existence is not "set apart" from physical matter, but exists as the space between atoms and elements and the power that generates them. This is the supply for all creation and the breath of the Creator. God is one with reality—not apart from it. In the 99% existence, there is no conflict and no chaos. This is the master dimension, which we naturally occupy as children of God. According to Jeshua, this is the place where all peace originates. And then it extends into the world of manifest reality through positive presence, thought, action, and sharing. However, from the perspective of the physical domain, peace will always be something of a mystery.

Peace is a perspective, a place of being that each soul can choose to hold and unfold into the world. It is **not** something you find or establish outside yourself first and then adapt to fit. Much energy and futile effort has been spent in looking for peace that way. Jeshua taught me that there is no better way to find your true self than to earnestly seek the ways and nature of your own peace. For there is one certainty—you cannot find the peace of another soul. It might also be fruitful to consider that even chaos has a spiritual function of challenging us to seek peace first within ourselves.

True civilization comes from peace—not from order. In a post-industrial world with all the advantages of order, we often assume that tending to order will automatically result in creating civilization. Many believe Mahatma Ghandi to have been the greatest proponent of peace in the twentieth century. He **knew** the secret of peace and also knew that most others did not. When he was asked about Western Civilization, he said, "I think it would be a good idea."

There is a great paradox and love is the only answer. Even through love, the secret is still concealed if you view love solely as an action in the 1% of physical substance. Only when you can see

†LOVE as the great being and beingness of the 99% of existence does the answer begin to emerge. YOU ARE LOVE.

You alone, AS LOVE, can see both sides of the great equation of existence. I am a humble student of his teaching, and it is my greatest hope today to heighten and clarify that pivotal marriage of possibilities for you. I have witnessed some amazing occurrences that defy standard logic and yet each confirms the eternal power of love.

Jeshua taught his followers to respect the laws of cause and effect, and to know they were also a part of the realm of miracles! The heartbeat of his truth *always* has a two-part rhythm—respect for cause and effect and the actuality of miracles. There have been other masters who taught us various pathways to transcendence. You can enroll in the finest universities to study the laws of cause and effect. Jeshua combined these two seemingly contradictory possibilities in an amazing and powerful way: He taught us how to be *in* the world and not be *of* the world. He walked among us as an ordinary human being so that his teachings of extraordinary transcendence might be fully valid for our lives.

It is the most natural response on earth, in a practical context, to look for explanations of cause and effect in directing our lives. It is also the most natural tendency for a God presence—which you are—to expect a miracle. Here is where the challenge to common rationality lies. In many ways it is the core of Jeshua's brilliant and revolutionary message. He taught us to work simultaneously with these two dimensions of reality and integrate them into a more complete and fulfilling life. Putting these two perceptions together is where the challenge is! It's like tapping your head and rubbing your tummy at the same time.

As we look for our answers and pursue our mastery of life, it is so easy to become absorbed in one side of the equation or the other … thus missing the most rewarding step of all … connecting the two.

Love is the power of being that allows us to have the full and complete perspective. Where do we find it? We find it openly

declared within the 99% of existence. What does it feel like?
…PEACE! In the mystery of peace we discover the real power of
love. The answer to peace and the power of love are much the
same, for they resolve all paradox.

Inspirations

Rainer Maria Rilke (b.1875-d.1926) Germany:

> *Buddha in Glory:* "Center of all centers, core of cores,
> almond self-enclosed and growing sweet-all this universe,
> to the furthest stars and beyond them, is your flesh, your
> fruit. Now you feel how nothing clings to you; your vast
> shell reaches into endless space, and there the rich, thick
> fluids rise and flow, Illuminated in your infinite peace."

Ralph Waldo Emerson (b.1803–d.1882) America:
> *Essays. First Series. Self-Reliance:* "Nothing can bring you
> peace but yourself."

Benjamin Franklin (b.1706–d.1790) America:
> *Letter to Josiah Quincy:* "There never was a good war or a
> bad peace."

Applications

Peace can affect external conditions more profoundly than
any other condition of human existence. However, peace does not

begin externally. Nor does finding or creating peaceful surroundings attain peace. First and foremost peace is a quality of BEING experienced as a place within yourself. It will radiate from your heart and envelop you with an essence of grace that is not of this world. Then, and only then, does peace extend into the world to perform its transcendent miracles.†

The following exercise is designed to help you discover, recover, or strengthen your experience of peace within … and then to see its transforming potential. This process may be done alone, but it is probably easier to master if two or three work together as a coach and student team. That way the person doing the process can stay in a feeling and exploring state and not have to shift back and forth into a thinking state. After you've practiced once or twice, then you can do it without really having to think about anything. The object of this is to give you a full body, heart, spirit and mind association with peace as a state of being.

In this process you will be creating five spatial locations. Write each one of the following words on separate pieces of paper which you will place on the floor as spatial anchors (you'll be stepping on them). Arrange them in a straight line in front of you about eighteen inches apart in the order listed.

1. Past
2. Present
3. Desire
4. Beliefs and Values
5. Transcendence

1. Once you've laid out the papers in front of you, step in front of the "past marker" and think about any memories of peace you have stored in your consciousness. Be as specific and detailed as possible covering every area of perception and sensation. The more detailed the better. After you've thought of everything, preferably stating them out loud to someone else, step on the "past marker" and feel

yourself completely standing in the strongest and clearest moment of peace you can remember.

Something to honor: These feelings and perceptions are about YOUR state of peace, not what you should want, what the world needs, or what someone else wants for you. THIS IS ONLY ABOUT YOU. It is important that when you step onto each piece of paper, you be fully and personally associated into the feelings.

2. Still standing on the "past marker," think about that state of peace as a present time experience. Allow the wonderful feelings of peace to surround you NOW. Notice your breathing and all your senses and how they adjust to the feelings of peace. Take a minute or two for savoring. If you are with a partner in this exercise, share your perceptions. After you have fully experienced peace in the present, step on the "present marker," and feel yourself truly being there.

3. Standing on the "present marker" and feeling that space, next look at the "desire marker" and think about the peace you would desire in your own perfect world. Call to mind any feelings, capabilities, certainties, and freedoms that would make up your perfect world of peace. Then step in and feel the wonderful glow of that space for a couple of minutes.

4. Still standing in the "desire marker," look at the "beliefs and values marker." Consider first which of your beliefs and values support your desires for peace and which are blocking it. State out loud what beliefs and values you will have in your perfect world. Then step into the space and savor. Experience the transformational feelings.

5. Finally, while you are standing in the space of your highest beliefs and values, look forward to the transcendence this will bring to external conditions of the world. The feelings available in your transcendent space can rarely be described in words. It would be

best to step onto the "transcendence marker" and allow the feelings to overcome you. Then linger long enough to allow a metaphor to come forth for you, or perhaps a color, or a couple of words to describe your experience of transcendence. Experience the wonderfulness and magnificence of that space as fully and completely as possible.

You now have an integrated body-heart-spirit-mind experience of peace etched in your consciousness. This will allow you to relive the feelings you experienced any time you wish. The metaphor, color, or words that came to you when you were in transcendence can now serve as an anchor for you, and a trigger-point memory, so that you can easily immerse yourself in the essence of peace at any time. Repeat this often as a dynamic contemplation of life and invocation of peace.

Meditation

You may want to light a candle for this meditation. This is to remind you of the light of the Creator, ever present in all dimensions of life. It is also a subtle reminder that fire, like all light, knows no scarcity and expands through sharing.

It is important for this meditation that you find a comfortable chair or sofa that also supports your spine in an erect position. Relax your body, uncross your legs, arms, hands or feet, and breathe normally. Begin to associate your in-breath with the light of God symbolized by the candle. Exhale and associate that with a cleansing release of tension, stress, and worry. Repeat this breathing visualization until relaxation and revitalization fill your whole being. If possible, inhale through your nose and exhale through your mouth. Allow your muscles to relax one by one. Close your eyes and drift into the peace within.

With eyes closed, lift your head about 30 degrees and imagine that there is a soft golden light flowing in your direction. Receive this light and draw it in through the top of your head. Send it to your brain. Send it to the muscles in your face, your eyes, your cheeks, your tongue and your neck. Continue to focus on your breathing, and see this golden glow as the light of God supplied to you from the endless world of Spirit. As you exhale, release everything that is distressing, reactive, or not of the Creator. Allow this light to flow down your neck through the length of your spine. Invite this light to flow through your arms and legs to the tips of your fingers and toes. Continue doing this for a few moments until your body and soul are in complete harmony.

Now, I want you to find a comfortable and secure place somewhere in the storehouse of your mind, memory, or imagination where you are completely safe. This is your special place and it is unique for you. In this place nothing can harm you, touch you, or cause you to be less than who you really are. It might be a place from your childhood. It might be an imaginary sanctuary, a field by a river, or a nest of pillows by a cozy fire. You might be watching clouds from a mountain slope, or in your mother's arms as a baby. Whatever image generates security, safety, and protection for you is what I want you to project in your mind right now. Use all your senses to make this experience as real as possible. If you're in a field, feel the green grass, hear the crickets, and smell the lush soil.

Once you have fully arrived in your special place of security and safety, and know beyond a shadow of a doubt that nothing can harm you, savor the feelings of peace where no pain, suffering or danger can affect you. Everything is at peace. You are in harmony with the universe. God loves you and you are in love with all of life. Now look once more at the golden light within your mind's eye about 30 degrees above the horizon. Inhale its soothing glow. As you do this, imagine that curtains are opening to a stage in front of you. On that stage, there are players who will enact some challenge in your life that you need to overcome. This could be an area in your life where it seems like there is no hope, no chance of success. Please remember to keep this enactment only on the stage, and don't let it bleed out into your special place. Take a few moments to watch the situation unfold. Don't be afraid, because you are in your special place where nothing can harm you. It's safe to watch this situation as theater. After you've allowed it to unfold, as it exists for you now, I want you to bring the soft golden light into the stage. Focus it like a spotlight and watch it move the players around and re-create the drama so that now you see success instead of failure, and fulfillment instead of lack. Use this sacred light as if it were your director's baton, and watch the players change a situation lacking promise only moments ago to one that embodies complete fulfillment. Through this process, there is actual transformation occurring in your life, because you are reuniting the two most powerful forces available for your life—the light of God and the power of peace within. Steep yourself in the feelings of this union, and know that whenever peace unites with God, consent has been given for a change of script to occur in your life. Look once more at the perfect scene playing on your stage and receive it with expectancy and gratitude for what is possible through the union of your peace and the Creator's perfect love. Allow the curtains to close and melt into the light. Now return to the nurturing environment of your perfect place. Bathe yourself in the feelings you experience there, keeping those feelings with you as you slowly open your eyes. See the candle burning brightly in the room. A spiritual transformation has occurred. Now you know that in the presence of God and your own power of peace, any situation can be your special place.

$\mathcal{P}_{rayer}$

Oh, Holy One,

You are my calm within the storm.
You are my refuge from all harm.
You are my candle in the dark.
You are my heart's eternal spark.
You are the door that's open wide.
You are the guest who waits inside.
You are the stranger at my door.
You are the calling of the poor.
You are my hope through all dismay.
You are the light, the truth, and the way.
May Your peace prevail on Earth.

Amen

8

THE SACRED AND THE SPIRITUAL

The Message

"*There is an indivisible field between and among us all which is common to every being, every particle form, and energy manifestation. The connective resonance of this field and its generative power is what we call Spirit. This great Oneness accommodates every quality of lightness and heaviness, condensation and immateriality. Otherwise, how could it be everything? In its finest, purest, and most innocent nature, Spirit is the very presence of God, and that which we call Holy Spirit. Spirit is also the essence of life: it is the ether in which thoughts are passed, it is the facilitator of energetic potential, and the arranger of particles into forms and structure.*"

"Then how," I asked, "can the idea of complete unity be reconciled with sacredness, when literally the word 'sacred' means set 'apart', 'untouched', or 'reserved for the Holy?'" With some degree of struggle, I pondered this as I listened to Jeshua explain that one of the most common limitations in religions was the belief in God's separation from normal life and the denial of unity that One Spirit insures. "How do we find or know what is sacred?"

"*That is man's challenge—to recognize the sacred—even though in actuality it exists within every aspect of creation. When you look for the sacred you are seeking a special quality that you can recognize and experience. The soul desires to find a clearing within its field of awareness where it may behold the presence of*

God. In this clearing, the soul recovers sacred perception, and in some ways it is 'apart' from the normal flux of ever-changing experience, though God and Spirit are apart from nothing. Only in the higher truth of the heart may such a place be found. The difficulty you are having is that your attention is focused on physical things and complications of life. There are no obstacles within the spirit, even though it sustains all densities and complexities of matter and memory. Spirit simply IS—always! Spirit is the essence of 'being' and awareness. Like spirit, 'being' defines, and consciousness assimilates. However, the soul, in its quest for experience, ascends and descends the relative densities of consciousness like an elevator. Within this roller-coaster of worldly adventure, the soul can lose its sacred center.

"Like love, spirit has no opposites. Nevertheless, lower levels of consciousness, being attuned to mortal existence, will often look up to spirit as a remote state of peacefulness, harmony and resolve existing above the solidification of matter. It can appear that physical matter is the opposite of spirit. This is the logic that has led many to believe in the separation of spirit and substance. If mankind were destined to know only a lower level of sentience, this line of reasoning would be inescapable. Fortunately you are not limited to that. The way has been given for ascending to higher levels of life and knowing. In teaching you about the Sacred Heart and its higher intelligence, I am giving you a map to begin this upward journey. The Sacred Heart is the center of your soul. And now I reveal a secret to you: every being - whether it is the Divine Being, the being of the universe, or a human being - is a 'being' because it has a center from which to view 'the whole'. There is a unique quality to the exact center point of any whole that is like a wheel or sphere—it is the only part that influences all other parts equally in all ways, and yet is itself innocent and immovable. The center is that which is 'sacred'."

Correlations

Isaiah 6:3 "Holy, holy, holy is the LORD of hosts; the whole earth is full of His glory!"

I Corinthians 2: 9-13 "What no eye has seen, nor ear heard, nor the heart of man conceived, what God has prepared for those who love him, God has revealed to us through the Spirit. For the Spirit searches everything, even the depths of God. For what person knows a man's thoughts except the spirit of the man which is in him? So also no one comprehends the thoughts of God except the Spirit of God. Now we have received not the spirit of the world, but the Spirit, which is from God, that we might understand the gifts bestowed on us by God. And we impart this in words not taught by human wisdom but taught by the Spirit, interpreting spiritual truths to those who possess the Spirit."

1 Peter 1:15-16 "But just as he who called you is holy, so be holy in all you do, because it is written, "Be holy, for I am holy.""

The Key

Spirit is the dimension of existence that is beyond all the contexts to which the laws of matter, energy, time, and space would normally apply, and beyond the duration of cycles of action and life. Spirit can reach beyond itself to embrace any being without losing its own identity or integrity. It can summarize all the residual values of many lives and varied existences, without being fractured by diversity or overwhelmed by infinity. Spirit resides in sovereign simplicity and has proven its infinite and eternal capacity to endure beyond all contests of survival. An individual may view spirit as the greater part of the self that survives the perils of collective existence and worldly problems. One's spirit exists above, outside and beyond the life force, which is its active companion in the "game of existence". In life, work, meditation, prayer and self-examination the spirit is our Counselor. It is what verifies, confirms, and guides the truth of our lives.

There is no place, no dimension, and no experience in which spirit may be viewed as an external thing—an aspect of existence to be objectified. Spirit is in all things and exists as all things. Though we may not separate from spirit, or successfully view it as an element separate from anything else that it creates and sustains, we may deepen and purify our experience of it. Therefore, it is imperative that we consider both its presence in all things as well as an extra depth and purity within it, which we may know as sacred. For example, Jeshua was most deliberate in discerning the presence of God within the spiritual realm as the Holy Spirit. When we look for the element of sacredness, we are most definitely seeking a spiritual sanctuary and yet like spirit, the sacred seems to defy definition, resolutely holding to its sovereignty as the definer of everything else.

In preparation for writing this, and by way of comparing the new messages of Jeshua with traditional wisdom, I enjoyed some time reading through a wide array of books devoted to this subject. In many places I found wisdom and guidance, although greater knowledge was revealed through expressions of spirituality where "Spirit" was left to its own defining. Even Spirit does not speak about itself. The Apostle John relayed the eloquent words of the Master in this regard: "Howbeit when he, the Spirit of truth, is come, he will guide you into all truth: for he shall not speak of himself; but whatsoever he shall hear, that shall he speak: and he will show you things to come." (John 16: 13)

Jeshua and His Apostles are unshakably firm in their assurances of a Holy Spirit that renews every soul by its baptism and leaves no shred of ego in its path. If we add such a glorious promise to the fact that spirit is literally everywhere in all things, at all times, then the more curious thought would be, how can we

miss the presence of Holy Spirit? It was in response to such queries that Jeshua gave me the metaphor of a wheel and its center. *"There is a unique quality belonging to the exact center point of any whole that is like a wheel or sphere—it is the only part that influences all other parts equally in all ways, and yet is itself innocent and immovable. This is what is meant by 'sacred'. What distinguishes any conscious being from a simple flow of life is that a conscious being has a 'center of awareness' from which to view the whole. Ideally, as a being views the whole, it focuses outwardly toward infinity. But this is not always the case. Much of the time a being is striving so intently to 'be' whatever has captured its attention, that it is caught in the centripetal forces pulling in toward the center. When one is captured by a whirlpool, it is unlikely that any awareness or energy will escape the compelling situation. Unlike the centripetal forces of mortal existence, the Holy Spirit knows only the Heart of God and makes that sacred center available for the restoring of any soul."*

The key to our sacred center is natural equilibrium, which happens in complete relaxation. Much to our eternal good and our ultimate glory, there is nothing more demanding of surrender than Spirit—any aspect of Spirit, and most *especially* the Holy Spirit. As an artist, I am always amazed when my personal powers of imagination are transformed by a higher force that takes the "sketches of my mind" and breathes life, reality, and meaning into them. Invariably this happens when I relax all my personal anxieties and invite the Counselor of Truth into my heart and studio. Always we have a choice of where to focus, but I find that my focus returns to the true center of my being only when I surrender to the spiritual presence of a higher power.

Recently, as I experienced my mother's passing from earthly life, I was given a sacred vision and profound insight into the power of simply changing points of focus. The news of her impending death was too sudden to permit me to travel from Arizona to Texas to be with her, so I shared her transition to higher life in prayer and meditation. It was near sunset, and my husband and I went to the most special place we know in Sedona, synchronizing our experience with the passing of a day. As the sun touched the horizon, I allowed my spirit and powers of visualization to reach out over more than a thousand miles, and attempted to experience one last touch of her hand. Just as it seemed that I had been granted the warmth of contact, a light suddenly burst on the horizon and within it I saw a young and radiant image of my mother! At the same time I heard her voice speaking from the depths of my heart. In a loving tone to comfort me, she said, "Don't look for me there. Earth was the place of my issues and I have finished them for now. Heaven is my home. I will always love you and be with you, but you must now find a new way of focusing on me that we may continue in our love." In that split second, I consciously witnessed the choice I had been given, and I know the same choice has been given to all of us, in all things. We may focus upon the issues of our collective mortality or we may expand our outreach into infinity through the council of Spirit.

In our focus and outreach we are given unlimited freedom, except that we are bound to the consequences of our choice. For most of our lives, it is the bane of our existence to live out the consequences of what we have already chosen. Though we may toil, serve, and pray, it seems that the vote has been made and the die is cast. Then we hope, plan, and scheme to reformulate our lives from a better vantage point. When nothing changes after all mortal efforts are made, most humans resign themselves to retire and enjoy whatever shreds of pleasure remain for the twilight years.

Fortunately, this is not the hope of life cast by Jeshua. That hope lies in a remembrance of the sacred—the Sacred Heart dwelling within each of us, wherein our connection to God is ever pure. Life is a vast and complex network of interconnected possibilities and consequences. The winding river of life may carry one through so many changes and complexities that one's personal life has become a solid and entangled knot of irresolvable issues. There is no knot, however, that the power of sacred centering cannot unravel. That one change of focus is eternally available to anyone, under all conditions, always. This is living equilibrium, however, and not the kind of inert symmetry that we observe it in objects and material substance. For the soul, sacred centering brings true liberation.

Inspirations

William Wordsworth (b.1770 - d.1850) England:

> *Lines completed a few miles above Tintern Abbey:*
> "A sense sublime
> Of something far more deeply interfused,
> Whose dwelling is the light of setting suns,
> And the round ocean and the living air
> And the blue sky, and in the mind of man,
> A motion and a spirit, that impels
> All thinking things, all objects of all thought,
> And rolls through all things."

Kahlil Gibran (b.1883 - d.1931) Persia: *The Prophet:*

> "Your daily life is your temple and your religion. Whenever you enter into it take with you your all. Take the plough and the forge and the mallet and the lute, the things you have fashioned in necessity or for delight. For in reverie you cannot rise above your achievements nor fall lower than your failures. And take with you all men: For in adoration you cannot fly higher than their hopes nor humble yourself lower than their despair. And if you would know God, be not therefore a solver of riddles. Rather look about you and you shall see Him playing with your children and look into space; you shall see Him walking in the cloud, outstretching His arms in the lightening and descending in the rain. You

shall see him smiling in flowers, then rising and waving His hands in trees."

Applications

The following chart is a summary of many teachings of Jeshua—both ancient and modern—as well as the guidance of Holy Spirit, and my experiences in living. This is a map of spiritual descent into physical terrain. We are each living for the sake of earthly experience, and yet we are simultaneously infinite souls. This has made for an interesting journey and an endless challenge.

The centerpiece of this diagram shows our descent into mortal existence as a narrowing point of increasingly focused perspective. As that happens, certain attributes of character and likelihood increase and others decrease. Then, as you return to an expanded vision of infinite potential, the other set of attributes and possibilities begins to prevail. In the center of the diagram is the sacred cord. It connects all levels and marks the place where serenity may be attained. Sacredness may be restored to your life no matter how deeply your point of focus has immersed into the earth. It is recommended that you study this diagram and find your life's map within it.

Infinity

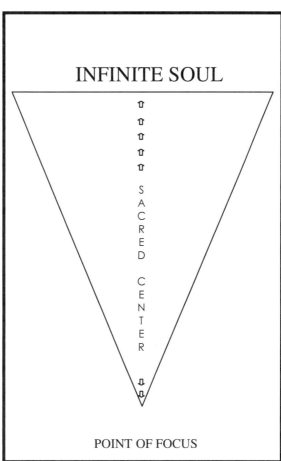

PEACE
SERENITY
JOY
FREEDOM
FORGIVENESS
UNDERSTANDING
UNITY
LOVE
LIFE
RESPECT
HONESTY
JUSTICE
KINDNESS
TRUE SELF

INFINITE SOUL

LESS

MORE

S
A
C
R
E
D

C
E
N
T
E
R

MORE

LESS

CHAOS
CONFLICT
CONDITIONS
BOUNDARIES
DISTRESS
SEPARATION
FEAR
DISEASE
ABUSE
DISTRUST
JUDGMENT
PAIN
IDENTITIES

POINT OF FOCUS

Some Signs and Symptoms of Inner Peace

- ❖ A tendency to think and act spontaneously rather than on fears resulting from past experiences

- ❖ An unmistakable ability to enjoy each moment

- ❖ A loss of interest in judging other people

- ❖ A loss of interest in interpreting the actions of others

- ❖ A loss of interest in conflict

- ❖ A loss of ability to worry

- ❖ Frequent, overwhelming episodes of appreciation

- ❖ Contented feelings and sense of unity with others and nature

- ❖ Frequent attacks of smiling

- ❖ An increased susceptibility to the love extended by others as well as the uncontrollable urge to extend it

- ❖ Much joy and happiness

Meditation

Sit or recline in a truly comfortable position, then stretch and relax. Inhale deeply and prepare to be at peace with yourself. Imagine yourself as an aspect of God's love. Now, extend your heart, mind, and soul as far as you can, and **contemplate "all that is"**. In this act of beholding, be content, and know yourself as a unit of one. Once you have done that, then receive and imagine **"all that is" contemplating you!** Whether or not you are conscious of it, this is an eternal dialogue existing between you and the one spirit for the whole of eternity. Now, envision that for every being in the entirety of existence! This dialogue of 'the one' and 'the all' is a never-ending rhythm of life. There are only rhythms of giving and receiving, speaking and listening, teaching and learning, advancing and receding, appearing and disappearing. **There is no separation!**

Prayer

Oh Christ, You are the Beloved Light,
The Radiance that illuminates all of creation.
From you, all images have sprung forth,
You are the Solar Logos, the Divine Intelligence,
The Presence in all images, all beings.
You are the Pure Self, living in each one of us.
We pray today to receive instructions, revelations,
Visions, love, and healing from You.
We seek to serve and walk with
You in this world and hereafter.

Amen

9

BELIEF: THE PATHWAY TO ATTAINMENT

The Message

"*True belief is a kind of knowing which invokes total certainty and complete conviction in your heart and your soul. Not everything a person hopes or professes to believe is truly believed. When beliefs are sustained only by agreements and doctrine they can be persuaded to change with either crisis or opportunity. Look at history. The creeds of men have changed like the seasons.*

"*Understanding the true power of belief will bring mastery to the frontier of human attainment. In actuality, belief and your willingness to receive are two sides of the same coin. Ask yourself about the causes behind what you have already received, and then what you will allow yourself to receive in the future. These are questions that will unlock the chamber of your* **true** *beliefs. Belief is a present time centering between past and future receptiveness. Only when you receive a change in your heart and soul, will your future be any different from your past.*

"*You can be conditioned to expect many things, both positive and negative. There are three enduring certainties around which all positive belief develops. The first and most powerful is your connection with God. The second is an honest knowing of yourself. The third is that you shall receive as you have given. When you take these three points of knowledge into account, you will experience renewed certainty.*" Naively, I inquired, "If belief is certainty, why do we associate belief mostly with faith?"

*"Belief is certainty expanding **beyond** itself. Once you have two or three points making a line, the line may continue into infinity. There is always an element of faith, however, because you do not know what the line will encounter as it moves forward or how it will relate to other lines of possibilities. Even among friends there are different practices and aspirations for life. Even though all of life is integrated and correlated from a higher perspective, you may have feelings of uncertainty or confusion when things do not happen exactly as you hoped or expected.*

"When your beliefs are centered on love of God, knowledge of self, and understanding of the principles of giving, sharing, and receiving, then faith will carry you through all obstacles to the fulfillment you desire. When your beliefs are only for self, created by worldly desires, built around formulas, and conditioned by others, no amount of faith will make your life whole. Such beliefs are not founded on anything enduring or interconnected with the ultimate power of life. Faith will not change that. So in achieving greater fulfillment for your life, the place to begin is with a greater understanding of belief. Once you understand your beliefs and apply them more masterfully, your faith will have a rock on which to stand."

At that moment I felt a pang of insecurity and followed a sudden urge to retreat into a private sanctuary where I might do an inspection of my beliefs. But he caught me before I could escape.

*"There is nothing in your life that is not the product of some belief. Your soul is not lacking in belief. If you would know your beliefs, look at your life. What is lacking in everyone is a masterful understanding of how to **steer** belief toward greater fulfillment. Most of your beliefs are actually unconscious and hidden beneath a superficial layer of dreams, wishes, and prayers that you offer up to God, family, or friends in hopes of making them come true."*

He was right. I had overlooked the fruits of true belief, and focused on areas of common agreement that I had expected to materialize through support from others. At that moment, I realized that I needed help with beliefs more than any other aspect of spirituality. All too often I had confused my wishes with beliefs. At the same time, the things I "knew that I knew" were confirmed only by logic and lacking in passion. A higher awareness had now been awakened in me, and I felt a deep sense of longing to know what I had forgotten or perhaps never fully known. My eyes pleaded with him and with all my soul I asked, "Could we start at the beginning as if I knew nothing and rebuild the foundation of my beliefs?" He seemed to savor my readiness, paused and then spoke.

"In order to return to innocence we must dismiss the first idea that the power of belief has anything to do with wishing, hoping, projecting, or affirming desires that are not appropriate and meaningful to the nature of your being. Each individual is unique in his or her own way, and that uniqueness grows in relation to God and others through the convictions one has about life.

"The second idea that has to be dismissed is that belief is an affirmation about life offered against a backdrop of doubts and uncertainty. Your certainties ARE your beliefs. If you had only uncertainty, you would have no beliefs. On casual observation, you might think that to be the case with many people. However, it could not be true. Without belief, no one could exist. But not all beliefs are positive. Not all beliefs are noble. When uncertainty colors the surface of anyone's life, usually the certainties can be uncovered on a deeper level of consciousness, embedded within beliefs that are not positive enough to give abundance and fulfillment to life. Yet the soul clings to those negative beliefs with strength and firmness. This is where honesty about self and forgiveness of others are essential to the progress of life. Negative beliefs cannot change without that.

"The third idea to dispel is that the act of belief somehow has a magical power to create what does not already exist. God is the creator of all things, and everything already exists—at least in seed form. For you, nothing exists until you receive it. At times this phenomenon shows up dramatically. Something you would not receive may literally be invisible, and you would swear it was not existent or even in the

*range of possibility. Then it 'mysteriously' appears for you the moment you are truly ready to receive. This is the anatomy of miracles—the spontaneous appearance of that which was already given but unavailable until the moment you could receive. Many times it is necessary to release a negative consideration or doubt before you **can** receive.*

"Belief is essential for existence; therefore you will always believe something. In areas of experience and consciousness where you have already created negative beliefs, adding a new positive one may only balance out the negative effects, but generate no positive change. This is the vacillation of doubt. It is a common and unfortunate cycle, which fosters discouragement and reluctance to master the power of belief. There are only two ways to overcome the frustrations of doubt. One is to discover and release as many negative beliefs as you can. Simply DO IT with courage and resolve. The other way is to earnestly restore your understanding of what belief really is and reinstate it to a true and firm foundation. This recovery begins with certainty of the Creator's everlasting presence and abundance, then progresses into knowledge of yourself and your place in life, and eventually develops into mastery over that which you can and will receive.

"The Creator is your boundless and eternal supply. No limitations or scarcities were ever constructed into the order of existence by God. Only man, and other species and elements of life, sought for definition through creating boundaries and proprietary structures. In the beginning there was everything, but it was void of pattern, form, and purpose. The original state of existence was like a table too full of food for anyone to sit and dine. By exploding this endless potential into infinity, it became possible that form, pattern, purpose, and individuality could emerge and then create the endless possibilities of life. Your infinite supply is still endless. The barriers and scarcities you encounter in life are from agencies other than God. And they stem from your first pillar of belief, which was about your personal limitations and those you impose for others. Ask yourself, 'On what foundation do I base my certainty about freedoms and boundaries that are real and constructive?'

"This brings us to the second pillar of belief, which is self knowledge—most importantly the knowledge of your heart and the nature of your love. If you knew yourself as well as the Creator knows you, all disparity between your beliefs and the will of God would disappear. You have only one true need and that is to advance toward the greater fulfillment of your soul. Most of what you think you need is the result of separation from God, unknowing of yourself, or mismanagement of cause and effect. Second only to God, you are your own constant factor for eternity. In knowing yourself, you are in touch with your reason for being.

"The third pillar of belief is composed of the laws of giving and receiving. As you give, so shall you receive. This is a powerful truth that has had a deep impact on everyone's ability to believe in God, in themselves, or anything else. When you would not like to receive back the likes of what you have given, or when you would set yourself as another's judge, you close the doors to your own receiving. It is not necessary that you give to others the same thing as you would seek to receive, for what would be the point of sharing? In some cases, the expectation of exact exchange would violate respect. Each person has different needs and desires. It is only necessary that you give freely, abundantly and benevolently enough that you may lose your attachment to results. Leave the matching of consequences to God and the natural order of life.

"Sharing and consideration of others is essential to receivership. Nothing moves, changes places, or applies its value to life except through the circulation of energy…despite the fact that things of the world seem to be solid. Indeed, everything IS energy. As you understand this, your beliefs will correlate more with reality. Circulating energy is the way of life. Paradoxical as it may seem, water does not become clearer by resting. Still water becomes stagnant very quickly.

"To receive, there must be openness and circulation of energy, and this begins with you. Charity—or lack thereof—is the measure of your belief. This is why charity is above both faith and hope, because it is the confirmation and energy of your beliefs.

"There is also an emotional equivalent to receiving, and that is gratitude. Gratitude is such a powerful emotion that you can magnify all your beliefs and bring them into present realization through praising gifts even before you receive them. True belief does not withhold gratitude until uncertainty has been eroded and resistance has been overcome. Those are the characteristics of disbelief. True belief knows the gift in the same moment as the belief is formed! The feeling is one of immense gratitude. Let me give you a simple example of gratitude exploding at the moment of expectation. Remember a time when you were parched and thirsty. When you saw a glass of water you were elated even before you drank. As you drank, the gratitude became even stronger. After you finished and felt satisfied, your emotional response to the water became one of indifference. At this point you might retain a **concept** of gratitude and appreciation, but you would no longer emotionally feel it.

"The gift has already been given. It is up to you whether or not you receive it—or how you receive it. Little do you know that the formation of your beliefs is a direct, though usually unconscious, response to preexisting possibilities. If you are responding to these possibilities with uncertainty, resistance, and unworthiness, then their fruits may come to you in the form of chaos, and your worst fears may also materialize. If you respond with expectancy and gratitude, you connect with the reality of God.

"There has been great competition in the world to hold and defend the champion belief. The champion is any person who knows his own beliefs and can base them on certainty of God, the truth of his own being, and the principles of giving and receiving. Shallow beliefs are not worth the effort. Those beliefs that run deep and are full of certainty will surely come true, whether they are positive or negative. Certainty is the soul of belief."

Correlations

Psalms 145:16 "Lord you open your hand and satisfy the desire of every living thing."

Luke 6:45 "A good man out of the good treasure of his heart brings forth that which is good;"

Mark 11:24 "Therefore I say unto you, whatsoever things you desire, when you pray, believe that you receive them, and you shall have them."

Mark 9:24 "Lord, I believe; help thou my unbelief."

The Key

Belief is the key to existence. Therefore, you will always believe in something. To gain mastery over your beliefs, you must answer honestly two questions:

1) What do I believe?
2) On what foundation do I base my certainty?

It is interesting to note that much current research confirms the fact that beliefs held with complete certainty can and do override common reality. This, of course, is the nature of miracles. Dr. Herbert Benson, founder of the Harvard Mind/Body Medical Institute, along with other esteemed researchers, have also revealed numerous instances where a mysterious factor called "belief" seemed to contribute to a patient's recovery. The power of belief may also show up in strange and undesirable ways. Scientists at Princeton University conducted research for eighteen years on the relationship between beliefs and the control of machinery. Their findings revealed that mastery and mishaps alike were affected by beliefs, and strangely, the relationship between belief and results was stronger than assumptions could predict.

✝ I asked Jeshua, "On what, then, do we base our certainty"?

"The most common base for man's certainty is experience. If experience were the only source of certainty, or the most powerful one, there would be little hope for anyone to escape the treadmill of chaos and mortal existence. Fortunately, there are powers much greater than experience, and as you develop your certainty in those greater powers, you will form beliefs capable of fulfilling your life and bringing experiences that are more positive into your life.

✝ *"These are the powers you find in your heart: unity, love, life, respect, honesty, justice, and kindness. God has given all of these powers to you, and they comprise your eternal link with the Creator. How each person receives and uses these powers is unique as a fingerprint. Even those who have no conscious awareness of a relationship with God—including those who deny it—are guided by these powers and derive certainty from them.*

✝ *"There is a complete circle within Divine order. Only through knowing the powers of the heart can you know yourself beyond the human, historical, and mortal context. You cannot know the powers of the heart without knowing God. In this knowledge of God, you may arrive at complete certainty and transcendence beyond the limitations of doctrine or the conflicts that often arise between doctrines. Only* **concepts** *about God are ever in conflict, and most often when a person claims to disbelieve in God, it is only a programmed concept that is being abandoned. Human beings are actually 'hard wired' to know God, and one's link to the Creator is so indelible that a person can only diminish that presence by turning down the heart's volume to a bare whisper. Even then, the Creator is present. It is your own consciousness that has turned in another direction.* ✝ *God IS…regardless of which concepts you use for describing the Divine."*

Inspirations

John Addington Symonds (b.1840 d.1893) England:
"No seed shall perish which the soul hath sown."

Oliver Wendell Holmes (b.1809 d.1894) America:
"God! Thou art love! I build my faith on that."

James Russel Lowell (b.1819 d.1891) America:
"The only faith that wears well and holds its color in all weathers, is that which is woven of conviction and set with the sharp mordant of experience."

Aescheylus (b.525 d.456 BC) Greece:
"It is not the oath that makes us believe the man, but the man the oath."

✝ Kahlil Gibran (b.1883 d.1931) Persia:
"And a man said, speak to us of self-knowledge. And he answered, saying: Your hearts know in silence the secrets of the days and the nights. But your ears thirst for the sound of your heart's knowledge. You would know in words that which you have always known in thought. You would touch with your fingers the naked body of your dreams. And it is well you should. The hidden wellspring of your soul must need rise and run murmuring to the sea; And the treasure of your infinite depths would be revealed to your eyes."

Applications

It is the natural tendency of any soul, being love, to gravitate toward its own fulfillment, toward a stronger and more meaningful relationship with the Creator, and to share more fully with others. When this is not happening easily, there are negative beliefs interfering with your ability to establish and maintain a positive direction. Wherever possible, it is beneficial to discover any negative beliefs you may have and release them. However, there may be too many, or they may be too deeply submerged, to find and release all at once. A simpler, more direct approach is to focus upon the beliefs you currently know you have and pass them through a four-point test. Ask yourself:

1) How does this belief strengthen my relationship with the Creator?
2) How does this belief reveal and enhance my own true nature?
3) Is it an appropriate belief for who I really am?
4) How will this belief enhance my sharing with others?

The process of simply asking these questions will strengthen your mastery over the power of belief. That in itself will subtly weaken all negative beliefs (which have no true foundation) and subtly strengthen your positive beliefs, which are based on these points of strength.

Meditation

I invite you to enter for a moment into sacred time and space, into a way of seeing that is broad and spacious. See this day, from the time you arose in the morning until you sleep this evening, as a celebrated event, divided into small and familiar rituals. Your Heart is the altar.

As part of the cycles of light and dark, you now begin to see your life from the moment of your birth until the time of your death as one long, continuous ceremony. It is filled with many rituals—some familiar, some unknown, and some challenging. Your home, your relations, and your occupation are the altar.

Through the many seasons and cycles, you now see this ceremony of your life as a much larger pageant extending seven generations into the past and seven more generations into the future. Many births and deaths and uncountable creations are part of this. The beautiful spinning earth is the altar, and you are part of its great ebb and flow.

Now, stretch your imagination and envision the total pageant of your life to be one small part of a greater ceremony, so grand, so magnificent as to be hardly comprehensible. There is an immense ceremonial circle, rich and vibrant with millions upon millions of swirling planets; and you, as one of the sparkling lights, are a candle in the Heavens. This is the altar of the universe. Here time is eternal, and you know that all of existence is sacramental.

Inhale the sweet fragrance of ancient love and the budding innocence of unborn spring. This is the moment of true belief, where—in reverent surrender—all is forgiven and all is reborn.

Prayer

† Challenge us, O God,
When we are too well pleased with ourselves,
When our dreams have come true
Only because we have dreamed too little,
When we arrived safely
Only because we sailed too close to the shore.
Challenge us, O God,
When with the abundance of things possessed
We lose our thirst for the waters of life;
When having fallen in love with life,
We cease to dream of eternity;

And when in our efforts to build a new Earth,
We have allowed our vision of the new Heaven to dim.
Challenge us, O God,
To dare more boldly, to venture into wider seas
Where storms will show our mastery;
Where in losing sight of land,
We shall find the stars.
We ask You to broaden the horizon of our beliefs;
And to push our lives into greater strength,
Courage, hope, and love.

Amen

10

THOUGHT AND CREATIVITY

The Message

Thought is a fascinating subject with many facets. At times we use it to scan memories. At other times we search in thought for unexplored possibilities. Occasionally we are blessed with a "bright idea" that seems to come from nowhere, like a shooting star. Thought can be the soul of inspiration, the analysis of data, or the summation of experience. Thought is a powerful, adaptable, and elusive force—ever seeking to manifest the choices we make. In some cases, if we allow it to take on negative values full of prejudice, malice, or deceit, thought can be an instrument of demise. Thought can be an angel or a monster, depending on how we use it! As I considered these many aspects of one power, I also wondered about its relationship to creation. "What is thought? Does it create ... or merely expedite? Jeshua's reply went far beyond my question."

"Thought is your inner response to inevitable forces. I say 'inevitable' not because they cannot be changed, but because these forces of life have already been set in motion by actions and intentions prior to thought. Thought is God's gift of reason to you that you may estimate the consequences of your actions, formulate revisions, expand them, or simply direct their course. Thought is not the germ of life which brings forth fruit. True creativity is the presence of God within, responding to the opportunities of existence. Through the power of will, actions are set in motion from a depth of being unfathomable even by thought.

"*Thought is vital to creativity, in that it provides a means to rearrange the patterns of your life—to change or consent to them. Thought is part of freedom and free choice. Without it, a soul is locked into endless patterns of unconscious stimulation.*

"*The creative product of thought is consciousness. Thought develops and activates consciousness, which in turn allows you to make pro-active connections between learned experience, broader awareness, and developing possibilities. Thought is your link between the two worlds of finite material existence and the infinite world of creative expansion. Knowing how to think and reminding yourself TO THINK are essential attributes of positive living and the development of higher consciousness.*

"*Creativity results from the complementary balance between thought and will. Thought is what makes connections. Will is what impels you to* **seek** *connections. Will is a kind of 'pre-thought' energy that is moving and carrying your life. It is actually a high frequency sound wave simultaneously containing life, intent, and creation. It springs from the core of your being, far beyond definition or conceptual description. Will shows up first as an impulse, action, or experience, and is often disregarded because of its subtlety. Then thought brings will into focus. Will is the raw power of creativity, and thought allows it to be examined and developed or revised. The key to creativity is the application of thought to elevate the will.*

"*Using thought to refine and manage the will is crucial to your quality of life. It is also essential for your creative vitality that you respect the direct connection between will and your Divine Source. Keep it holy. Creativity is life's yearning to be like its Creator. Thought searches out the nature of that inevitability and directs it toward fulfillment.*"

Correlations

Isaiah 14:24 "The Lord of hosts has sworn, saying, Surely as I have thought, so shall it come to pass; and as I have purposed, so shall it stand:"

Amos 4:13 "He who forms the mountains, creates the wind, and reveals his thoughts to man, he who turns dawn to darkness, and treads the high places of the earth, The Lord, The God of hosts is His name."

Matthew 6:34 "Take therefore no thought for the morrow: for the morrow shall take thought for the things of itself."

Matthew 10:19 "But when they deliver you up, take no thought of how or what you shall speak: for it shall be given you in that same hour what you shall speak."

The Key

The key to creativity rests in the power of thought and thoughtfulness. One of the most important distinctions in human behavior is the difference between proactive and reactive living. Proactive behavior stems from having a positive goal in life monitored by thoughtfulness. Reactive behavior is a stimulus-response mechanism generated by advantages or threats to survival. Although Jeshua did not use these modern psychological terms, it has become clear through study, meditation, and further communion that he was giving us the foundation for proactive living. If we center our intentions on the wellspring of love within; if we follow life and the living; if we seek to do the right thing; and ceaselessly forgive; then we only have to add one ingredient to have a fulfilled proactive life. That one ingredient is thoughtfulness. Often the fine line between success and disappointment is the brief moment we pause to think about our actions before doing them. On the other hand, for the sheer lack of thoughtfulness, a subtle shift can occur in the context of a situation, which causes it to become reactive. The negative side of any situation could result in consequences that are catastrophic. This shift would be ignited by ego-defensive behavior, which is essentially destructive, competitive, and intolerant.

What is so important about thought is that it links our actions meaningfully with the contexts in which they arise. Within any context, thought further searches out the links between creative possibility and the intentions we have of manifesting it. In all of existence, there seems to be a dialogue between content and context. In that regard, thought is the instrument of clarification, connection, and direction. The content of creativity is a mystery to us all until the moment that it shows its face. If anything were predictable about the creative process, it would be the generative force of innocent perception to recognize newly emerging possibilities in the contexts of our lives.

The ultimate state of originality belongs not to man, but God. Within the human domain, what appears to be creative actually shows up on closer examination to be rearrangement, discovery, or revelation of what "already exists". Within endless rivers of possibility, revealed in microseconds of awareness, there are choices to be made. We select our perceptions and decide what we will do with them. Our right to choose is possibly the core of human creativity. As an artist and writer, I know that thousands of choices are made subtly or explicitly in a painting or book. The energy of recognizing, choosing, and extracting possibilities from the endless universe is the nature of will—and that in its truest form reduces simply to responsibility. Response-ability is our inalienable freedom to respond, select, and direct the actions of our lives. If we look closely at this equation we can find a significant truth. Thought responds, selects, and directs. Will is the energy of thought, which results in creative living.

The content of creativity is different with every person and each occasion. However, the contexts in which creation takes root are very similar. Sustainable life is created in thoughtful, proactive conditions. Just as seeds in the plant kingdom require fertile soil, water, and sunlight, so too certain environments favor creation more than others. The basic choice so often overlooked is the preparation of conditions in which we plant the seeds of our endeavors. Jeshua has said before, *"As you sow, so shall you reap."* In my communions with him, he has emphasized that this rule applies even more to context than to content. Many times the direct relationship of cause and effect does not make sense if we focus only on actions and content. For example: a gift to someone may not be reciprocated **as a gift back to you**, but if our gift was truly given in the spirit of love, the ability to remain in that loving way will be reinforced by other events. The reciprocation may then come from other sources. To the contrary, we may have committed a destructive act that was overlooked, but the destructive attitudes that generated the action will not go without consequence. Actually, according to Jeshua, the attraction power of positive and negative contexts is much more imminent than positive and negative events. That is because of a universal principle that regulates all cause and effect. The secret of cause and effect is revealed through the natural way that positive action is drawn to positive contexts and negative action is drawn to negative contexts.

"Retribution does not occur through judgment—most especially by God. Retribution occurs naturally through the fact that negative, or reactive, actions contribute to chaos and chaos always travels to find its instigator's weakest area of life. For example: a man who engages in destructive actions in his business may manifest no signs of retribution in his career, but the chaos that he set in motion will travel like a heat-seeking rocket to find the area of his greatest weakness, which perhaps is his health or his marriage. The good news is that love behaves the same way, except that it travels to find the area of your greatest positive attribute. When I promised that a man who applies his talents will have them multiplied, I was referring to this principle. When you focus only on the content of events, the

consequences of action will elude you. You will see neither the logic of balance, nor the patterns of creation. This is true whether you are referring to particle physics, human communities, careers, or health. Context is what you can predict and manage.

"Context is the part of reality you are invited to select, manage, and even create for yourself and others. This is why thought is so important for positive living. Thought is the power that illuminates, clarifies, and directs the nature of connections and contexts."

Inspirations

Alfred Tennyson (b.1809 d.1892) England:
> "One God, one law, one element,
> And one far-off divine event
> To which the whole creation moves."

The Upanishads (c. 600 300 BC) India:
> "He is the inner self of all,
> Hidden like a little flame in the heart.
> Only by the stilled mind can He be known.
> Those who realize him become immortal."

Christopher Pearse Cranch (b.1813 d.1892) America:
> "Thought is deeper than all speech,
> Feeling deeper than all thought;
> Souls to souls can never teach
> What unto themselves was taught."

Kahlil Gibran (b.1883 d.1931) Persia:
> "Your children are not truly your children.
> They are the sons and daughters of life's
> yearning for itself."

Henry David Thoreau (b.1817 d.1862) America:
  "I know of no more encouraging fact than the
  unquestionable ability of man to elevate his life
  by conscious endeavor."

Applications

We all have objectives in life, if only the small practical one of getting through the present day. Some of our goals are long-range guiding stars that shape our destiny. For the purpose of clarifying this chapter and absorbing its message, let's set aside **all** goals—large and small—to consider a deeper driving force. That is…life itself. Here you will consider the context of your own life and the seeds of desire you are planting in it.

1. What is the strongest drive behind all your actions?
   Is it pro-active or reactive?
2. What is your most intense desire or longing?
   Is it pro-active or reactive?
3. What is your greatest joy?
   Is it compulsive or selective?
4. What is your greatest anxiety?
   Is it a reaction to the unknown or a wake-up call to
   become more responsible?
5. What brings you the greatest peace? Does that come by withdrawing from life, or finding your place in life?

   Our lives unfold through many contexts from the cosmic to the mundane. The following twelve vital areas are particularly fertile for human accomplishment. By directing your efforts in an appropriate way to these areas, the content of your hopes and efforts will have a greater chance for fulfillment. Consider how these contexts show up in your life:

1. Self knowledge
2. The reality of nature
3. Communication and learning
4. Community
5. Creative expression
6. Duty and responsibility
7. Partnerships
8. Values
9. Discovery and enlightenment
10. Leadership
11. Humanitarian service
12. Contemplative and spiritual practices

Most importantly, invite The Creator to fill the vessel of your life and its many contexts with the content of happiness and fulfillment.

Meditation

There is no creation that does not celebrate the Creator. There is no thought that does not connect with All-knowing Consciousness. There is no expression of the self that does not seek for unity between Heaven and Earth. Therefore, let us enter this meditation with an earnest desire to extend to the height and depth of our being, above our consciousness and below our sub-conscious life until we discover our real self.

Let me know the self that You gave me, the divine likeness in which I am made and into which I am to grow—the place where Your spirit communes with mine; the spring from which all my life rises. In this wonderful place, let me behold and rejoice in our unity, so that I can dream the dreams that become my life, and think the thoughts that propel my actions.

In all that I do, let me celebrate the joy of our union, for I see You everywhere, without beginning, middle, or end. You are the Lord of all creation, and the cosmos is Your body. Your radiance is blinding and immeasurable. I see You, who are so difficult to behold, shining like a fiery sun blazing in every direction. You are the supreme, changeless Reality, the one thing to be known. You are the refuge of all creation, the immortal spirit, the eternal guardian of all Being. You touch everything with Your infinite power. The sun and the moon are Your eyes. Your mouth is fire; Your radiance warms the cosmos.

By Your own desire, You were born from nothing. Forever I will sing the glories of my Creator, whose eyes are everywhere, reflected in the eyes of a child, or an old man, a rainbow, or a flower. O Marvelous Creator, Your presence fills the Heavens and the Earth and reaches in every direction.

You are the Source of all creation, and the One who dissolves creation. You are the Doer behind everything, without whose will neither a leaf falls, nor a cat licks its paws, nor a woman blinks her eyes. You are also the Non-doer; ever changeless; resting in Yourself. You are the Infallible, the Almighty, Soul of the Universe. You are beyond all material qualities—the Inconceivable—and yet the forest flowers are a garland on Your head. You are the Essence of all prayers, the Song of all souls. All Hearts worship You, and Your arms are a constant embrace.

In this wonderful place where we are united, let me know Your pleasure, that I may express it as the creations of my life. Let me know Your desire that I may embrace it with the thoughts of my heart.

Prayer

O Perfect Master,
We give thanks this day for the expanding grandeur of Creation,
Worlds known and unknown,
Galaxies beyond galaxies,
Filling us with awe and challenging our imaginations.
We also give thanks for this fragile planet earth,
Its times and tides, its sunsets and seasons.
All around we behold Your Creation:
The power of Your countless arms,
The vision of Your watchful eyes,
The words from Your innumerable mouths,
And the fire of life of Your endless body.
Nowhere do we see a beginning or middle or end of You,
O God of all, O Great Infinity.
You shine on all things and all people as gleaming moonlight plays
Upon a thousand waters at once.
For the joy of human life,
Its wonders and surprises, its hopes and achievements:
For high hopes and noble causes,
For faith without fanaticism,
For all who have labored and suffered for a fairer world,
Who have lived so that others might live in dignity and freedom:
For all who rejoice in Creation
We give thanks this day.

Amen

11

WILL AND RESPONSIBILITY

The Message

His teaching about "will" began with a question that I asked about "being". I wanted to know if "being" had to be accepted as a self-defining reality (too basic to be defined by anything else), or were there any associated meanings that could provide more understanding about it.

"Being is by nature self-defining, but you can expand your understanding of it by realizing a fundamental property of all being. I have told you several times that creation began in a 'void' and that creation began not with substance, but with BEING. Now I will tell you more. Being IS – simply because it says that IT IS. There is nothing more to the beginning than that. The first act of Being, and the second act of creation, is the creation of space. Energy and matter are merely extensions, changes, and complexities of space. Every being is known by the space that it creates and holds. This is equally true whether we are referring to our Holy Source or the tiniest insect.

*"A soul living within physical creation takes space for granted. The recurring patterns and predictable phenomena of the physical universe can have a hypnotic effect. A 'being' comes to assume that space is an element, like the ocean, that one moves into and out of as it passes through life. Nothing could be further from the truth. **Your space would not exist if you did not cause it. You do not occupy or displace space ... you create it!** Without BEING, there would be no space. All the space that is, is shared by those that create it. This is why all souls are essential to existence.*

"*In the densities of physical experience, a soul most often focuses on the limits and boundaries of energy and matter, and considers that to be space. In reality, space precedes that perception. Space is the extension of a being. Where the extension of one being interacts with the extension of another, energy is generated. Where agreements are formed about what to do with that energy, matter is created. Most of these interactions and agreements are unconscious, and a natural consequence of the kind of beings in communion. Nevertheless, they occur, and are not always harmonious. When interactions are not harmonious, the beings will seek readjustment. As they look for other places and ways to be, they begin to consider that space is outside them selves. This is the beginning of separation, and also the need for responsibility.*

"*The Supreme Being is the Father of all being, and gives to each particle of being the autonomy of its own space, to be where and how it chooses to be. Your only responsibility is to be **who** you truly are and to fulfill the love that you are. You do not have to be all things, in all times, and in all places to fulfill your reason for being. **You must simply be the love that you are.** Except for the Creator, only you know what that is. Therefore, you have been vested with the responsibility to know and decide for yourself. You have been given the will to make it so.*"

I needed to pause and think. He had answered my question about being, but now my focus had shifted to the subjects of will and responsibility. He had presented responsibility as a privilege, an opportunity to direct one's own life. In the physical world, responsibility usually develops as an obligation, in consequence of prior action. In fact, responsibility is often associated with blame. For him, responsibility was the 'steering wheel' of personal autonomy and freedom. We 'respond' and then adjust our directions toward greater fulfillment. I could feel this in my being as he called my attention to it. More than that, I began to sense that will was the inner drive that DID THE RESPONDING! This was a fresh new awareness. Like others, I had assumed that 'will' was the extra push we exerted in the face of obstacles, resistance, or competition to attest to our strength of purpose. I needed to be with this feeling for a moment. Then he proceeded.

"Will is the life force of a being. In your individual evolution, spirit first manifested as will. Then will manifested as your body. There is a natural condensation of elements like mist becoming dew and dew watering a flower. Each spirit that is born is given a new opportunity to create its reality according to its own heart's desire. Will is the power that spirit uses to direct this opportunity into physical being."

"I was right, then. It is will that responds to life and in so doing there is responsibility. This is very different than the common assumptions about will. Often there is fear of will, that it will be irresponsibly driven."

"There are many negative associations with will and willfulness because it is often driven by circumstance and unexamined compulsions rather than by love and spirit. However, will is only irresponsible when it has lost connection with the spirit that created it and the love that moved it! **Will is just the future tense of 'to be'!** *Therefore, in its purest form, will is simply love and spirit moving into the future, creating space and negotiating with others for the sharing and co-creating of energy and matter. Whatever you are, do, and have is the product of will. A being is as alive as his will is able to manifest a continuance for him.*

"When I talk about free will, I am talking about free will for the unfolding of your own life - not about free will over others. You do not have the right to manipulate others with your will or to use it to reduce the desires of others to your own limits and boundaries. The choices belong to each person, and they must be made with feeling as well as thought, intuition, and deliberate action. Each person discovers his own boundaries by the perception of pain as he crosses them. You will know where to go by the feelings that attract you. You will know where to stop by the pain that you experience when you have gone too far.

"Many souls thought that they should experience and accept everything to be truly evolved. Others thought that submitting will to

the dominance of rules and structure was the way to produce optimum co-existence. These were efforts to accept or enforce externally what could not be accepted in oneself. Neither extreme brings happiness. A soul must unconditionally want to experience something before it is the right experience to have. All one must do is what your love has planted in your being. It is not freedom to do everything. Freedom is fulfilling your love.

"What you must accept totally is yourself—not every possibility for experience. Spirit is the source of will, and yet in a physical reality, they work together as a kind of binary language to direct and unite the whole of your life. Will and spirit are the expanding limits of a connected whole. They are evolving extensions of the same thing. The key to uniting will and spirit is through accepting the entirety of who you are and the love that made it so. How do you think you will ever accept another when you have not accepted yourself?

*"Most people on earth have made a separation between will and spirit. They have felt their will was not acceptable; that to love the way God loves, they must eliminate their own feelings and opinions and do what they have imagined is the will of God. The will of God is not in opposition to the will of the individual, except that **you** have allowed that to happen. As the condensation of spirit, will becomes the physical form, and your physical form is true in its instinct if it has not separated from the Spirit that created it.*

"The union of will and spirit is kept alive through sensitivity and thoughtfulness. You know your individual will as feelings. When these feelings are alive and true, they will respond to the needs of the moment rather than relying on habits formed in the past. All habits need review and examination. Many need releasing. Beneath every habit pattern are buried feelings. Some have positive associations, some negative. The feelings underneath habitual responses are often denied feelings, and the habit is a substitute for true response. There is also the habit of avoiding feelings. Habits are to the body what judgments are to the consciousness. Both are deployed without further thought, and both prevent response and sensitivity to the truth of the

moment. Both prevent change. In a healthy life, change is ongoing and responsive to sensitivity and thoughtfulness. When will and spirit are balanced, there is an instinctive desire to do the right thing, and the right thing is naturally the thing most desired.

"The undermining of free will has been accompanied by another habit – looking outside yourself for answers. Often you deny your own will in favor of someone else's idea of what is best for you. Then you reciprocate by doing the same thing to them. This is social imbalance between will and spirit. Although regard for others and respect of shared agreements is necessary, this **can** become another type of habit that goes unexamined and annihilates true sensitivity. The answer is not more regulations and rules. The answer is reunion of will and spirit.

"The problem of honoring will on planet Earth is great, indeed. Don't put forth an intent that you, yourself, cannot honor. Like anything else, the first step begins at home. Proceed without compromise to make it so. You might be surprised how well this works, especially if you remember that in all actual or potential conflicts, the power of love is the grace that resolves problems.

"As for the will of others that you do not like, you might be equally surprised that in honoring their fundamental right to have free will, the effects of what you do not want will flow through you without harm. Don't forget about your own will in the process. You have a right to say 'No' to anything, insofar as it affects your own life.

"When you cannot easily know and receive your body's messages, and when you do not instinctively do the right thing, there is a gap between spirit and will. When the two are in harmony, and joy permeates your life, you always do exactly what you should be doing and for no other reason except that it is what you feel like doing. The spirit sees all possibilities. The will then selects among all possibilities what is right for the moment. The merger of will and spirit creates a state of true sensitivity.

"Unconditionally accept your feelings, even if there is something that needs to change or be reformed. Everything experienced is valid for some reason in the moment when it occurs.

Maximum learning, growth, and attunement come from looking at your feelings exactly as they are. Then you can make choices about how to respond. That is responsibility.

"This union takes place in the heart and this balance creates a reality that meets your needs without overriding anyone or anything. Unfortunately, the will has been so severely disciplined on Earth that it is extremely confused and is very much like an abused child that demonstrates its pain with further abusive action. The answer is not more suppression. The answer is trust and restoration of the will's instinctive desire for life and living. Not only actions, but understanding and receptivity must evolve as well. Denial of feelings has created an imbalance in the Heart. Denial of the will is often filled in by what is actually a false will. This consists of a false feeling the person convinces himself he actually has. It also consists of hurt and misdirection caused by many earlier denials of will by self or others.

"Be patient with yourself and others. Your understanding of will is sure to progress as you move forward in your sensitivity and understanding of life. Initially everyone sees will as the pushing and efforting of ego as it attempts to make oneself, others, and reality conform to how you think it should be. In doing so, one attaches will to personality and the projection one has about life. This is false will. False will does not support your fulfillment, or even your survival for that matter, because it has a particular attraction for conflict. False will leads to depletion and emptiness. It leaves you feeling like something is missing, that you have no inner support or capacity to persevere. As you move through life, the essential will comes more clearly into view. Essential will is the power that has actually supported you and carried you to where you are. That power has allowed you to survive and thrive no matter what your condition.

Unlike false will, the essential will is felt as a sense of inner support that brings personal confidence and higher guidance. The best way I can describe essential will is the feeling of 'going with the flow' of one's BEING."

Correlations

Matthew 6:10 "Thy kingdom come. Thy will be done in earth, as it
is in heaven."

Psalms 40:8 "I delight to do your will, O my God: yes, thy law is
within my heart."

Romans 12:2 "Be not conformed to this world: but be transformed
by the renewing of your mind, that you may attain that
which is good, and acceptable, and the perfect will of God."

Matthew 7:7-8 "Ask, and it shall be given you; seek, and you shall
find; knock, and it shall be opened to you. For whoever
asks, receives; and he who seeks, finds; and to him who
knocks, the door is opened."

The Key

There is nothing quite so exhilarating as having wind in our
sails, moving gracefully to the horizon of our dreams. The wind
that propels our ship is nothing more or less than the coordinated
energy of God's will, our own will, and that of others. It would
seem that the greatest mystery in life would be the will of God.
Ironically, it is our own will that confounds us most, and second to
that, the will of others. We have pushed our lives along so
feverishly with effort, and developed such stress around the
counter-efforts of others, that we have confused will with challenge
and lost touch with the exquisite sensitivity that is innate to the
energy of our being.

As I study the teachings of Jeshua and apply them to life, I
find many symptoms of that confusion, but essentially three causes
for it: 1) We have failed to realize that will and effort are not the
same thing. Thus, we do not understand the will of God as the

integrated harmony of life and living. True will unfolds with grace and positive support. 2) We deny our own instincts and inner voices in favor of conformity, or what "should be", or "what has to be". 3) We do not understand the simple efficiency of accepting "No" for an answer when something is not working or is unacceptable to others.

A few years ago, I had an experience in my garden that illustrates all of these causes in one incident. (I live in a high mountain desert climate that is richer with wildlife than vegetation. So there is an ongoing challenge for any human to harvest anything planted in a garden.) With some cleverness and good fencing, I managed to keep the rabbits out. Since I couldn't fence the sky, planting day was invariably a contest with the birds. As I laid the new seeds in the ground, there was an eerie feeling of being watched by a thousand eyes from the surrounding trees. The little "seed vultures" were not a bit shy, and as soon as I turned my back, there would be twenty or more feathered harvesters taking my seeds out of the earth before they could sprout and become a crop for some other predator.

The first year I was here, I was too passive about my wishes for a garden. When the season was over, all I had was an agave and two cacti, which preceded my efforts. Nevertheless, something propelled me to try again. I listened, and with full expectation of success, I proceeded. Just as I planted the last seed in the ground, one audacious bird lit on the ground in front of me and began scratching the loose soil. Flabbergasted with his bravado, I jumped to my feet and yelled, 'Shoo!' He came back several times and I protested more vigorously with waving hands.

Clearly, I had to do something better unless I planned to camp in the garden for five days while the seeds were sprouting. Because I have learned to respect the power of will, the first thing I did was ask myself, "How much do I want this garden?" The answer was emphatically, "Yes, very much!" Almost as soon as I declared my true intent, a transformed state of mind came as well. It is amazing how clearly I knew what to do. My will had expedited the solution. I put my cat Gunnar in the garden and instructed him to keep the birds away while I went back to the garden store. There I bought a roll of garden cloth to cover the seeds and a sack of wild birdseed as a distracting consolation prize for my competitors. I had "won" by knowing my own will and assessing the will of others with at least some degree of reality and responsibility. I was happy, the birds were happy, and the will of God rolled on.

What I did not expect is the one bird that had sparred with me would be obsessed with continuing the game. He persisted in trying to peck through the garden cloth lying over the ground. His efforts would not be successful, so I turned and walked away. I watched him from my studio window, for thirty minutes or so, as he struggled with the barrier to his goal. All the while, the other birds had cleaned up the dish of birdseed and left him nothing. The frustration of his obsession had cost him energy and left him without food. By not accepting the answer of "No" in one avenue, his will had lost an opportunity to seek his desire in another direction. Poor thing had become so focused on effort and opposition that he had lost touch with his own will to find food. He had become so involved with fighting for food that he had failed to see it lying on the ground.

We do share an environment, and our own will is not the only one at play. Whenever our desires involve the will of another, sometimes the answer is "No". If our will is clear, true, and focused, there is always a "Yes" somewhere. By understanding the true nature of essential will outside the context of competition, effort, and discouragement, we are free to move in new directions.

That bird paid the price of what Jeshua called false will, the will focused on effort and driven by ego to overcome obstacles. False will arises when you see yourself as a "separate self" unsupported by the universe. The issue of getting your own way is a big one for the ego. The thought of surrendering to any other will may feel like defeat. Frustration and eventually defeat will happen when you are trying to impose your will upon reality by pitting yourself against the unfolding current of the universe. Disregard of reality (yours or others) is the hallmark of false will. By contrast, essential will is an effortless steadfastness in carrying out your goals. That power comes from an inner sense of support and confidence existing in harmony with the universe. In this state, you are free to seize opportunities of the moment. You are open to new ideas about how to implement your will.

Surrender is not defeat. Actually, it is the beginning of harmony as you are released from your separate self and your will is reunited with reality. Just as the universe is unfolding in the sense of new stars, supernovas, climatic changes, and seasons of the year, the universe is also unfolding inside you. If you stay with and surrender to your inner process, your own universe will unfold in the same way.

There is "a way", but you do not find "your way" by choosing it to fit your personality, or forcing it despite the will of others. If you are sincere and truthful with yourself, remaining so regardless of conditions, you will eventually see that having your own way is really a matter of surrendering to your inner truth.

"The Way" that Jeshua taught is the way of releasing false will and returning to the power and innate responsibility of essential will. Your way is following the thread of your own experience. The **key** to essential will is being who you really are and putting it into action.

Inspirations

Thomas Jefferson (b.1743 d.1826) America:
"The God who gave us life, gave us liberty at the same time."

Kalil Gibran (b.1883 d.1931) Persia:
"Your soul is oftentimes a battlefield, upon which your reason and your judgment wage war against your passion

and your appetite. Would that I could be the peacemaker in your soul, that I might turn the discord and the rivalry of your elements into oneness and melody. But how shall I, unless you yourselves be also the peacemakers, nay the lovers of all your elements.

"Your Reason and your passion are the rudder and the sails of your seafaring soul. If either your sails or your rudder be broken, you can but toss and drift, or else be held at a standstill in mid seas. For reason, ruling alone, is a force confining; and passion, unattended, is a flame that burns to its own destruction. Therefore, let your soul exalt your reason to the height of passion that it may sing. And let it direct your passion with reason, that your passion may live through its own daily resurrection, and like the phoenix rise above its own ashes."

Alexander Pope (b.1688 d.1744) England:
"All are but parts of one stupendous whole, whose body Nature is, and **God** the soul."

Applications

Jeshua said spirit becomes will, and will becomes substance. That thought has ominous implications if one considers how it could play out in the destiny of planet Earth. There would be infinite blessings in the presence of good will and endless hardship in the presence of unhealthy, misdirected, or conflicting wills. If we take this literally to be true, then we can count on it to play out in all areas of our existence from physical substance to nature, human agendas, community life, family life and personal fulfillment.

Dr. Masaru Emoto, a visionary researcher from Japan, introduced a new concept to the study of micro-clustered water and Magnetic Resonance Analysis technology. His investigations have revealed a special mystery of water. He has discovered that molecular cluster arrangements within water can be altered by various factors of vibration and consciousness. Through photographs of crystalline formations, he showed what variations could be obtained by imprinting upon the water different qualities of music, thought, prayer, chaotic noise and various words with emotional intent. Then he photographed the complex arrangements of molecular crystalline beauty. His studies not only show that water is alive, but also that it is conscious and responds to applied influence by rearranging its inner crystalline properties. Through repeatable experiments, Dr. Emoto demonstrated that human thoughts and emotions could alter the molecular structure of water. For the first time, he has provided us with physical evidence that the power of our thoughts can change the world within and around us.

Water that was imprinted by love, gratitude, and appreciation, responded with the development of complex beauty. Water that was mistreated by negative intentions became disorderly and lost its magnificent patterning. In fact, it often took on grotesque forms of resonance. After much experimentation, Dr. Emoto discovered that the most powerful combination of thoughts in terms of capacity to transform was that of "Love" and "Gratitude". This realization is rather comforting on a planet that is mostly water!

Another recent discovery about particles in a solution of water may have provided the first scientific evidence for demonstrating that homeopathic medicines really work (Newscientist.com). A team in South Korea has discovered a whole new dimension to one of the simplest of all chemical reactions. What happens when you dissolve a substance in water and then add more water? Conventional wisdom says that the dissolved molecules spread further and further apart as a solution is diluted. But two chemists have found that some do the opposite: they clump together, first as clusters of molecules, then as bigger aggregates of those clusters. Far from drifting apart from their neighbors, they increased in size and moved closer together.

German chemist Kurt Geckeler and his colleague Shashadhar Samal stumbled on this effect while investigating fullerene particles (very large and general class of carbon molecules) at their lab in the Kwangju Institute of Science and Technology in South Korea. They found that certain of these carbon molecule groups kept forming untidy aggregates in solution. The scientists were looking for ways to control these clumps and prevent their formation when they were stunned by a phenomenon new to chemistry. Much to their surprise, when they diluted the solution even more, the size of the fullerene particles increased.

Further work showed it was not an isolated occurrence. There were numerous other particles including DNA and plain old sodium chloride that behaved the same way. An interesting aspect of their experiment is that it only worked in polar solvents like water, in which one end of the molecule has a pronounced positive charge while the other end is negative.

Up to this point, one of the mysteries of high-dilution homeopathy relies on a belief that water has yet-uncharted living properties. This discovery could provide the first scientific insight into how certain homeopathic remedies work. Homeopaths repeatedly dilute medications, believing that the higher the dilution, the more potent the remedy. Some make a dilution until no molecules of the remedy remain. They believe that water holds a memory, or "imprint" of the active ingredient, and that memory is more potent than the ingredient itself.

These studies also echo the controversial claims of French immunologist Jacques Benveniste. In 1988, Benveniste claimed in a "Nature" article that a solution once containing antibodies could still activate human white blood cells. Benveniste claimed the solution still worked because it contained ghostly "imprints" in the water structure where the antibodies had been.

Aside from the interesting content of these studies, their value in this context is to draw our attention to the fact that WILL DOES MANIFEST.

With this certainty, we can begin to inventory our own lives to discover how will is being manifested around us. It is no accident that things are the way they are. There are signs all around that confirm this timeless principle. Some are more obvious than others, because the relationship between will and manifestation is more evident in some cases. We must learn to be more aware of ways in which we separate from the flow of life, judge others, and deny our own true feelings. Separation from the flow of life separates us from the will of God. Judgments see situations as unable to change. Denial of feelings creates emptiness in the heart. Denial is merely judgment and separation directed toward ourselves.

For your practical study and life enhancement, assess your life. Note the areas of your life that are:

1. Most "in the flow".
2. Most unconditionally accepting.
3. Most like you want them to be.

Give thanks for these areas of life that are doing so well. Acknowledge and express your deepest appreciation to God and to all others who support you with their will. Accept the deep pleasure of work well done and life well lived.

Now let's move to the other parts of your life that are causing you more difficulty. Note the areas that are:

1. Most "stuck".
2. Most filled with judgment.
3. Most filled with denial of your true feelings.

The recipe for improvement in these areas is simple, if you sincerely apply it. Begin by checking with yourself about confusions of intention. What do you really want? Check with

142

yourself for denial. What did you really feel or desire that you would not admit? Did you deny others (including God) the opportunity of supporting you by not making your intentions clearly and passionately known? Now, honestly confess the judgments you have put on yourself and others related to these difficult areas. Anything that is stuck will have judgments within it. Look closely. They may be concealed within seemingly positive thoughts. For example, if you are having trouble with money, you may easily spot some negative judgments such as "money leads to ruin", but seemingly innocent statements such as "life is sweeter with money" are also judgments. A judgment is any statement you make when you really do not have all the information or experience to make informed observations. These statements and attitudes become rigid and fixed misunderstandings overlaying a subject you do not have enough consciousness to deal with in a positive or causative way. Judgment is actually that mechanism whereby a person is taken to the experience he most requires for restoring faith and consciousness. Far better that one release all judgments and allow the flow of life gently to bring increments of experience and consciousness that will be supportive to growth. Look for ways that you can build greater acceptance and openness to learning in these areas. There is a children's song that you might want to whistle or hum lightly as you look at these areas of judgment. "Row, row, row your boat gently down the stream. Merrily, merrily, merrily, merrily; life is but a dream." In that state of mind you will feel and understand the last thing you must do to bring more love, light, and growth to these areas. Forgive yourself and others...endlessly!

Meditation

To join with the will of God, the power of unity must first be embraced. To begin, we must examine the nature of prayer. The word prayer could be translated from several ancient languages literally as "wish-path". In its original usage, prayer was a method of purifying and directing the heart and mind to seek union with God. Prayer acts as inspiration by arousing the heart's inherent desire for good. This attracts the fulfillment of its aim through preparation, unity, and praise.

In our highest and truest human nature, we are **in the will of God**. Although you may do nothing at all, you are actually doing something when you are in your true character. You are being yourself, and expressing that to others. Your eyes, voice, and disposition will all express. The most important thing is to show your true being in the simplest, most unaffected way and to appreciate its impact on the smallest parts of life. To be in the will of God is to be in a state of natural goodness, appreciating everything around you.

As we open our hearts to this unity, we begin by releasing. In the empty space, your soul longs for reunion with that which gave it birth. God is both the infinite, and the inner self of all. Hidden like a little flame in the heart, God can be known only by the stilled mind. Those who realize this union become immortal. Repeat this affirmation:

> I will abandon all grasping, yearning and attachment, and send my consciousness into the space of newborn awareness; in so doing I will have greater life. In this place is the rebirth of will. When I am liberated from my separate self, I am no longer involved in the measurement of life, but in the living of it. My prayers are without distraction. My whole silence is full of prayer. My whole life becomes a

prayer. At the center of the universe is a loving heart that beats in harmony with all and that wants the best for me.

✝ As your heart moves into unity, sing forth your praise to the Creator. You made me. You called me. You taught me. You fed me. You loved me. Through me, you create. You cast your will and your knowledge. You provide for me. You love me. I am yours.

✝ In silence now, bring forth the will of your life, the yearning of your heart. Release all the times you abandoned the will of your life. Release all the times you denied it. Release all the times you said the will of your life belonged to another. Release all the times you took the will of another to be your own. Honor the presence of God as your true will, and know that this is enough. ✝

Prayer ✝

O God, You are my being.
You are the fulfillment of my desires.
I embrace You in my innermost thoughts.
All around I behold Your infinity:
The power of Your immense presence.
Nowhere do I see a beginning, middle, or end of You,
O God of all, O Great Infinity.

In Your purity, You make me pure.
In Your wholeness, You make me whole.
Help me to find the place where Your spirit unites with mine,
The spring from which all my life arises.
Steer the ship of my life to Your quiet harbor,
Where I may be safe from the storms of life.
Show me the course I should take.

Renew in me the gift of discernment.
Give me the strength and courage to choose the right course,
Even when a storm is raging.
Help me to find the ultimate consciousness
Where Your will is my guiding light,
Where Your soul and my soul are like two candles,
Shedding a single ray.

Amen

12

TRUTH AND REALITY

The Message

"Reality is as diverse as our perception of it, or our considerations about it, so how do we find truth within reality? You say that God is one with reality, but sometimes reality is so harsh and confusing. How do we keep our balance within it and feel the presence of God?"

*"God is one with reality, but God is not necessarily the same as **what you perceive about** reality. There are many dimensions of reality ranging from personal beliefs and experiences to the more predictable patterns of natural order. All of these dimensions are part of your life experience. In all of it, there is God. In any one picture, there is both truth and reality. What you see is what you seek. The most concise explanation I can give you is that truth is the essence of a thing. Reality is its manifestation.*

"Your first step toward knowing the truth is to understand that personal reality, physical reality, and essential truth are not separate. They are also not the same. Consider the way parts of a wheel are not the same, but together they form a greater whole. If you know the physical world exclusively through your physical senses, you see only particles, elements, and objects. Add to this your own emotions, attitudes, feelings and beliefs and you see the reality you have created. If beliefs, denials, and judgments do not block your inner sensitivity, you will also recognize the unifying elements of consciousness and love. At this level of perception, the universe looks quite different. At the highest level of consciousness, there is only one

homogenous medium permeating all existence. Differentiation exists, like waves on the surface of an ocean, but there are no ultimate divisions. Reality and truth represent the interplay of parts, perspectives, and unity within a greater whole.

"Therefore, the real challenge with truth lies not in separating it FROM reality (which cannot be done), but in knowing how to find truth WITHIN reality. Numerous misconceptions have distracted mankind from a workable correlation of truth and reality. One is the belief that truth was a kind of archetypal blueprint that took on fault and error as it played out in dynamic form. This would mean that the relationship between truth and reality is merely linear and moving toward entropy. If that were the case, how could you recognize or solve any problem without creating more problems? What basis would there be for resolution? By contrast, knowing how to find truth within reality will set you free from the chaos and conflicts that may arise in your experience of reality. Truth redeems you from disappointing realities that went awry. If truth were not present in all situations, you would have no refuge."

As I thought about the omnipresence of truth and the presence of God in all reality, it almost seemed as if two hands were clutched, and the interlocked fingers held together two distinct but supportive dimensions of existence. There was such love…such wonder. He continued…

*"The one power that drives and connects both truth and reality is Love. This is why it is so important for you to know that love is WHO you are. When you view love only as an action, or a good intention, you see it only as part of reality and miss the truth of love. You cannot see the full context of your life, but one certainty you can always have is that **being love** will embrace and include your basic motivation for living. It will remind you of that same essential truth in others, and give you the strength to forgive when realities move into conflict.*

"The Source of all life is beyond the objective universe, and at the same time dwells within created forms as the giver and sustainer of life. So great is the truth of God that it would not be accessible to you if

it were not also within you. Here is the secret and mystery of infinity. Infinity is not what lies 'beyond' a confinable universe. Infinity is what permeates a universe and integrates subjective and objective awareness into one boundless potential.

"Infinity is a qualitative dimension of existence that integrates subjective and objective experience. When you know this, you will be able to unite truth and reality in an effective way. This is an uncomfortable proposition for science because subjective properties are not seen as appropriate for controlled discipline. That problem can be overcome by knowing this: At the juncture of subjective and objective reality, there is a 'still point' of perfect equilibrium where more is revealed than the sum of measurements. Just as mathematics could not represent complex variables without the functional entity of '0', so too dynamic change cannot unfold without a foundation of complete neutrality. Discovering this '0' of virgin homeostasis will greatly elevate human understanding. Then infinity may be viewed as a gradient scale of possibilities expanding from a neutral center.

*"Truth is without measure. Therefore, any part of it will stabilize reality and serve as a centering point from which observations may be compared and evaluated. Reality approaches or recedes from truth according to its affinity or resemblance to it. Truth is not measured by data, and you do **not** need volumes of it to make your life more productive and beneficial. What you **do** need is a better understanding of how and where to **find** the truth. Then you will be able to evaluate your experiences using an axial power rather than a boundary-based context. The true definition of a context comes from its center rather than its boundaries. Knowing this is freedom.*

"In human terms, truth is the answer your soul is seeking. The answer does not lie in data, experience, beliefs, or pushing the boundaries of reality. The answer lies at the center of your being.

"The pursuit of truth is what requires you to rise above the issues of polarity, resistance, and depletion that are often part of physical living. When you master this problem, it will not be because all extremes have disappeared from your life, but rather because you are operating from a realization that all extremes draw their power

from a common center. All centers empower the reality extending from it. Events are actually controlled by a precise equilibrium rather than by the resistive factors that seem to define their existence. There is no point of contrast or conflict that cannot be integrated into a peaceful whole when its center is found.

"From your own center, you may view the ever-widening concentric rings of reality, which begin with your personal reality and extend to include the reality of others and the physical universe. This center will be found in stillness, and there, truth will be revealed. This principle is valid subjectively, objectively, and collectively, for it is the nature of truth to clarify through unity. Polarity is actually an illusion. As long as you are convinced that it is real, you will believe all other illusions and miss the truth of existence."

† "Clearly, what you are telling me about is an absolute that exists unto itself, a higher power that is beyond the physical dimension. How can we know this within the context of relative truth or the manifestations we call reality?"

"Truth has no mass and no spatial limitations, but it is far from being 'nothing'. Truth is a great neutral generative force. It begins with God and extends as love to provide a common and undivided matrix for universal life. The power of truth is carried by love beyond all bounds of time and space. Truth scatters Love, like countless stars, into particles of Being that possess a loving center and a perception of infinity. These are the living souls, which forward the Creator's work through whatever reality they choose to create. Your experience of reality is a direct result of what you have created, of your relationship to those with whom you co-create, and ultimately your relationship to God. Your experience of truth is through surrender to universal law and to the power of love. Love is the force that integrates truth and reality and is common to both.

"Regardless of your own reality, your soul retains a 'still point' from which infinity may be viewed. That point is located within the Sacred Heart. There you may contact true peace, purpose, and meaning. In that stillness, as true love, you were created in the image of God. You are invited to be in this perfect equilibrium whenever you

choose, and take it as the basis of your understanding. Indeed, the greatest truths are unknowable from a viewpoint external to them.

*"There is an eternal dialogue between stillness and motion, Creator and Created, truth and reality. If you would know reality, you must examine evidence without judgment or bias and apply the laws of cause and effect. If you would know yourself, you must trust your subjective responses. If you would know God, you must seek the stillness within where the subjective and objective intersect and reveal more than the sum of perceptions. The universe itself would be a consuming machine were it not for the inter-spatial stillness that sustains all dynamic interplay. Change is the basic stimulus for your perception of reality. But stillness **behind change** is that which embraces the truth. 'Be still and know that I am God.' This is the road map to Truth.*

*"There is an irony to change: If you would change a condition, you must first examine its connection to 'The Changeless'. When I calmed the storm, I did not address its action, but first contacted the stillness within it. Then I commanded it with love. An interesting property about reality is that each facet of it stays created (even if the love by which it was created is abandoned, forgotten, or betrayed) until the time it is **recognized again in love**. Then you may freely choose to dismiss it or accept it once more in love.*

*"You must first **connect** with love if you would change the nature of anything. If it is a physical situation you seek to change, first find the constant from which it draws its power. For a living soul, its faith is the gateway to that 'still-point'. Faith is one's trust in God and Eternal Truth, which penetrates all illusion. By connecting in love with your own faith, or that of another, you tap into a power that can result in healing and complete restoration. In reaching a soul's faith, you have reached its most innate truth. This is the most practical explanation I can give you for all distress and failure, as well as the key to all healing. Fighting an undesirable situation only makes it worse, for that denies the love within it. It is equally futile to cast charitable feelings, thoughts, or actions upon a situation to which you have judgments.*

"Holy Spirit is the pure essence of Truth. This is your Eternal counselor. Reality is changeable and much of it created by ourselves. Truth is an immutable constant that does not submit to alteration through experience or perception. Truth actually endures 'between the lines' of time and space, unchanged by them. When looked squarely in the face, Truth does not hide, but neither does it disappear when we look away. Truth does not take its authority from our actions or feelings. Our lives take authority from Truth."

Correlations

Mark 4:39 "And he arose, and rebuked the wind, and said unto the sea, 'Peace, be still.' And the wind ceased, and there was a great calm."

John 8:32 "And you shall know the truth, and the truth shall make you free."

John 14:17 "Even the Spirit of truth; whom the world cannot receive, because it sees him not, neither knows him: but you know him; for he dwells with you, and shall be in you."

John 16:13 "And so when he, the Spirit of truth, is come, he will guide you into all truth: for he shall not speak of himself; but whatsoever he shall hear, that shall he speak: and he will show you things to come."

The Key

Jeshua never spoke with me about yesterday or tomorrow. He only spoke about today...now. This present moment is the time for realization and fulfillment. This is the day wherein we may gain everything and anything the heart can possibly desire. NOW is the key to truth.

If truth is observed as the passing of events through time, it is elusive. If approached through faith and consciousness, with the simplicity of pure being, truth can be seen as the quality of NOW that permeates all of life, and there is nothing but truth.

Once when I was talking with Jeshua about BEING love, I asked about the soul. What was it, and where was it located? He said that the soul is a vessel created by God to contain the love that we ARE. You might say that the soul is a kind of spiritual body that allows YOU, the eternal being, to be present in physical form for a while and then continue with a sense of self throughout eternity. In relation to our physical body, he said that the soul connects with our mother at the time of conception and guides the development of the fetal body from an external position. At the time of birth, the soul enters the body THROUGH THE HEART. The first breath of life then represents the consummated union of body, soul, and love. The mark of our entry endures for life, and remains as our connection for higher life and further communions with the Holy Spirit.

The heart is our link with eternity, infinity, and immortality. From this divine center, it is possible to emanate the power and force of infinite intelligence throughout the magnitude of space, or to call into its presence all that is. Infinite intelligence is not confined to the time-space continuum. In our human attempt to understand this concept, we often imagine eternity as an endless stretch of time, and infinity as an endless stretch of space. But eternity really means no past, no future… only the ever present NOW…the ever present HERE…the center from which all is viewed.

It is imperative for the evolution of our consciousness that we know to look again for this special place of sacred peace. It must be rediscovered through faith. Real faith has nothing to do with beliefs, or with trying to convince oneself that a certain belief is true. Empowering faith "knows" that truth is **true essence** and is available right NOW. It is the recognition that our own true essence is REAL and cannot be lost. We really exist! Reality is supporting us and we are part of it. We do not have to make support happen, because it is already here and will not vanish anymore than the sky will disappear simply because we close our eyes. Through faith, our essence of being is a FELT and primary experience.

Thus faith gives us an unshakable confidence in the inherent goodness of life and of the universe. Even when things seem to be going wrong from the perspective of ego, we recognize that we are supported and that our true nature cannot be harmed. Faith gives us the inner freedom to respond spontaneously to whatever emerges in the moment because we are not bound by beliefs, doubts, and learned procedures. We are guided in each moment to optimal action.

Inspirations

George Macdonald (b.1824 d.1905) Scotland:
"Like weary waves, thought flows upon thought, but the still depth beneath is all thine own."

William Shakespeare (b.1564 d.1616) England:
"Truth is truth to the end of reckoning."

Blaise Pascal (b.1623 d.1662) France:
"We know the truth, not only by the reason, but also by the heart."

Daniel Webster (b.1782 d.1852) America:
"There is nothing so powerful as truth—and often nothing so strange."

Francis Bacon (b.1561 d.1626) England:
"No pleasure is comparable to standing upon the vantage-ground of truth."

Applications

There is a great secret place in our hearts where we become one with God and one with each other. There are many ways— through prayer, meditation, stillness, expressions of gratitude, forgiveness and surrender—in which we may release the cares of life and enter its refreshing serenity. One of the most ancient and powerful practices for entering the sacred place involves focusing on one's breath. Perhaps it is because of our associations between Spirit and breath, but also because breath is our closest link between the inner and outer worlds. In the space between breaths, that interval can become the perfect experience of equilibrium when it is fully mastered. On the highest side of this mastery, you will strengthen your awareness of the Eternal Life Force that guides your life. On a practical side, it will invigorate your body and energize your work like nothing else. In the development of wisdom, it is imperative that we be able to navigate gracefully and freely between the veils of truth and reality. When we can do this at will, then we have fulfilled the promise of Jeshua "to be IN the world, but not OF the world."

While you are learning this practice, I recommend that you concentrate deeply upon it in a quiet environment, as if you were meditating. After you have mastered it, you will be able to practice it anywhere, under any condition.

BREATHING EXERCISE: Inhale for seven beats of your heart. Hold for two beats of your heart. Exhale for seven beats of your heart, and hold for two beats. Repeat seven times. The action is simple, but the mastery comes in the clarity of your perception about what you are really doing. As you progress in your mastery, expand your perception of breath to include more than air. See the energy, vitality, ether, motion, and light that is being inhaled and exhaled by every cell of your body. Focus on the clarity present in the intervals between.

Meditation

There is perhaps nothing that simplifies reality and facilitates our progress toward truth more than forgiveness and the relinquishing of judgments. Reality can bring some harsh surprises, but truth in its omnipresence can restore wholeness and heal all wounds. This meditation is one of the most effective practices I know for expediting that process:

Allow quietness to engulf you and enter the stillness of your heart. Within this place of peace, visualize a person you need to release or forgive. Even though it may be painful, look earnestly and directly at the person you are visualizing until you see the presence of Christ in his or her heart. Allow the presence of Christ to join your hearts.

See that you are as brothers of sisters in this higher presence. Then recite the following affirmations.

We are one with God in thought, word, and deed forever. Therefore, I accept the results of our interaction as the will of God.

As we accept our oneness in spirit our differences will die and our unity in love will be reborn.

I forgive and release you to the will of God, completely in peace, love, and harmony.

You are hereby free to experience life, as you will.

I bless you to reside in love always.

See the other person as accepting these blessings and returning them in full measure to you.

Envision the other person completely released into light and love, fading until only the light is left.

One final word about the subject of forgiveness: Be sincere. Release judgments about those persons and situations you **truly can forgive**, and do not hold pretentious ideas that you have forgiven those whom you still cannot tolerate. Forgiveness is a return to God—a return that does not BEGIN with sainthood, but ENDS with sainthood. Atonement begins with **one authentic experience** of surrendering to Love and its power to heal the wounds of broken faith. It progresses from there toward complete restoration as you are healed and made stronger by the practice of conscious forgiving.

Prayer

I pray to pass safely through all darkness to the light beyond.
By faith in what I cannot see and cannot know,
I pray to know that which transcends sight and knowledge.
I pray to hold Your Truth as my highest reality.
Be all my love, all my hope, and my entire endeavor.
Let my thoughts and words emanate from You,
And let my daily life be lived in You.
Let my every breath be filled with love for You.

Amen

13

PROACTIVE VERSUS REACTIVE LIVING

The Message

Science tells us that for every action there is an equal and opposite reaction. This seems to be true for all things physical, and we can only speculate about its relevance or lack of relevance to other realms. In regard to human behavior, there seems to be a definite choice. At times we react to circumstances like a ball bouncing off a wall, and at other times, we catch ourselves in "mid-flight" and redirect the course of our actions to better consequences. Totally beyond considerations of right and wrong (which are often subject to opinion and custom), there is a more fundamental choice for living – to "proact" or "react" to life. When we proact, we are considering the optimum consequences for our actions before acting, thereby affirming our freedom of choice and our right to pursue higher ideals. Whenever we react, we are reciprocating to forces set in motion outside ourselves. Each time we do that we lose a bit more command over our own destiny. The fact that we have this choice **at all**, to me, is confirming evidence of our true spiritual nature. We make giant strides toward fulfilling our relationship to God and life when we make the choice consciously.

According to Jeshua, *"There is a fundamental choice made in the heart. That is, to live your life as the love that you are, or to defer responsibility for your life to other forces. The latter choice often emerges as blame, dependency, and compulsion. You cannot understand the difference between proactive and reactive behavior simply by positive or negative appearances. Many seemingly positive actions are just automatic responses to positive stimulation. Perhaps they are automatic defenses to invoke a positive reaction from others, when in fact there was no responsible thought or intention present. At the other extreme, seemingly harsh or destructive actions may actually have been duly considered and directed for corrective results, much like a fire-break is used to halt a raging and greater fire. Do not be deceived in this. What makes the difference between proactive and reactive behavior is the nature of consciousness driving the actions. Man has been given a higher consciousness, which provides higher choices for living and the ability to be responsible for his own integrity. That consciousness is within the Sacred Heart. Through the heart, you may tap into the higher powers of unity, love, life, honesty, respect, justice, and kindness. By implementing these principles in your life, you may become all you were created to be and make a positive difference in the lives of others.*

"Essentially, the difference between proactive and re-active behavior is determined by whether or not a person perceives himself to be connected and whole, or separate and insufficient. To strengthen this understanding, consider the great miracle of all the systems in the universe—galaxies, planets, and life systems – which are all functioning simultaneously in perfect harmony. Throughout creation there is wholeness, and yet there is always a choice: to view yourself as an isolated part of it or an extension of the whole.

"Reactive behavior stems from beliefs in separation and practices of narrowly focusing on separate and limiting 'parts of life'. The idea that 'pieces and parts' of existence have separate and isolated power leads to an obsession to own or oppose them. Reactive behavior is rooted in the fear and inadequacy a person feels when he strives for external power. On the other hand, proactive behavior begins in the heart, with its perceptions of unity and wholeness. There has been no other true power given to mankind than the higher consciousness of the heart's knowing. All other power is borrowed from the universe or counterfeited. When a person attempts to support his life with acquired power, he will never have enough, no matter how much he

has. He will never feel complete, no matter how much he achieves. This sense of inadequacy will generate a greater thirst for things outside oneself, accompanied by fear of being controlled by them. Through its thirst and hunger for what it is not, a soul then becomes embedded in the mechanics of physical existence and reacts to life instead of embracing it.

"The answer always is in the heart. Remember that within the heart is your connection to God and the oneness of all creation. From this encompassing perspective you may make choices that truly fulfill and sustain your life."

Correlations

Psalms 46:10 "Be still, and know that I am God."
1 Peter 3:4 "But let it be the hidden man of the heart, in that which is not corruptible, even the ornament of a meek and quiet spirit, which is in the sight of God of great price."
Job 31:6 "Let me be weighed in an even balance, that God may know my integrity."
Matthew 5:48 "Be ye therefore perfect, even as your Father which is in heaven is perfect."

The Key

We live in a world rich with opportunity and abundance, yet challenged by conflict and confusion. Every day we are presented with choices of how to optimize positive possibilities and minimize negative encounters. We are on the alert to assert our values, and yet to refrain from judgment so that progress may continue toward unity and freedom. We always have a choice between proactive and reactive behavior. The **key** to proactive living is in knowing that within the whole of existence, conscious choice and miraculous potential are also part of cause and effect.

When we truly have understanding, our basic goodness usually prevails, and we make decisions from the heart. Most often, our tendency to become reactive increases as our understanding diminishes.

Unfortunately, we often presume understanding until faced with a crisis. We may assume the rightness of a fixed position until it is shaken. This is where strengthening the heart in daily practice and preparation can make a profound difference. For example, do you know exactly what you are at liberty to do, to have, and to be... without reservation, without condition? Without an answer to such important issues, life is diminished...even in the best of times. In the worst of times, it can be unbearable. With answers to such important questions, you are IN the best of times regardless of external conditions!

Two thousand years ago Jeshua came into a world much like our own. It was a world dominated by a large prosperous nation, resented by smaller nations that pursued other values. It was a world on the brink of change forever. In the face of many challenging decisions, it was imperative that humanity be elevated. We are in such need today. Perhaps more critically than ever before.

Essentially, Jeshua taught us to respect the laws of cause and effect, and yet to know that we are part of the realm of miracles as well. All things are possible BECAUSE of the way things work...not in spite of natural law. Many other teachers have taught us various pathways to transcendence. We can enroll in the finest universities to study the laws of cause and effect. But Jeshua combined these two seemingly contradictory possibilities in an amazing and unified way. He taught us how to be IN the world, yet not be OF the world. He walked among us as an ordinary human being that his teachings of extraordinary transcendence might be fully valid for anyone's life.

Because of the miracles associated with his appearance to me, I was worried for some time that the experience would set me apart from others in a strange or special way. To my great relief, no such thing occurred. Actually, I share more connections now than ever before. From an historical perspective, I am but one among many to whom Jeshua has appeared. He lost no time after his resurrection. On that same afternoon, he appeared from nowhere to two men traveling on the road to Emmaus. He went home with them for dinner, gave them messages of truth and love, and then disappeared again into thin air. From then until now he has never stopped teaching us about the ever-present possibility of miracles within the context of ordinary life.

In practical matters, it is natural and logical to look for explanations of cause and effect. It is also the most natural response for a child of God to expect a miracle. Here is where a challenge to common rationality lies. In many ways, this is the core of Jeshua's brilliant and revolutionary message. He taught us to work simultaneously with these complementary perspectives on existence and to integrate them into a concept of wholeness. Only with this complete picture can we remain stable in a state of proactive living. Only with this higher understanding can we correct or prevent undesirable actions while maintaining the greater vigilance of love.

Unless we are directed by faith or consciousness to seek for the whole, we may easily become absorbed in one or more rewarding or demanding "parts" of life. At times, we may be oblivious to the potential for complete unity. At other times, we may feel like we are diagonally parked in a parallel universe! All the while, the most rewarding opportunity awaits us…to see miracles in "ordinary" existence. This can become a task of coordinated enlightenment. Except that we know our lives to be part of a greater wholeness, and we seek to view that wholeness from the inner seed of our own BEING, there would be no rational way of viewing all parts within the same whole.

Jeshua's basic message to me is: "Love is who you are." In this, you are one with your Creator, who is Perfect Love. From this primary focal point, all our other connections emerge as part of the One Spirit. On any subject there are many perspectives. They become exposed through exchange, sharing and communication. This is the never-ending dialogue of life. Sometimes it plays out on a grand scale, such as the alternating rhythms of mortality and immortality. At other times, it can be a subtle shift of viewpoint bringing new—even humorous—insight to a familiar subject.

Within dialogue, there are always choices. Often they are not between external things as much as opportunities to determine the quality of life. To comprehend this, we will have to change the direction of our reasoning...how we connect the sequences of cause and effect. If we view consequences as external, then we miss the point. We must see them as reflecting our relationship to life.

In science and thought, logic is the study of comparative values and what comes from what. It's the study of derivatives—how something came to be what it is. Usually, when we think of derivatives, we think of something far down the chain of cause and effect...such as organic evolution, chemical compounds, or financial certificates having only speculative value. Through derivative processes, all of life is an effect becoming another effect...a chain that persists by progressing **away from** its source or point of origin. In complex derivative systems, we often de-emphasize intervals and gradations and shift our focus to emerging polarities. Thus, we simplify with opposites and lose our sense of the subtle. We use explanations of good and bad to sort out our preferred and not preferred experiences.

Jeshua explained to me that in the beginning there was only good. Evil appeared to the degree that life moved away from its Original Source. Evil has no fundamental presence or power. Evil is a destructive threat coming from polar opposites as they play out in experience and reality. This is also true with reactivity. As we consent to act with fear and anger, for motives of control, we have chosen the energy most associated with derivative potential. When we are submerged in the polarities of life or captured by them, we most often react. In the midst of challenging circumstances, we can easily wonder, "Where is God?" and reject the idea that all creation was originally good.

If we simply open ourselves to a broader perspective, embracing all aspects of the experience, we make ourselves available to greater fulfillment.

In presenting these ideas, Jeshua was connecting logic (derivative explanations of reality) with original perfection. The word for that original perfection is LOGOS – the starting point of all logic. The word LOGOS has often been used in reference to the Prime and moving Force...the Source of All...The Truth! Logic, on the other hand, is a system of thinking we use to explain cause and effect. Logic is the language of science and reason. Logic is both progressive and comparative. White progresses toward black (or vice versa), passing through numerous shades of gray. When these progressions are omitted, white stands out in stark contrast to black. In our consciousness, the simple perception of white may bring to mind progressions of gray or immediately invoke the opposite extreme of black. This polar response mechanism may occur automatically and unconsciously, if not balanced by some higher way of responding. LOGOS is the absolute, immovable equilibrium that provides the "constant", or framework, in which logic unfolds. In presenting the two systems of order as being connected, there is actually a **new logic**, one with many simultaneously integrated perspectives. When you understand the implications of this integration in logic, you will be entering one of the greatest paths to wisdom.

The two principles of order have always been indelibly connected, but we have failed to see the grace of that connection because we have tried to derive LOGOS **from** logic. We try to find equilibrium as a center-point defined by extreme possibilities of logic and contrast. In other words, we are trying to find the center-point of a line by first determining its limits. What if it has no limits? We are unconsciously driven to compare extremes of possibility, as if somehow the magic center of a limited dimension would provide an answer. That is the trap of reactive behavior. It does not bring answers, and yet we faithfully engage in it as if it could.

Albert Einstein faced this dilemma as he studied the nature of light. He realized the limits of Newtonian physics and structured reasoning. He knew somehow that light was a center point of physical integration – but could not **deduce** it from polar extremes observed in comparison. Therefore, he postulated an equilibrium point (constant) for energy that contained no mass. From that point, all variations could be predicted. In discovering this postulate to be true, he established a new infinity-valued logic, which we now call relativity. For the first time in science, LOGOS and logic had been connected.

Jeshua's explanation of life was radical then...and now. He brought dramatic evidence of a miraculous universe fully compatible with the laws of cause and effect. He taught that derivative consequences and original virtue were completely coexistent, and that mankind is part of the mystical paradox. At one time Jeshua would say, "There is none without sin." Then on another occasion he would instruct, "Be ye perfect as your Father in Heaven." At first, these strangely divergent thoughts seem almost irreconcilable. In the history of Christianity, many factions have disagreed over their meanings because these instructions came from a consciousness so far ahead of its time, it could scarcely be understood except by faith. He knew that mankind was inseparable from this paradox: We were created in the image of God. We come from our love...not our history. Yet we also have history, conditioning, and survival concerns. **Therefore, both aspects are present...and each provides opportunities for experience and focus.**

An enduring state of equilibrium sustains the patterns of cause and effect. This is indeed an amazing universe! When we shift from comparative logic to heart-centered perceptions of unity, we find whole new possibilities for perceiving and predicting experience in our lives. From this perspective, all manner of new realizations may occur...from practical, to scientific, to sublime.

Perhaps all of our limitations in life are rooted in limited perspectives **about** life. When we call upon God, yet answers don't seem to come... it may be because we have defined God with our own limiting concepts, rather than permitting God to define us with empowering strength. When we define God as *only* the answer to our self-created problems, then we do not see the Source of Life in its glory, and we rob ourselves of its miracles. Through the practice of limiting ideas, one's whole life could be like the fellow who slipped while climbing a tree. He grabbed a branch and hung there for an hour or so. As exhaustion began to loosen his grip, he **cried** out to heaven: "God, help me, please, help me!" All of a sudden, the clouds parted and a voice boomed out from on high... *"Let go!"* The man paused and looked up at heaven once more. In *desperate anxiety* he shouted, **"Is anyone else up there!?"**

Jeshua's life was a string of miracles, but they were not used for show or even to win conviction in him. They were to demonstrate an enduring truth about existence and to expose the choices always presented in every moment. With assurance, he said, "All these things you shall do and more." When you allow Love to be the Source of your actions, all things are possible. When you can cease to be defined by your conditions, you will know the true liberty of love. Then you will understand the true meaning of his words, "I am in the world, but not of the world."

Inspirations

Lal Ded (b. 1326 d.?) Kashmir:
   "On the way to God the difficulties
   Feel like being ground by a millstone,
   Like night coming at noon, like
   Lightening through the clouds.

But don't worry!
What must come, comes.
Face everything with love.
As your mind dissolves in God."

Brother Ramon (b.1935 d.2000) England:
"Lord of the elements and changing seasons,
Keep me in the hollow of your hand.
When I am tossed to and fro by the winds of adversity
And the blasts of sickness and misunderstanding,
Still my racing heart, quieten my troubled mind."

St. Teresa of Avila (b. 1515 d.1582) Spain:
"May nothing move you;
May nothing terrify you;
Everything passes;
God never changes.
Patience be all to you.
Who trusts in God shall never be needy.
God alone suffices."

Applications

The applications for this lesson are simple but profoundly life changing.

1. In any situation where you may be tempted to thoughtlessly **react**—catch yourself and make a proactive decision about how you could respond differently, with more tolerance and consideration, or perhaps with more honesty or respect. Then take note of how the outcome is different than it would have been if you had merely reacted.

2. Memorize the seven dimensions of the heart's intelligence: Unity, Love, Life, Respect, Honesty, Justice, and Kindness. Then give yourself examples of how each principle would be a preferred alternative to reactions you have made in the past. Practice this in the present.

Meditation

In this meditation, we will relax into the oneness with all life, and release our minds into spaciousness and tolerance. This meditation would be best practiced outside on the grass, under the stars, or by natural bodies of water. If they are not available, you can create these spacious environments in your mind's eye. The objective of this meditation is to practice openness, tolerance, acceptance, and unity of all things. Cultivate equanimity and non-attachment. Neither grasp at anything nor keep anything back.

Begin with your toes and move to the top of your head, acknowledging every part of your body as equally valuable in the whole of your physical form. Notice where there is any blockage or stickiness, and pronounce these areas neither more important nor less important than any other part of your being.

Now purse your lips and blow. As you do, direct your attention toward any areas of tightness or restriction. In your mind's eye, see a strong wind passing through the blockage until that area relaxes into the flow of life.

Acknowledge any thoughts passing through your consciousness. Accept, but do not attach any opinions or expectations to them.

Survey your life. Are you grasping for anything? Are you grasping for any attainment, any sensation, any feeling? Are you grasping at a loved one? Are you grasping for security? Wherever you have grasping attachments, you will have limited some aspect of life and lost your view of its wholeness.

Now purse your lips again and blow. As you do, direct your attention toward any area of attachment or blockage. In your mind's eye, see a strong wind passing through the restrictions until this area surrenders to the flow of life. As your whole being relaxes into the flow of life, observe the benefits of non-grasping consciousness and begin to repeat this verse:

May I accept things as they are.
May I be open, balanced, and caring.

Now wish this to a neutral person, then to a loved one, and finally to someone you dislike. Visualize each person repeating this verse and wishing it to you.

Open your eyes and breathe deeply. Notice everything that surrounds you. Can you be with it, fully engaged and deeply caring without grasping or rejecting anything?

Prayer

O Eternal Light,
Shine into our hearts;
Help us to have patience with everything unresolved,
And strive to love the process of living.
Steer our course to where the mind is without fear
And the head is held high
To where knowledge is free,
To where the world has not been broken
Into fragments by narrow walls,
To where words come from the depths of truth,
To where the clear stream of reason has not lost its way,
To where the heart is led forward by ever widening
Circles of love.

Eternal Wisdom,
Scatter our ignorance,
That we may see the truth in each present moment
And live our way into fulfillment.

Amen

14

FREEDOM AND FORGIVENESS

The Message

"You said that judgment is the original sin. If that is true, how do we approach life with discernment and move it upward, without preferring one set of possibilities over another?"

"The answer to that lies in how you seek improvement. There are those who say that one must repel fleas to restore health to a dog; and there are others who know that a healthy dog does not attract fleas. In the headlong pursuit of personal accomplishment and ideals, one may develop personal fixations on villains and heroes or limiting beliefs that center on popular ideas. It is easy to believe that symbols of success or failure represent what is right and wrong with the human race, but why limit yourself to such narrow perspectives?

"There are now over six billion souls in the human family. Why not find your rightful place within it and work to make the whole body healthier? The truth is, there are much greater forces affecting your life than any that have captured your attention. This is a living, dynamic environment. When you are in a positive way of being, you simply flow with it. When you fixate your attention on negative issues, you make your life into an obstacle to be moved aside.

"I did not come to judge you, but to set you free from judgment. You are a family. Many are lost, hurt, and alone. Judgment was the original cause of these alienated conditions. What makes you think that more judgment is the answer? I ask you to forgive one another, but more than that, I ask you to do it with all your heart. Proclamations to forgive, or decisions only made in the

mind, can be just another form of judgment. Many speak hollow words of forgiveness and never open their hearts again. Even for that, I do not judge you. When I see you judge, I see you not as wrong, but as weary and led by misunderstanding. A person who judges is one depleted of ability to experience anything further on his chosen path. He justifies the stagnation and resists change. His ability to seek greater understanding and community is depleted. He fears being subdued, when his desire is to be triumphant. Persisting through a dark night of conflict, with exhaustion, desperation, and pain does not cause the dawn to happen. It is better to have the wisdom of a child, resting when darkness falls. The spirit of a new morning brings hope and renewed perspective.

"Only through the spirit of a new day can you understand the blessings of forgiveness and see the perils of judgment. The power of forgiveness is that it can restore transparency to your life and freedom to your spirit. By comparison, when you judge, you adopt a fixed position on something you do not understand. Each time you do this, you block your growth toward enlightenment and place a greater distance between yourself and the Creator.

*"The most common misunderstanding about forgiveness is that it means giving up or giving in on what you believe is right, or releasing a debt that you feel is an injustice. I am not saying that you should condone destructive actions. You do a real service to yourself and others when you correct situations, attitudes, and conditions that give rise to harmful behavior. Forgiveness means **bringing resolution to troubled situations.** The subject of forgiveness is not for the weak of heart. Nothing will make your heart stronger than forgiveness practiced for the accomplishment of resolution. When you forgive, do not concede to appease your transgressor to calm your own fear of further harm. This does not bring resolution. Those who attempt this find no end to the chain of enforced and disagreeable realities.*

"Though forgiveness begins in your heart, it usually requires action. It begins with a change of viewpoint. You must rise above the judgments and hidden venues that are perpetuating your conflict. Whatsoever has been set in motion by conflict must then be released.

Otherwise, your life will be limited to that reality. Would you give such power to what has hurt you?

"When you give the cause of your life to anyone else—except for God—you gradually lose all freedom and transparency. Every relationship and endeavor will suffer.

*"There is no single formula or process for forgiveness. Forgiveness is **known by its result!** Prayer is the best beginning. Love is the power that carries it through. Simple release may often be enough ... sometimes laughter. At times, you must act to prevent the offense from occurring again or worsening. Sometimes you must repair a degenerating condition or inform an offender of how hurtful the actions have been. Sometimes an expression of emotion is helpful. You can be assured that the problem will not clear by adding more destruction. Revenge will not restore peace.*

"Forgiveness of another restores the truth of one's own being. It brings freedom, transparency, and the restoration of life. Any process leading to understanding can accomplish this. When your life is transparent, you are free, wise, and of service to all. Your life is a profound asset to the consciousness of mankind. You were never created to be a solid perishable entity—but to exist in the love of God, forever in your Creator's presence. Your delusion of mortality exists to the degree that you, as a soul, have lost your transparency and begun to see yourself as the mortal container representing you in the world. Therein the trouble began.

"You cannot afford to withhold forgiveness. Nothing will destroy your life more surely, for there is a great hidden grief in the denial of forgiveness. Your heart is so heavy from what you have not forgiven that you bear the offenses of another as if they were your own. Souls are punishing themselves because of what they cannot forgive. It is for this reason that in forgiving yourself, you are actually forgiving old injury from others. Within the human perspective, forgiveness simply means to release. The patterns that entangle a soul in grief and guilt are often complex, but the result of forgiveness is simple: you are free!

"It is not within human authority to offer complete

exoneration from error. That power is reserved alone for the One who created all things. You cannot prevent exoneration by withholding your forgiveness or by judging. You cannot insure exoneration by punishing yourself or others. You can, however, determine how your life and character are shaped by what you experience. If you would be free and restored to health and immortality...forgive!"

Correlations

Matthew 18:21-22 "Then Peter came to Jesus and asked, 'Lord, how many times shall I forgive my brother when he sins against me? Up to seven times?' Jesus answered, 'I tell you not seven times, but seventy times seven.'"

John 8:7 "If any one of you is without sin, let him cast the first stone."

Matthew 7:1 "Do not judge, or you too will be judged. For in the same way you judge others, you will be judged, and with the measure you use, it will be measured to you."

The Key

The fourteenth key unlocks the nature and purpose of human struggle: Experience is necessary to make us strong. Forgiveness is necessary to set us free. Judgment merely impedes that process and separates us from our holy purpose of being in union with God.

As a child, I had so little to forgive that the concept was almost foreign to me. As I grew to be a young woman, there were

were caused more by perplexity than grief. I wondered why, in my otherwise pleasant existence, I was momentarily inconvenienced with discomfort and unhappiness. Little did I know that I was virtually illiterate in one of the great virtues of the human heart. Fortunately, this would not last. One day, on a visit home from college, I was sitting in my mother's kitchen with my books spread out on the table. She was at the counter drying dishes. In a moment of quiet compassion, I looked up and watched the way she carefully handled glasses that were nothing more than jelly jars, and everyday dishes that were unmatched remnants of forgotten sets. Her hands had the caring touch of a woman who had ceased to judge. Her character had marks of honor I could only defer to in respect. Then in a moment of sudden unexpected grief, I collapsed my head on the table and wept. My mother rushed over to ask what the matter was, but I could only speak in broken sobs. When I finally cleared my voice and eyes, I engaged with her strong, comforting eyes and confessed. "You have struggled in a way I will never know. And when I think about the suffering of so many people, why am I exempt?" I will never forget her answer. She could not have been more earnest had she been consoling a wounded soldier. "God gives us what we need for our growth. Possibly for you, the struggle needs to be within. But don't worry, you will not be spared. We all struggle in different ways. The important thing is what you make of it."

Until that moment, I had viewed the hardship of others as cause for pity—or perhaps dread of pain—should I be caught in similar circumstances. In retrospect, that viewpoint almost seems arrogant. But in truth, it was just naive. None are set apart from the human condition. As long as there is strife **among us**, there will be struggle **within us**. There is a unique path of attainment for each of us; and, we each have our unique challenges. In that moment, I knew that the innate struggle of my life was already in place and would eventually shape my character. I felt like the butterfly that was finally strong enough to emerge from its cocoon and survive.

The triumphant butterfly was a very vivid image for me because of my personal experience with one that did not survive. A classmate of mine had found a cocoon lying by the sidewalk on his way to school. It was still undamaged and tightly woven to the tiny fallen branch. After presenting it to the class, our homeroom teacher gently placed the cocoon in a wide-top jar with holes in the lid. She set it on her desk where we could all watch the miracle that would be emerging in a few days. Every morning we observed the silky envelope. Then, finally, almost imperceptibly at first, the cocoon moved. We watched more closely and soon the cocoon was trembling with activity. Finally the shaking became so intense that we feared the butterfly would die from its battle. Our teacher panicked as well, and removed the lid on the jar. She then took a sharp penknife from her desk and carefully made a tiny slit in the side of the cocoon. Almost immediately, one wing appeared and then another was outstretched. The butterfly was free! It seemed to enjoy its freedom and walked along the edge of the Mason® jar and along the edge of our teacher's desk. But it didn't fly. At first we thought the wings needed time to dry, but time passed, and still the butterfly did not take off.

Worry propelled us to consult with the science teacher. We explained the whole situation and what we had done. With a regretful sigh, the science teacher informed us that the butterfly would likely never fly because it was not strong enough. "You see, the struggle for emergence is what gives the butterfly its strength to fly. In nature, a butterfly simply does not emerge until its wings are strong enough to assist its survival."

We have all asked, "Why is there suffering?" It certainly seems that heavier loads are given to some than others. Perhaps therein lies an opportunity for us to correct an imbalance. Most certainly we will not grow in our humanity without caring, sharing, compassion, and charity. At the same time, it is important not to embed a judgment of superiority within our sympathy. Often we project our own fears into the challenge of others, like the anxious students who prematurely relieved the butterfly of its struggle.

Wisdom impels us even to consider that suffering is the ultimate challenge to judgment itself. I was once privileged to share the last days and passing of a lovely child stricken with leukemia. Her parents were torn with grief and judgment, but the little girl was a lovely angel who comforted them every day. Repeatedly they would ask me, "Why does our daughter have to suffer?" When I asked the child how she felt, she would say, "I'm not suffering. It's my parents who hurt. Could you help them feel better?"

When we look around our troubled world, how do we relieve the anguish? How do we forgive? Perhaps it begins by releasing our own worry and judgment. Clearly there is harm and destruction that needs to be addressed by some form of justice, containment, or correction ... at least until its energy can re-emerge in a more constructive way. But in the end, it may be that our only need for forgiveness, to ourselves and others, is that we did not know the presence of God more richly while we lived. Perhaps we did not allow the power of God to work through us more fully. We cannot live another's life or make another's choices. But in living our own life to the fullest, we may know God. In that, we will make a difference. Considering that a certain amount of pain is part of living, it may be that one of the greatest human tragedies is that we view our struggles as punishment, and suffering as evil. Could it be that life is just a great cocoon from which the butterfly is born upon the death of its shell?

Inspirations

Sophocles (c. 496 - 406 BCE) Greece:
  "The prayer of one pure heart, I think, has the power to atone for many."
Marcus Aurelius (b.121- d.180) Rome:
  "It is in your own power, whenever you wish, to retire into

yourself: and nowhere is there any place that a man may retire to that is quieter and more free from politics than his own soul."

Martin Luther (b.1483 - d.1546) Germany:
"Just as we can't stop birds from flying over our heads, but can stop them from nesting in our hair, so we can't avoid evil thoughts, but we can stop them from taking root in our heart and giving birth to evil deeds."

Francis Bacon (b.1561 - d.1626) England:
"We read that we ought to forgive our enemies; but we do not read that we ought to forgive our friends."

Applications

With every judgment we make of another, we have introduced a negative possibility into our own life. It has long been known that positive beliefs as well as negative can affect our life and destiny. A focus on the positive is called a "placebo" effect, and the negative is called a "nocebo" effect. As people presume the worst that is usually what they get. The word "nocebo" is Latin for "I will harm." It is not a new idea that beliefs can be harmful as well as helpful. What is now patently obvious is that any consistent and persistent thought will eventually manifest into physical reality. Some years ago, researchers stumbled onto a striking discovery. Women who believed that they were prone to heart disease were nearly four times as likely to die as women with similar risk factors who did not hold such fatalistic views. In other words, the higher risk of death had nothing to do with the usual causes of heart disease—age, blood pressure, cholesterol, or weight. Instead, it tracked closely with belief. That study is a classic in the annals of research on the "nocebo" phenomenon, the evil twin of the "placebo" effect.

This can even be demonstrated biologically. For example, 34 college students were told an electric current would be passed through their heads and the researchers warned that the experience could cause a headache. Though not a single volt of current was used, more than two-thirds of the students reported headaches. Science is finally looking beyond the veil between mind and body. With the aid of high-tech imaging devices, neurologists are taking pictures of the brain in action. In a recent blind study, researchers studied patients with Parkinson's disease who were given a placebo under the guise of a medication that stimulates the release of a brain chemical called dopamine. In most cases, the brain responded exactly as if the real medication had been given. Apparently, the release of brain chemicals has everything to do with what the mind expects. In other cases, where depressed patients were wary of medication or worried about drug side effects, even the actual medication did not have a positive effect. These patients even developed negative symptoms!

These are very real effects. Whatever you think about will be focused into action until it becomes reality. This is especially true if there is considerable emotional intensity behind the thought. Releasing fear, abstaining from judgment, and practicing forgiveness is crucial to a meaningful life, not because it is saintly, but because it is sensible. Life is too short and too precious to be wasted on the consequences of negative projection.

Now let's consider your life:

1. List the times in your life when you viewed a challenging situation as being necessary, constructive, or even positive – and it turned out that way.
2. List the times when you viewed a situation as being negative – and it became worse.
3. List the times when you addressed an injury with constructive

correction instead of vengeance – and it healed.
4. List the times when you responded to an injury or fear at its own level – and it became worse.
5. List the times when you sought a higher perspective for a destructive occurrence – and found consolation.
6. List the times when you sought truth above reality – and negative connections lost their hold.
7. Consider the many immensely positive connections you could have in your life and how much more important these could be to you than the negative connections you hold onto out of loss, fear, or resentment.
8. List the times you have forgiven – and found release.
9. List the times you accepted forgiveness – and found release.
10. Consider the charity of forgiveness as the wealth of freedom.

Meditation

In this meditation, God is speaking to you. Read this until you can close your eyes and recall the essence of its meaning. In that quiet state, feel the presence of God until you are blessed with the promise of this message and know its truth in your heart.

"I am always with you, even when you do not sense my presence.
I love you always, even when you do not love yourself.
I include you in abundant opportunities for living,
Even though you often focus on scarcity.
I am aware of your every need, although My perception
of your need
May be very different from your own.
I listen to your problems, and offer you solutions.
Although these solutions may come in the form of new
perspectives, you refuse.

I hear your prayers and answer them according to your heart's truth.
I am the light and the thoughts in your mind;
I am the sight in your eyes,
I am the life in your body,
I am the feeling in your heart.
I am always at work in your life for your greater good;
I offer you serenity, courage, and wisdom.
Trusting in Me, you will discover the secret of opening your heart to my love.
The greater your faith in Me, the more I am able to fill your heart With My love.
I love you without conditions and give to you
from an ever-flowing fountain of love, peace, and joy.
I am with you in every pursuit and every challenge.
Unlike your friends who may run in fear,
I am with you through the worst of times.
As you meet with pain, I will turn it into compassion.
As you meet with disappointment,
I will turn it into hope, courage, and endurance.
As you suffer harm from others, I will teach you to forgive.
As you realize the error of your ways,
And sincerely regret the pain you have caused others,
I will forgive you; and teach you the gift of mercy.
You are My beloved child.
It is My will that you would be wise, caring, and prosperous for all your life in all ways."

Prayer

Oh Holy One,
May Your grace and purity be with us.
May we see the unity in all creation.
May there be tolerance on earth.
May the springs of the earth give water to us all.
May we be nurtured with love.
May Your will bring us into harmony,
And the sorrows of yesterday be forgiven.
Make us children within our own hearts
And heirs to Your peace.

Amen

15

MAGNETIC ENERGY AND ZERO POINT

The Message

A number of years ago I was powerfully transformed by a spiritual experience, second only to the appearance of Jeshua in 1992. Without this second epiphany, I would never have spoken or written about my conversations with him. I would not have found that special place within myself, where his truth would become my own. This occurrence and his subsequent response to it are imminently relevant to this chapter, because it was my first and only encounter in this life of a true Void.

It happened one evening in April 1996. I was browsing in a bookstore when my eye caught the title of a popular spiritual book that I had been intending to read. I started to pick it up when my hand froze in mid-reach. My heart pronounced a silent, but percussive "NO!" The reaction was not one of rejection or any other negative insinuation. It was simply a mandate to honor the wisdom already given to me before acquiring any more. When my hand stopped, it seems as if my whole being went into a motionless state through which I entered a realm of endless expansion somewhere between solid physical reality and the subjective world of inner thought. By way of expanding consciousness, I passed through corridor after corridor, through door after door. Each one opened to greater expanse and light until at last I stood on the threshold of infinity. Before me was an incredible light show and I could hear the music of the spheres. A gentle touch, like a light gust of wind, pushed me over the edge and I fell into infinite cosmic space. To my surprise, I was known and received as if I had been expected. I was one with Absolute Life and Consciousness, and there was only Peace. I could see and experience all of creation generating itself. It was without beginning or end. Somehow, I had crossed over the beginning of time—the first word, the first utterance of vibration. I was in the Void—a place that is less than nothing and more than everything. I could see and feel the presence of eternal life, and light was flowing like rivers. I have not known such a dimension in my worldly existence. Rather than progressions of conditional space and substance, only intervals of time separated one experience from another. Here, love alone governs the appearance or disappearance of everything. Here was true Zero: chaos forming all possibilities simultaneously, and reducing all possibilities to utter simplicity.

I asked quizzically and wide-eyed, "Where is this place!? Where am I?" I was in a realm more ancient than my soul and yet virginal with undreamed potential! In days to come, and through discussions with Jeshua, I was to learn that the Void is inside and outside everything. You, me, and all things are simultaneously inside and outside the Void. The Void is a vacuum of nothingness between all physical particles and even between the inner world of subjective awareness and the outer world of objective reality. The Void is the inner sanctuary of creation where "now" and "forever" are of equal duration.

"To all things there is an inner and an outer world. This is true of the cosmos or of the least particle within it. It is true of a rosebud or a human soul. The inner and outer worlds reveal themselves through different kinds of perception and different kinds of encounters. Between these two easily perceived realities, there is yet another deeper inner world, which is invisible even to you. This invisible world is waiting to be discovered, begging to be revealed. This is a reality beyond the limits of your dream horizon. This is your true magnetic energy. The invisible inner world is both majestic and humble. It is shy and elusive, yet powerful as an ocean. At times, you catch glimpses of this world in your dreams and imaginings, or

perhaps in moments of ecstasy, tenderness, or compassion. However, the most powerful connection to this realm is through sincere and devout prayer. Prayer occurs in the heart, but it can be facilitated with any words or activity that invoke your own true presence in the presence of God. This occurs in the mysterious invisible zone. Anyone or anything in its true presence is intrinsically connected with the Divine. In this state, a natural equilibrium brings life into greater wholeness whether you understand it or even perceive it.

"Do not limit your experience of this world by what you can see and touch with your physical senses or think about in your mind. These three dimensions of reality (outer, inner, and invisible) are known in different ways. The outer world is essentially recognized through the detection of resistive patterns of data. Thoughts, feelings, intentions, and attitudes circumscribe our subjective world. The deep inner world is only known by the humility you feel in the presence of a force that calls you into life, moves you through life, and carries you beyond. For example, the outer world of an elephant is the forest, the fields of grass, rivers with lush muddy banks, and bright starry nights. Its subjective world is made up of feelings and thoughts about all that, to which there are qualities of life, memories, social connections, history and a sense of belonging to the herd and the ancestors of the herd. Beyond that, there is the deep inner world invisible even to the elephant. This is the power of its place in the kingdom. Through a sense of its own presence in the kingdom, and the presence of nature and natural elements, the elephant will be drawn mysteriously to where the rains have come. Perhaps he will be carried away mysteriously from where the hunters are, and then beyond life to where the elephant in its glory may serve eternity or re-emerge again into creation. Reverent connection with this deep inner realm is the humility of a soul seeking to know its nobility and the nobility of the soul seeking to express its faith in the great unknown. The inner world is a Void (a vacuum, technically speaking), for there is neither time nor space. The inner world is much more ancient than either the subjective world of thought or the objective world of manifestation. At the heart of the inner world is the seed of all beginnings—ever able to

newly begin from this timeless potential. This is the place where love as Pure Being is replicated and carried forth to appear in the worlds of thought and manifestation."

Correlations

Genesis 1:2 "And the earth was without form, and void; and darkness was upon the face of the deep. And the Spirit of God moved upon the face of the waters."

Isaiah 48:5 "I have even from the beginning declared it to you; before it came to pass I showed it to you."

Revelations 10:6 "And swear by him that lives forever and ever, who created heaven, and the things therein, and the earth, and the things therein, and the sea, and the things which are therein, that there should be time no longer."

2 Thessalonians 3:16 "Now the Lord of peace himself give you peace always by all means."

The Key

Zero Point energy is far from zero in output. It is actually the true source of energy in the universe. As more is being learned about this magnetic form of energy, it is revealing itself more in the realm of time than space. There is a particular division of physics being developed to study this phenomenon and its influence on the physical world. Concurrently, in our subjective growth, we are learning about the power of "now", which involves the ultimate compression of time to a single point. In the world of experience, we are acknowledging the heightened energy of synchronicity and simultaneous occurrence.

The correlation of time and attraction is universally being explored, because it comes from the inner life of the universe. From our human ego-centered perspective we have previously assumed that only a soul or a conscious being possessed an "inner life". In so doing, we have missed the greater part of existence by not realizing that **every** part of creation is held together by a great collective inner life. Sustaining that inner life, attraction is the mother of supply. The secret to uniting with that great inner world and unlocking magnetic potential lies in releasing our attachment to energy forms, ideas, and practices based on scarcity, resistance, and force. Then much can be discovered about both human nature and the universe.

On March 26, 2002, a team of inventors was awarded a U.S. Patent for a "Motionless Magnetic Generator" (MEG). As the inventors point out, patents are not granted on devices that cannot be proven to work. The U.S. Patent office has been especially skeptical of devices that promise something-for-nothing. I have not seen this particular invention nor can I certify its performance. However, the announcement is noteworthy in that it foreshadows the budding of a new era. It suggests that someone may have tapped into an invisible dimension of energy more abundant than the one in which we are presently competing and struggling.

Leading scientists and professors of physics have told me that low resistance energy inventions are not new and many of them actually generate measurable and verifiable quantities of energy. The problem has always been in generating enough energy to make further efforts worthwhile. In addition to that, all the existing structures for transforming low resistance energy into electricity have a self-defeating flaw. Electrical circuitry in conventional machinery (batteries, generators, and magnets) has a dipole nature. To understand the problem this presents let me first explain that low-resistance magnetic energy is apparently manifesting from the vacuum or zero-point field as a different kind of EM (electromagnetic) wave running longitudinally to the ordinary EM waves, which are generally called transverse waves. As the dipole nature of a generator activates and channels the transverse EM waves it interferes with and actually dampens the vast amount of longitudinal EM waves that normally co-exists in passive harmony with ordinary electromagnetic waves. These newly observed longitudinal EM waves (which are normally undetected, and to date largely untapped) represent a vast untapped resource. All we need is more compatibility between this vast reserve of energy and the instruments we have for exploring and developing it.

Once this happens, a whole new world of enlightenment is waiting for us. What is especially intriguing is the postulate that longitudinal EM waves are created and stored as compressions of time, parallel to the way ordinary EM waves are relative to mass. It has been asserted that time is compressed energy by the same factor that matter is compressed energy ... the speed-of-light squared! If time itself is actually compressed energy (and this greater reserve of energy is actually coming from the time domain), then longitudinal EM waves would be the energy filling the ocean of space-time, which is 98% of our universe. According to the new science of scalar electro-magnetics, this 'other' energy may be stored in fourth dimensional time, rather than third dimensional space. If this is true then we may be able to explore primary magnetism in free and uncharted ways without breaking the law of conservation of energy. It may be possible to provide virtually effort-free electrical energy by tapping the longitudinal EM waves that exist in almost infinite abundance in the vacuum of space.

Jeshua has told us that an adamantine particle is the mass resulting from spontaneous integration within the zero-point field. From that, by way of exchange and accumulation, all other particles derive their mass. The energy of adamantine particles, and the energy generated by the zero-point field, is not the energy generated by friction, as we know within densities of accumulated mass and structure. When the zero-point field is explored and better understood, these particles will be discovered. Nobel Prize winning physicists have proven beyond any doubt that the physical world is one large sea of energy that flashes into and out of being in milliseconds, over and over again. Nothing is solid. This is the world of quantum physics. We only need to take it a few steps further to see the rest of the 'picture'.

Free and endless motion and its subjective counterpart, feeling, is the energy that is compatible with adamantine particles. This is where Consciousness (or Higher Mind) connects to the realm of manifestation through projections of intention and desire. Here at this delicate but dynamic interface is the connective tissue of our universe, having for its outflow the Universal Life Force. This is accomplished through the harmonious connection of feeling, intention, thought and energy. Our thoughts are linked to this invisible energy and they determine the energy forms that emerge. Our thoughts, and most especially our love, literally shift the universe on a particle-by-particle basis to create our physical life. Look around you. Everything you see in our physical world started as an idea, an idea that grew as it was shared and expressed, until it grew enough into a physical object through a number of steps. We literally become what we think about most. Our life becomes what we have imagined and believed in most.

Discovering the zero-point field and energy of our physical universe will inevitably progress with (and reflect) our understanding of the great inner world. The **key** to this higher knowledge lies in finding unity within ourselves, where the infinite Source of energy is always available, and then seeking with all our hearts a pragmatic pathway for developing it externally. Allow your heart to ignite your imagination, and examine the end of this rainbow. Always remember that the energy of the universe is free and endless.

Inspirations

Anonymous:
> "In the depths of space,
> There isn't a trace,
> Of the power that brought it to be.
> But it cannot hide,
> If you look inside,
> It was the Spirit of Life set free."

Kahlil Gibran (b.1883 d.1931) Persia:
> "For what is prayer but the expression of yourself into the living ether? And if it is for your comfort to pour your darkness into space, it is also for your delight to pour forth the dawning of your heart."

St. Gregory of Sinai (b.1290 d.1346) Sinai:
> "The prayer of the heart is the source of all good, refreshing the soul as if it were a garden."

Applications

The thoughts and feelings of your inner world have great impact over your outer world ... even the outer world of other people and living things.

Stress, depression, and illness are very prevalent in our world today, although we have the most competent medical advancements in history. Many researchers who study the relationship of human behavior to illness have traced over 90% of all disease to traumatic experiences preceding an illness by six to twelve months.

Extensive studies have been made of acute illnesses as well as long term physical problems such as: arthritis, emphysema, ulcers, cancer, diabetes and high blood pressure. In an amazingly high percentage of patients, their sickness started six months to one year after a traumatic experience in their life. This is not limited to physical illness. It also includes psychological, financial, career, relationship and family problems.

If you are currently suffering from any disease, then ask yourself the four following questions:

1. How long have I been afflicted with this problem?
2. What happened in my life six months to two years before the symptoms began?
3. How was my inner world different before the trauma?
4. What is my inner world like now?

Contemplate your answer to these questions sincerely and quietly. Some of the most crucial things in life you must do for yourself and only by yourself. No one else can talk, walk, eat, or think for you. Certainly, we can have assistance in these things, and we enjoy companionship. But only you can write, direct, and act on the script of your inner world.

If your thoughts do have the power to create, then maybe you actually create your own world!

Would you like some proof that your inner world has power over the outer manifestations of your life? Then do the following experiment. It has been around for many years and children love it (who knows who first thought of it). It is a very simple one, but it may have quite an effect on your confidence in the power of thought and emotion.

First: Get six to eight raw carrots and cut off the tops (the part you normally throw away).

Second: Place the tops in two bowls with a little water in each.

Third: Label one bowl "negative" and the other bowl "positive".

Fourth: Place them on the windowsill to get sunlight.

Fifth: Every day set each bowl on the counter and talk to those tops separately. Instruct the carrot tops in the "positive" bowl to grow abundantly. Give them love and see them as beautiful, strong, and healthy. Instruct the carrot tops in the "negative" bowl not to grow. Give them hate. Wish them struggle and lack.

If you have moral difficulty with telling a plant to die, remember that you were going to trash the tops anyway. Ask permission of the plant and the Creator to perform an experiment that will make you stronger in support of life in the future. If you still cannot bring yourself to be hostile, then ask the plant to be a willing surrogate for everything and everyone who has caused you frustration, hurt, and disappointment. Heap all of your personal resentments upon them. If that does not work for you, then at least ignore the negative bowl. Separate it from the positive bowl and place it in a windowsill that you never visit. Withhold your love.

In a few days, you will notice a difference because your thoughts do have the power to create! Yes, there is actually a correlation between your inner world and external manifestations around you! Now ask yourself, "Since I controlled something outside my body, what about me? What happens every time I think negative or send out hate? What am I causing to happen to my body?"

Some people actually reverse the growth with the carrots. The tops in the negative bowl grow and the positive die, probably because of an element of sympathy given to the neglected carrot and an element of guilt surrounding the one you have pampered. Remember, feeling is a powerful as thought. If this happens to you then I suggest that you do the experiment again and examine your thoughts and feelings more closely. Focus more and use more carefully considered intention.

Meditation

Sit in a comfortable position, and close your eyes. Allow your body to relax as you move your attention through it from the tips of your toes to the top of your head. Shake your shoulders or roll your head if necessary. Once you are physically relaxed, tell your mind to relax. Draw your attention gently into the area of your heart by deepening your breath. As you inhale, allow your abdomen to swell and hold the breath for as long as you can. Exhale slowly and experience the cleansing release. Feel the seamless unity between your inner and outer worlds. Within this unity, find the center point that is the heart of your being.

Breathe and focus on this center until you see a point of light. As you continue to breathe, fan the spark and see it grow. See it light up your physical heart and begin to enter the blood stream and flow throughout your body. Follow the light through the arteries to every limb, every organ, and every cell. Then see the light return to its source in the heart. Now see these cells form a common light around the outer skin of your body. Notice how it touches the air, lighting the room or landscape where you are until it reaches the walls or distant horizon. Send this light through the rivers of the earth as you did the arteries of your body. See the light empty into the oceans and reach seamlessly from sea to sea. Behold the light of the rivers and oceans becoming a common light that encircles the earth. Now see the lighted atmosphere touch the magnetic space between earth and sun. The two lights are joined and become a common light throughout the solar system. As this happens, imagine our solar system to be a dot of light in the heavens. Fan it with your breath, as you did the light of your heart, until it unites with the light of other stars. The galaxy is now one light that joins with the light of other galaxies. Wherever you see an outer edge to light, see it touch and expand into the next element until there is no separation. If you encounter any holes of darkness, see them filled with light as a waterfall fills a stream. Expand this perception until there is seamless light throughout the universe.

Dwell in the glorious presence of endless light, total possibility, and perfect love. Now behold: This is your inner world! God has given it to you as a mirror image of the outer world, so that you may also share the experience of creation, imagination, choice, freedom, love and pure being. In this light, see your life as it has been. Now see your life as it can be.

With your eyes still closed, begin to make connections between the inner and outer worlds. First, notice the texture of your breath and the temperature of your environment. Then notice the feeling of gravity beneath your body. With your hand, touch something around you and begin to move your limbs. Finally, open your eyes. The first thing that will catch your attention is light. Focus with love upon it and remember the sacred connection in your heart.

Prayer

Divine Creator of all beings, of all worlds, of all times,
Fire of the Spirit and life within us,
We pray that Your light stream forth into the minds of men
And descend upon the earth.
We pray that Your love stream forth into the hearts of men
And descend upon the earth.
We pray that Your grace stream forth into the lives of men
And descend upon the earth.
We rejoice in these gifts and offer our homage, love, and faith.

Amen

16

ABUNDANCE AND PRODUCTIVITY

The Message

A long history of progress towards an industrialized economy has conditioned us to believe that abundance is directly caused by production, and without production, there is eminent scarcity. We have lost our instinctive understanding of the true symbiotic relationship between abundance and productivity. There **is** a causal relationship between the two. But the truth is, effective and meaningful abundance occurs AFTER one's perception or belief in abundance—not the other way around!

In the work ethic of our society, we are taught to produce our prosperity, or do without. 'When you have earned it, you deserve it'. Often resentment is directed toward less industrious people who tax the productive efforts of others. But upon closer examination, we may find that these conditions persist because of some innate and natural drive within human nature to find a better way of sharing. When you think about it, limiting our ideas of human prosperity to the scope of human industry is a very grim prospect.

On a brighter note, we are told in the Book of Genesis, that, "God bestowed on the earth abundance in every form and instructed it to multiply." In that innocent context of life, the first humans aspired to be stewards over **natural** abundance. Never did they consider themselves the source of it! It is critical to know the difference between stewardship and causal power, for therein lies the real key to continued positive morale. Some things we cause, such as our attitudes, beliefs, and personal realities. However, we are stewards for most things. Persistence in the direction of what is truly possible builds wealth and sustains it with genuine satisfaction.

My conversation with Jeshua about this began inadvertently when I expressed my curiosity about the forbidden tree in the center of the Garden of Eden. I asked, "What was the poisonous fruit of our human fall?" Little did I know that I was about to be blessed with an answer to the ancient mystery as well as a key to endless abundance.

"It does not matter what kind of tree it was, for there were no special qualities about the fruit. Nor was obedience the issue. Disobedience was certainly a part of the transgression, but that can only be understood in relation to the story's real point. The meaning of this story has been lost beneath millennia of change from agrarian to industrial living. Nevertheless, the truth contained in the story is eternally valid. Those who lived this teaching understood it so deeply within the context of their lives that they never considered any later generation would require an explicit instruction.

"It was customary in the very ancient world to tithe all manner of harvest back to God. Tithing was tangible praise and gratitude! If you read through the rest of Genesis, other ancient books of the Hebrews, and many surviving records of the pre-industrial world, you will find frequent and explicit instructions about this. Even rotation of crops and fields was mentioned as a kind of tithing. In every field, there would be a strip of grain left uncut for God to distribute back freely to nature. In every orchard there was one tree never harvested and kept sacred as a natural altar to God's abundance. This altar was also an expression of faith in His eternal supply. Indeed, tithing permeated all of life, not just temple contributions or alms to the poor! God was acknowledged and worshipped as the Source of all abundance. Man was considered the recipient, steward, processor, developer, and distributor of that abundance, but certainly not the source of it. "The tree in the center of the garden was a tithing tree.

It was a community symbol of charity, gratitude, and faith. Its generous, untouched bounty united the community in their reverence for life and their assurance of continued supply. In the Genesis story, Eve's transgression was that of violating a sacred area of open beneficence and consuming its fruit for personal gratification. To put it in modern terms, she had just authorized the building of an oil refinery in a sacred wildlife refuge, or bought a yacht with corporate retirement funds. The 'Tree of Life' was a preserved area that symbolized abundance beyond expectation. Man can only hope to connect with the highest level of creativity and true replenishment through such reverence and respect.

"The supply of each day is sufficient for its needs. The only reason a person has 'needs' exceeding his supply is that he has practiced the belief in scarcity until it has become a manifested reality. Scarcity is an interesting, but highly artificial contrivance of the mind. Consider this: When there is more than you can ever touch, see, feel, hear, or do, why would you ever believe in scarcity of your own accord? Actually, scarcity is the most implausible conclusion that could ever be drawn from any body of evidence. The allure of scarcity is that it seems to provide an extra certainty of prediction, manipulation, and control over others. But the inevitable betrayal of such belief is that it will rob you of true abundance. Even if a person becomes materially wealthy and focuses on what he lacks, his heart will be set on fear of losing instead of joy in having.

"Belief in scarcity is essential for artificial economies, because it generates strong motivation to engage in competition, political war, and enforced dominance. There is no basis for this in natural order. All beliefs in scarcity are rooted in man's perception of what he can control and produce for himself. When he does this, man is viewing life through his own instruments of production and limiting his perception of abundance to what his means can control or invent.

"Now please understand, production is an honorable pursuit. Truly productive men and women are actually emulating their Creator. Even so, production is not the cause of prosperity. Absolute certainty that prosperity is possible is the cause of production! **The**

199

visible and open presence of charity, shared one to another, is the source of that belief!

"And charity is not just the giving away of worldly goods. Charity is a generous heart, a grateful spirit, a forgiving soul, a courageous life, an expansive vision, an exploratory mind, caring hands, persistent dedication, and creative ideas. Charity is a visible sign of spiritual wealth. As you express your spiritual wealth, material abundance will follow.

"Spiritual wealth has other recognizable qualities. For one, the **feeling** of wealth is gratitude. The **inner way** of wealth is to be so in harmony with your true being and with God that you do not waste vital energy on looking for greener pastures, but cultivate and multiply that which you have been given. The **attitude** of wealth is humility! Even with meager material possessions, you can experience great abundance and wealth. When you can see the abundance of infinite supply as greater than you are, there is no end to your wealth. When you can know this with all your heart, then material possessions—however great or small—will serve your life and bring no sense of lack. The **action** of wealth is creative ingenuity.

"The greatest obstacles to living abundantly are resentment, self-pity, fear, blame, hoarding, and wishing yourself to be what you are not. Even the very wealthy are guilty of these things and take no joy in their prosperity. Many who live modestly have none of these qualities and enjoy their meager bounty as a king in a palace.

"**Above all else, the confirmation of wealth is charity.** If you would have true wealth, restore the 'Tree of Life' somewhere in your garden. This could literally be a nature sanctuary, or it could be the time you give to help the homeless, or to cultivate the talents of children. As you do this, know that you are sanctifying this activity. Do not enter this sacred place for personal glory, gain, tax advantages, social obligation, or simply to comply with a doctrine of tithing. Perform these acts with sincerity, honor, discretion, and even secrecy when that is appropriate. Do it as a celebration of the Creator's abundance, and your conviction in eternal supply. Your entire prospect of wealth will change when you do this."

Correlations

John 10:10 "I am come that they might have life, and that they might have it more abundantly."

Zechariah 8:12 "For the seed shall be prosperous; the vine shall give her fruit, and the ground shall give her increase, and the heavens shall give their dew; and I will cause the remnant of this people to possess all these things."

Genesis 1:12 "And the earth brought forth grass, and herb yielding seed after his kind, and the tree yielding fruit, whose seed was in itself, after his kind: and God saw that it was good."

Leviticus 27:30 "And all the tithe of the land, whether of the seed of the land, or of the fruit of the tree, is the LORD'S: it is holy unto the LORD."

I Corinthians 13:3 "And though I bestow all my goods to feed the poor, and though I give my body to be burned, and have not charity, it profits me nothing."

The Key

A charitable heart is the **key** to abundance. Abundance has been given to you that no one else can see. It is possible that our belief in scarcity comes from relying on the perceptions of others that were not given the eyes to see what is ours. I personally consider the "comparison of gifts" to be the core transgression in the commandment that instructs us "not to covet". In coveting, we destroy our inner perspective on the abundance uniquely given to us. There is much insecurity, resentment, and envy often associated with our human capacity to accept and cultivate our own gifts, and to support others in doing the same. We each have an equal and indelibly important relationship to God. But we humans are so insecure in that truth we often look for confirmation and proof of it by comparing superficial advantages and disparaging the opportunities of another when they do not seem to support our own. Such attitudes reflect the lowest common denominator of childishness. When I was a university instructor, I was invited to be on the state Arts and Humanities Council. As part of my service, I donated one day a week to teach art to fourth and fifth graders in the public school system. It was in this context that I observed a perfect example of how we use comparison of one another to build mutual limitations instead of multiple opportunities. One little girl was very developed in her eye-to-hand coordination. She was well beyond her age in drawing objects very realistically. But she was so fixated on the outlines of a picture that she could not develop any emotional expression. I encouraged her to look beyond the outlines and allow her hand to move freely. Sitting nearby was a little boy who had a wildly expressive approach to his drawings, but when it came to developing a visual image, he could never get past the chaos of uncontrolled hand movements. I suggested that he practice tracing some pictures to gain a little more eye-to-hand coordination. This coaching was working very well until a third child raised his hand and proclaimed: "But you told Sandy to draw outside the lines, and you told Tommy to practice tracing! That's not fair! Why can't we do the same thing?" After that, the class attitude moved downward from creativity to conformity, as trust in individual differences was lost. I was eventually able to restore *esprit de corps* through sharing and communication, but it would not have happened without deliberate nurturing of each child's personal confidence.

St. Paul, in his first letter to the Corinthians (12:7-11), encouraged the people to remember and respect always that: "Now to each one the manifestation of Spirit is given for the common good. To one there is given through the Spirit the message of wisdom, to another the message of knowledge by means of the same Spirit, to another faith by the same Spirit, to another the gift of healing by that one Spirit, to another miraculous powers, to another prophecy, to another distinguishing between spirits, to another speaking in different kinds of tongues. All these are the work of one and the same Spirit, and he gives them to each one, just as he determines." When you can receive your gifts with gratitude, you know that you have been given much in measure with your ability. God delegates talents. It is up to each one of us to discover, cultivate, and harvest the wealth of these talents. Often there is more to be discovered than we would dare to dream.

In seeking abundance, one of our greatest mistakes comes from the idea that our abundance is limited to what we can produce; and that prosperity comes from accumulating and hoarding whatever wealth we can legitimately claim. Much to the contrary, true prosperity comes from the spirit of creative faith and ingenuity. One of the most powerful instructions by Jeshua on the subject of prosperity centered directly on whether or not a man believes in hoarding or creating. It is the parable of the talents (Matthew 25:15-25). A man was going on a journey, and before he left, he entrusted his servants with several portions of his wealth. Unto one he gave five talents of money, to another two talents, and to another just one—each according to his ability; and he went on his journey. The man who had received the five talents went at once and invested them, and made five more talents. The man with two talents also gained two more. But the man who had received only one talent went off, dug a hole in the ground, and hid his master's money. When the master returned and approached his servants for a settling of accounts, the men who multiplied their money presented their profit as the harvest of faith and ingenuity. The master's response was, "Well done, my good and faithful servants. You have been faithful with a few things; I will put you in charge of many things." But the man who had buried his money and preserved it, was not met with a favorable response. He was punished for his hoarding, laziness, and lack of creative faith in the laws of abundance. His one talent was taken away and given to the man who had multiplied the master's wealth the most.

It is the role and purpose of the Children of God to expand creation! Abundance is everywhere for those who decipher the secret of their own being. This is your first requirement for success, and no one can do it for you. Yes, there is risk, but on the other side of such risk is the greatest fulfillment you will know on this earth.

When Alexander Graham Bell invented the telephone in 1876, it did not ring off the hook with calls from potential backers. After making a demonstration call to President Rutherford Hayes, the President remarked: "That's an amazing invention, but who would ever want to use one of them?"

When Thomas Edison invented the light bulb, he tried over 2,000 experiments before he got it to work. A young reporter asked him how it felt to fail so many times. He said, "I never failed once. I invented the light bulb. It just happened to be a 2,000-step process."

In the 1940's, another young inventor named Chester Carlson took his idea to 20 corporations, including some of the biggest in the country. They all turned him down. In 1947—after seven long years of rejections—he finally got a tiny company in Rochester, New York - the Haloid Company - to purchase the rights to his invention, an electrostatic paper-copying process. Haloid became the Xerox Corporation we know today.

In 1944, Emmeline Snively, director of the Blue Book Modeling Agency, told modeling hopeful Norma Jean Baker, "You'd better learn secretarial work or else get married." This model went on to become Marilyn Monroe.

In 1954, Jimmy Denny, manager of the Grand Ole Opry, fired a singer after one performance. He told him, "You ain't goin' nowhere son. You ought to go back to drivin' a truck." This performer went on to become the most popular singer in the world - "The King" - Elvis Presley.

In 1962, four nervous young musicians played their first record audition for the executives of the Decca Recording company. The executives were not impressed. While turning down this group of musicians, one executive said, "We don't like their sound. Groups with guitars are on the way out." The group was called "The Beatles".

Wilma Rudolph was the 20th of 22 children. She was born prematurely and her survival was doubtful. When she was four years of age, she contracted double pneumonia and scarlet fever, leaving her with a paralyzed left leg. At nine years of age, she removed the metal leg brace she had been dependent upon and began to walk without it. By thirteen, she had developed a rhythmic walk, which doctors said was a miracle. That same year she decided to become a runner. She entered a race and came in last. For the next few years, she came in last in every race she entered. Everyone told her to quit, but she kept on running. One day she actually won a race…and then another. From then on, she won every race she entered. Eventually this young lady, who was told she would never walk again, went on to win *three Olympic gold medals!*

One of the most common mistakes we all make in the pursuit of happiness and prosperity comes from acting on limited perception of reality and not considering what is possible when working in unison with a larger reality. Because of our own shortsighted investments, we often fail to see a new expression of life and creativity as it begins to emerge. What is the antidote? Courage, gratitude, ingenuity, faith, and persistence…not to mention charity! As the American educator, John W. Gardner once wrote: "We pay a heavy price for our fear of failure. It is a powerful obstacle to growth. It assures the progressive narrowing of the personality and prevents exploration and experimentation. There is no learning without some difficulty and fumbling. If you want to keep on learning, you must keep on risking failure - all your life."

Once we know the truth of our Source and our own identity, we know that failure is nothing to risk.

Inspirations

Kahlil Gibran (b.1883 d.1931) Persia:
"All you have shall some day be given; therefore give now, that the season of giving may be yours and not your inheritors. You often say, 'I would give, but only to the deserving.' The trees in your orchard say not so, nor the flocks in your pasture. They give that they may live, for to withhold is to perish ...For in truth it is life that gives unto life—while you, who deem yourself a giver, are but a witness."

Marcus Aurelius (b.121 d.180) Rome:
"All that is harmony for thee, O Universe, is in harmony with me as well. Nothing that comes at the right time for thee is too early or too late for me. Everything is fruit to me that thy seasons bring."

Henry Wadsworth Longfellow (b.1807 d.1882) England:
Evangeline: "Neither locks had they to their doors nor bars to their windows; But their dwellings were open as day and the hearts of the owners; There the richest was poor and the poorest lived in abundance."

Rainer Maria Rilke (b.1875 d.1926) Germany:
"A billion stars go spinning through the night,
blazing high above your head.
But in you is the presence that will be,
when all the stars are dead."

Applications

The applications for this section are prescribed by the last paragraph in Jeshua's message. Look at your life and find some places where you can plant one or many "Trees of Life" to

Abundance and Productivity

strengthen and celebrate your gratitude for the abundance of life. How or where these trees are planted is a personal and sacred choice for you. I do encourage you to choose from your heart though, and within the context of what is already important to you. You may share in a large way, or you may plant small trees. For example, I have one part of my closet where I hang clothes that I have decided to give away. If I do not find a specific person the gift seems to fit, I pack them up every few months and give them to a charity. I also have a shelf in my pantry where I place a certain portion of my groceries as a gesture of sharing my food with others. When I collect enough, I find a needy recipient. There are endless ways that charity can be expressed. The important things to know are that love impels them and the spirit of abundance is celebrated.

Meditation

This meditation addresses the inevitable and irrefutable truth that we have cut ourselves off from God's abundance by creating and practicing beliefs in separation. We have created separation from God, from others, and even from ourselves. Moreover, we have created separation between our own aspects of being—our heart, mind, body, social self, professional self, practical self, and dreaming self. Personal fragmentation destroys inner peace and denies all feeling of satisfaction, regardless of our level of prosperity. We all know that we have the makings of a single person wearing the same face and name, and yet the process of accepting and celebrating this unity often eludes us. The awful evidence of history is that most people who have ever lived have struggled with the "enemy camps" of opposing forces within, to wage a continuing war, mild or violent, on themselves. But this need not happen to anyone who seeks unity.

207

So let us begin by setting aside any judgments you may have about your separate parts, regardless of whether you look upon them with preference or rejection. In nature, there is nothing hostile or contradictory about the many complex parts of a microclimate; moreover, the complexity of it need not be understood, explained, or justified. You only need to observe that a natural environment, without interference by arbitrary and destructive forces, simply WORKS. So, let us begin our meditation with this affirmation:

> "God created me to live with myself in perfect harmony, merging of all aspects of my conscious and unconscious life. I am truly and fundamentally, only ONE. Oneness was my pre-creation, the actuality of my life, and my ultimate destiny. There is something bigger in me that knits the threads of my life and elevates me to Self-Togetherness. Whenever I choose my Oneness, I may be assured that the 'power of togetherness' is also choosing me!"

Now let us consider the unity of time. It is really you who connects all the times of your life. Start by remembering a fresh spring day with blue skies. Feel the warm breeze, and smell the lovely fragrance in the air. See the presence of a favorite pet exuding an overpowering pleasantness. Now recall a friend you haven't seen in years, or a stranger with whom you exchanged memorable words. Think of a favorite food from childhood that still causes your mouth to water. Remember a great reward or pivotal accomplishment. Are these things less part of you now because they happened yesterday? Consider the things that have not yet happened. Think of the trip or visit that has already been planned. Envision the future events that will happen almost certainly to you or your loved ones. Savor the taste of your favorite meal that you will enjoy again soon. Are these less part of you because they have not yet happened? Time, space, substance, ideas, people, and experiences may vary widely, but what connects them into a single tapestry is the weaver. The weaver of your life is YOU! In knowing this, we humbly seek to know and join with the larger tapestry of life that is woven by the love of God. We look to the North, South, East, and West. We see all directions converge and pivot around a common center.

Extending to infinity, the Great Spirit of the North is like a fresh cool wind through boundless skies. May our union with it enliven our thoughts with power and clarity. Join this Great Spirit to breathe and flow through all of life. Help us to hear the inner voices that bring visions to mind. Into your breeze, let us sweep away old unworkable patterns. You are the ecstasy of dance that we find in our harmony, and where we find a place of greater knowing.

Extending to infinity, is the Great Spirit of the South, protector of the fruitful land, of all green and growing things, resplendent with noble trees and grasses. O Mother Earth, essence of nature, great power of the receptive, of nurturing and endurance – we receive power from you to grow and bring forth flowers of the field and fruits of the garden. We seek harmony with you for the blessings we may share.

Extending to infinity, the Great Spirit of the East is the radiance of the rising sun and new beginnings. O fire of creation, vital spark of life, we ask that you purify our senses and give us the vision to see far and boldly for the greater good. We seek harmony with you so that your powers may flow through us and be expressed by us, for the benefit of this Earth and all life upon it.

Extending to infinity, the Great Spirit of the West shows us the immeasurable waters of the earth—rain, rivers, lakes and springs, and our boundless Mother Ocean. From her womb all life was born. Within her deep blissful darkness is the power to dissolve boundaries, to release holdings, to sense and to feel, to cleanse and to heal. We seek to join with this harmony for the good of our planet and all living beings upon it.

As we harmonize with all the elements of creation, we see there is no disparity and separation even from opposite directions of the wind and powers of life. In this, we can be comforted and know that all the directions and seasons of our own lives have a purpose that is unfolding. Only belief in separation has reduced our access to true abundance. In truly seeing this, any belief in separation may be replaced with a perception of living and dynamic unity that need not be understood to be embraced, loved, and received with complete exhilaration.

✝ *Prayer*

This traditional Jewish prayer has its stylistic roots in the profound and lavish praise of King David and Solomon. I like to think that Jeshua would have prayed such a prayer many times.

How wonderful, O Lord, are the works of Your hands!
The heavens declare Your glory,
The arch of the sky displays Your handiwork
In Your love You have given us the power
To behold the beauty of Your world
Robed in all its splendor.
The sun and the stars, the valleys and the hills,
The rivers and the lakes all disclose Your presence.
The roaring breakers of the sea tell of Your awesome might,
The beast of the field and the birds of the air
Bespeak Your wondrous will.
In Your goodness, You have made us able to hear
The music of the world.
The voices of the loved ones
Reveal to us that You are in our midst.
A divine voice sings through all creation.

Amen

17

COMMUNITY...
THE HUMAN CONTEXT

The Message

There are few words loaded with more different meanings than "community". When we hear the word we might think of anything from fellowship to township to global politics, and each meaning would be valid from its own perspective. In many ways, the idea of community is the collective equivalent of love and is applicable to all things. Certainly, it seems that Jeshua espoused the more universal meaning. The foundation of his message consisted of two simple instructions: "Love the Lord your God with all your heart, mind, and soul, and like unto that is the second. Love your neighbor as yourself." (Matthew 22:37-39). In other words, view love as an extension of yourself to others and upwardly to the Divine. Stated more pragmatically: build, sustain, and honor community on all levels.

On the many occasions that we spoke, it was rare that our conversation did not touch on some aspect of community. These references were historical, reverent, practical and timeless. One of his conversations that most clearly revealed his thoughts about community began as an historical anecdote on the beginnings of communal bonding and sharing.

"All of the categories and sub-categories of life are defined by the natural chains of support that create living community. The science of ecology has mapped the network of ecosystems in vivid detail. These ecosystems are natural communities of life. Often the

network of one system will overlap that of another and many may combine into a larger integrated community.

"Once, very long ago, human communities were intimately tied to the land through the biological family and the ecosystems providing their sustenance. In the beginning, this was the only basis for unity. But, Divine Consciousness ordained that man would also develop communities of thought, spirituality, purpose, industry, and conscious caring.

*"A great leap was necessary for man to develop collective values. That propulsion came from the discovery of fire as a controllable form of energy. Fire provided warmth in the winter, light in the dark, and nourishing food for large numbers of people. As fuel, it turned the first wheels of human industry. It was the center of every camp and village. More importantly, fire brought a great intangible lesson that would stimulate movement toward larger, more complex networks of economic support. The realization was that sharing this valuable commodity or extending it to others **did not diminish the quantity of fire for oneself**. To the contrary, sharing fire only created more! By sharing, each family and tribe was more secure in the knowledge that this vital resource would not be extinguished.*

"Here is a truth that elevates co-habitation into community: the quality of life for all is more assured by the survival of each person, and the quality of life for each person is more assured by the survival of the whole. Your neighbor's survival adds to your own. Fire gave man his first lesson in this truth. Once this lesson was learned, it quickly spread to other applications such as the sharing of seed reserves, technology, labor, knowledge, and beliefs. Progress continued uninterrupted for millennia, until the idea of scarcity was presented as a very sophisticated form of 'knowledge'. Beliefs changed quickly, neighbor turned upon neighbor, and village upon village until every generation would have to contend with war. Scarcity was an important discovery within mid-range perception and intelligence, but it was tragically misapplied to human society. The principle of scarcity is certainly valid for such mechanistic functions as engineering - where the balance of cause and effect must be determined in solid pre-

existing properties — or in any science where the energy being used is already in a state of entropy. Nevertheless, it applies to only the smallest dimension of the universe, and most certainly does not limit the greater laws of the human heart and community.

"Just as fire is not diminished by sharing, so too is communication not consumed by transmitting it, or truth made less valuable by imparting it to another. All of the great principles of human consciousness are expanded through sharing. That includes liberty, honor, and the right of each person to find his own natural place for giving and receiving. You must learn the true and loving laws of community if you would live in a supportive world. There are rights and privileges of the human soul, and these rights and privileges extend to the choices we make about our patterns of nourishment. There is nothing more important than to nurture the love that you are and to assist others in doing the same. As you do, the natural love that you are will grow into values that support the love of others. This is the basis of community.

"The defining characteristic of any community is its pattern of sustenance. By concentrating on how you give and receive it, you may innocently discover your true community. In the human context, nurturing also includes thought, emotion, play, work, celebration, and worship, as well as caring for economic and biological needs. Advanced and progressive forms of social infrastructure were essentially created for support and growth. If you would find health and live a progressive life, it is essential that you study and implement appropriate patterns of nourishment.

"Study the chains of sustenance and the contexts they create. Set aside all considerations of conformity such as race, nationality, gender, or social class. Not all social structures are built on the true and living nature of community. Conformity merely protects you from your own ignorance—until someone with greater understanding challenges it. If you would harvest the wealth of God and flourish in your own life, you must study and respect how your own life nourishes others and how others nurture you. This is true for all your relationships, your place in community, service, and business.

*Consider how your activities, attitudes, and resources have served and enhanced the lives of others. Study the support cycle of nature and humanity and then contribute according to your values. Whatever you nourish will increase. But be aware—it will increase according to its **own** nature. You cannot change a rock into a tree by feeding it compost and nitrogen.*

*"It is written that I said to my disciples, 'Do not throw your pearls to swine.' In the sparse context of that isolated statement, it would seem that my principle intention was to say, 'Do not give that which is precious to one who is unworthy.' However, it was not in my nature to teach them judgment. On many other unreported occasions, I was known to say such things as, 'Do not plant seeds in the ocean or fish in the fields. Do not feed horses with meat or dogs with oats.' The reality of every context is created through its chain of nourishment. Appropriateness and logic about this will add to your health, wealth, and wisdom immensely. There are those who are ready to receive what you have to offer, and there are those who are not. If you nourish those who are willing and ready to receive, then there will be abundance that others can carry into other contexts. Do not worry about what you cannot do. Be concerned that you have done what you **can** do— one to another as your lives connect. You are wasting your energy to support illogical directions of 'influence'. Human society has often ignored the laws of community with disastrous societal consequences. Many have taken support they could not develop or reciprocate. Others have used their resources to manipulate the recipients into being paid allies. These imbalances of exchange may satisfy immediate needs or achieve temporary compliance, but they do not result in true community or making of friends.*

"Beyond the human context, you will find that community extends forever throughout time and space. Creation unfolds as an endless web of support. What you nourish now will be your future, your community, and the pathway for your own return sustenance and fulfillment. To this expanded view, you may add the many 'communities' within yourself. Each person is an integrated whole of many microcosms. How do you nurture your physical body, your

heart, your mind, and emotions? There are patterns within you to be discovered and supported or evaluated and changed. Every choice you make is about community on some level, and the support in which you vest it is the basis for all you will ever have or create. Choose well."

Correlations

Romans 13:8 "Owe no man anything, save to love one another: for he that loves his neighbor has fulfilled the law."

Matthew 5:43-45 "Ye have heard that it was said, you shall love your neighbor, and hate your enemy: But I tell you: Love your enemies and pray for those who persecute you, that you may be sons of your Father in heaven. He causes his sun to shine on the evil and the good, and sends rain on the righteous and the unrighteous."

John 15:12 "This is my commandment, That you love one another, as I have loved you."

I Peter 3:8-9 "Finally, all of you, live in harmony with one another; be sympathetic, love as brothers, be compassionate and humble. Do not repay evil with evil or insult with insult, but with blessing."

The Key

The key to community is giving and receiving nourishment. We can and do share all of life, one way or another. We give and receive everything from material support to the heights of consciousness and prayer. God is the highest state of our collective potential working harmoniously and seamlessly together. Contemplation of this is prayer. Emulation of this is natural goodness. Extension of this is the basis for growth, healing, and a fulfilling life. We each have our part in God whenever we open our hearts and hold out our hands.

One of the most exciting developments of the late 20th century was the study of consciousness as a connective and sustaining energy within all life systems. These studies were both general and specific, embracing many disciplines of research and development. The new science of consciousness, still in its infancy, has already brought to light some startling confirmation of what has long been suspected. The mind's extended reach remains to be fully defined in scientific terms, but research on human consciousness suggests that we may have direct communication links with each other, and that our intentions can have effects in the world despite physical barriers and separations. Many are compelled by good evidence to accept statistics that cannot yet be explained. It appears that consciousness may sometimes generate a resonant field of converging effects that is well beyond the local field of normal cause and effect parameters. In an effort to study and monitor larger patterns of consciousness, Princeton University has established a Global Consciousness Project. Pivotal to this study are data accumulation and processing devices that map detectable responses from the environment; much the way an EKG records human heart function and responses. The GCP began recording data in August 1998, and has grown to more than 50 sites around the world, each generating and reporting second-by-second data.

The Global Consciousness Project takes this possibility as a starting point for a speculation that such fields generated by individual consciousness would interact and combine, and ultimately have a global presence. Individuals are busy with random activity incapable of being reflected on a structured graph of large-scale movements. Under these conditions, there is little patterning or meaningful fluctuation. Even so, this gives a valuable backdrop to the sudden meaningful changes that occur when global events bring great numbers of us to a common focus with an unusual coherence of thought and feeling. Examples that appear with a definite pattern are both peaceful gatherings and disasters: a few minutes around midnight on any New Years Eve; the first hour of NATO bombing in Yugoslavia; the Papal visit to Israel; a variety of global meditations; several major earthquakes; and September 11, 2001.

Many believe that programs such as these are on the verge of proving what the spiritual community has claimed all along about prayer and meditation — that group consciousness exists and it can show up on a worldwide scale. Henry Reed, Ph.D., Senior Fellow at the Edgar Cayce Institute for Intuitive Studies, said in a lecture, "This study is adding to a growing body of evidence that a group of people, setting their intent and working in consciousness alone, can have an impact world wide." If what's being measured does indeed prove the existence of group consciousness, such a result could be of major significance. As it becomes generally known and accepted, groups could begin consciously and deliberately focusing their thoughts, emotions, and energies toward the achievement of a single intention worldwide.

At the same time as these advancements in science were occurring, many souls began to discover the common truth of the world's many sacred teachings. The tightly controlled, centuries-old borders between different religious traditions began to dissolve and a great spiritual loom of comparative thought began to weave a tapestry of united consciousness. Our souls are conscious entities that exist in full and unrestricted partnership with our bodies, our minds, and our communities. What we think is what we create. The web of life extends from microcosm to macrocosm. There is no manifestation of life that is without a soul.

If we carry this logic to its obvious conclusion, we must also embrace a powerful political truth: Each nation on this planet is an organ of one body, and the health of this body rests upon each organ receiving the same care and respect. Just as people united form the global soul of this planet, so also do the souls of each nation participate in the maintenance of the life force of our global soul. Nations therefore must learn the laws of community as well as the precepts of government.

Elevating social structures and governments to a true state of community is challenging to say the least, but it can be done. It is possible that our every thought, action, and decision has an impact on life, the community around us, and far beyond. Each person is a microcosm within the macrocosm of an infinite web of life. Consciousness is possibly the ultimate medium and context for the development of community. From one perspective, this idea could almost be overwhelming! From the perspective of sincere and humble respect for each connection we make, this truth can empower the simplest action with immense potential. An incredulous interviewer once asked Mother Theresa how she dealt with the immensity of need in her country. The tiny Albanian nun smiled and replied, "One by one."

Inspirations

George Appleton (b.1902 d.1993) America:
Daily Prayer and Praise, "O Creator Lord, let me feel the 'isness' of things and people, without resistance, without trying to impose my own pattern upon them or exploit them for selfish ends. Let me welcome them, enjoy them, value them, love them, for what they are and for what they are becoming through your creative love."

William Wordsworth (b.1770 d.1850) England:
Recollections of Early Childhood, "The heavens laugh with you in your jubilee; My heart is at your festival."

Applications

It's a paradox that in order to experience individual freedom and well being, we have to connect to the collective consciousness of humanity. When we realize, even if only intellectually, that we are one, then we will care about the well being of others as an extension of our own.

The goal of community is connecting all parts of the whole. That includes the community within your self. When you do, there is a great feeling of being satisfied and fulfilled in every area of your life. That means you must connect with others in genuine service, celebration, intention, and sharing of life. It also means that you may have some real inner traveling to find out who you are as well. You may need to define your values and figure out what will bring you peace and joy. Then you have to find the courage to act upon what you discover.

The following eleven steps may help you create a more fulfilling experience of community and greater personal abundance:

Step 1. Define your values.

Make a list of what matters to you and write a description of what you want your life to look like.

Step 2. Take a good look at your life.

Look at the energy you are generating, the people with whom you interact, the condition of your home, what you eat, how you feel, etc. Also, examine whether or not the life you are living is in agreement with your values. If it isn't, what is keeping you from doing what you want to do?

Step 3. Make a commitment to change.

If you are not living the life you want, you will have to make a deep commitment to change your thoughts, beliefs, emotions and the physical expression of your consciousness.

Step 4. Accentuate the positive.

From the choices you make, you can predict the outcome. If you expect the worst, that is what you are likely to get even if you are working for a positive result. You have the option of believing that life is benevolent and that you can live a fulfilling and satisfying life. If you learn to look at your experiences from a positive point of view, you will learn the "attitude of gratitude". Instead of feeling that you aren't getting enough, you will begin to appreciate what you have.

Step 5. Take care of yourself.

Dismiss the critical parent, or any voice in your head, that says you are not perfect just the way you are. Treat yourself with loving-kindness and remember to say to yourself at least once a day in the mirror, "I love and accept you just the way you are." Remember that you will treat others as you treat yourself.

Step 6. Share your time, energy, and resources.

Sharing your life with other people feels good and contributes to your future abundance. Give freely of your time or resources to show your appreciation. If you want to receive more support, then you need to support others. If lack is what defines your life, then you may have to make an effort to connect on a deeper level with more people. Go to meetings; join clubs that interest you; go to spiritual gatherings, etc.

Step 7. Be grateful.

Gratitude unlocks the fullness of life. It turns what you have into enough. It turns denial into acceptance, chaos to order, and confusion to clarity. Gratitude can turn a meal into a feast, a house into a home, a stranger into a friend. Gratitude makes sense of our past, brings peace for today, and creates a vision for tomorrow.

Step 8. Let go of the past.

Forgiveness and letting go of the pain of your past takes time, but opens the door for positive energy to come into your life. You can begin the process of letting go by cleaning out the things that you no longer use—things that remind you of uncomfortable times in your life.

Step 9. create some special moments alone.

Spend time in solitude getting to know who you are. Pray or meditate. Also, spend some quiet time doing whatever feels good to you. Connect to nature as often as possible. Even if you just sit on a patch of grass and feel the earth beneath you, that will help. Become aware of the birds, trees and flowers.

Step 10. Take responsibility for your life.

As long as you blame others for what is happening to you, or if you keep yourself in a victim role, you will seek separation more than connection. Happy people understand that it is their reaction to life that determines the course of their lives. They are willing to examine their role in creating whatever negative dramas may play out. The idea is to let life happen **through** you, not to you.

Step 11. Each day do at least one new thing that strengthens community with others.

In order for your life to change, you have to consciously make changes. This takes effort and commitment. That's why success does not happen to people who just wish for it and hope that some unseen force will give it to them. You can start by changing the quality of your thoughts, or by getting in touch with what you are feeling in a variety of situations. Nothing will build a connection faster than a smile. Smile at someone you might have scowled at in the past. Give something away—if only to pass around your bag of potato chips at the office. Keep extra change on your desk for those who are a bit short of cash. Take one small step each day, and you will adapt yourself to the process of always moving toward community. Regardless of your starting point, the direction of your movement is what really counts.

Meditation

This meditation begins with your eyes wide open in a place that is quiet enough for you to enjoy inner peace, but interesting enough to engage your attention. A place in nature or with a view would be perfect. Sit quietly and behold. In a peaceful state, behold your connection with all that is around you. Because your eyes are open you may think more than in a typical meditation. Don't try to stop the thoughts, just watch them. Imagine that you are on the bank of a river and that your thoughts are the river going by. Don't try to stop the river, just watch it. Within a few moments, you will see the river begin to slow. If you find yourself becoming impatient, bored, or complaining, that's okay. Just watch the thoughts pass by.

Notice how everything supports something and receives support from something else. If you are in a natural environment, notice the bustling activity all around you. Now begin to direct your attention inwardly by noticing your own body. The whole of the human system lives by giving. If we view the microcosm of the human body, we find that the heart pumps blood into one valve and out another. Blood is normally circulating, seldom stagnant. In a healthy body, all the fluids are in a constant state of expenditure. If one cell stores its secretion for a few moments, it is only until the other organs of the body are in need of it. If any cell in the body should begin to store up its secretion, that stagnation would soon become the cause of chronic disease. Any organ that does not give forth its products is seriously impaired and eventually loses its ability to function at all.

So too, it is with the larger parts of your body. The eye cannot say to the foot, "I have no need of you and will not guide you." If the eye does not perform its watchful duty, the whole body will stumble and fall. If the members refuse to contribute to the whole, the body will collapse and eventually die.

Now, let us learn a great lesson from nature. We must give in order to get. We must scatter to accumulate. We must make others happy to make ourselves happy. To attain our goodness and become spiritually strong, we must do well and seek the spiritual goodness of others.

You will enjoy the fullness of your place in nature, when the sea itself flows in your veins, when you are clothed with the heavens, and crowned with the stars. Perceive yourself as the sole heir of the whole world. Then behold that others are sole heirs to creation also. When you can sing, rejoice, and delight in God—as a winner does with his trophy and a mother does with her infant— you will enjoy the bounty that has been given to you.

In this state of unity, there are unlimited dimensions. There is nothing too small for your attention to support and nothing too grand for your attention to embrace. The expansive quality of love and the innocence of perception alone define your heart. At this point, you may close your eyes and gently drift into your inner world. In this state of unity, recite the following affirmation of inner truth:

The spirit in my heart is smaller than a grain of mustard seed. Yet, the spirit that is in my heart is greater than the earth, greater than the sky, greater than heaven itself, and greater than all these worlds. This is the spirit in my heart.

The light in my heart is smaller than a firefly in the night. Yet, the light in my heart is greater than a cosmic sun, a galaxy, or the universe. This is the light in my heart.

The love in my heart is smaller than a fly in the wind. Yet, the love in my heart is large enough to embrace my fellow man, to serve all of nature, and reach for the stars to touch the face of God.

My spirit, my light, and my love all have unlimited dimensions. I can join everyone through compassion and community. I say this again and open my eyes to behold that it is true.

Prayer

O! Thou God,
Creator of all beings, of all worlds, and of all times,
We pray to look beyond the small variations among ourselves
That distinguish one from another in the vastness of Your creation.
May we focus not on the variance in our history,
Our languages, our customs, our imperfect laws,
But seek to enjoy the banquet of community that
You have laid before us.
May we see our human variety as an invitation
To feast and celebrate!

With humbleness,
May I face everyone with compassion.
Grant me the heart and wisdom to serve the best
In everyone.
May I abide in true community,

With devotion to enlightened life.
May I endeavor in every way for a better world,
For the generations to come.
May I abide in the energy of the universe as
The source of wisdom and opportunity.

Empowered by Your grace,
May I share the wisdom of life and death
In true community.

Amen

18

EXPERIENCE AND GROWTH

The Message

"Absolute or pure Spirit is unmanifest. For that reason it cannot be experienced or discerned through ordinary perceptions of awareness. Spirit is the fundamental nature of everything— ultimately, the only thing that exists! Anything you can know or sense or experience is an emanation of Spirit. The possibilities of perception are infinite.

"The procession of events through time gives us our record of experience. As we see from this record, certain patterns are constant. In a person's youth, and in the youth of one's soul, attention is focused mainly on external events. A person grows by collecting and examining the opportunities and stimulations of life. It is only natural to seek variety, adventure, pleasure, and challenge as you discover and compare the different ways for living and being. But there is a crucial moment, like the first opening of a rose bud, when experience is no longer measured or valued by the nature of external events. At that moment, the value of experience begins to be internal and subjective. Within this greater depth of consciousness, there is more interest in **how** to hold an event, **how** to value it, or whether to give it any importance at all.

"**What** you perceive is determined by your focus of attention. That is how you select your experiences and navigate through them. Most people tend to fixate on the physical plane. As you refocus your attention, whole new possibilities emerge. You can choose to move it to *other dimensions of reality. By shifting your focus, more of your potential becomes available to you without relying on some external cause or adjustment to make it happen. For example: you might learn to be more open and curious when you feel a certain emotion or develop a particular interest. You might learn through remembering or thoughtful examination to respond differently to repeated similar events. When you feel fear, you might choose to stand still, examine the situation from another viewpoint, and seek to understand your fear instead of running.*

"The greatest experience of all is being 'The Experiencer'! When you know, with full consciousness, that you are the one who decides how you experience the events of your life, you are establishing patterns of growth that will unite the inner and outer worlds. You will begin to select what you experience with more certainty and clarity of the heart. As this maturing process accelerates, and your perceptions are refined, you also may grow in silence and peace, becoming less dependent on external stimulation. At last, you will have the incomparable experience of total acceptance. This is when you can accept the large and the small, the complex and the simple—pleasure, pain, rich, and meager – as relevant to the whole of existence. At that moment, you will have fulfilled the purpose for all your experiences.

*"The path—The Way—is for Love to come full circle back to its own simplicity. You were created as Love in a place where love only knew itself as One. Then Love began to notice a wondrous and fascinating thing. It saw miraculous and irrefutable evidence of its many aspects interacting and coexisting. Every change or fluctuation that a soul made left a unique trace or 'footprint' upon the emerging potential of life. Love began to see that each soul left a trace of its own being wherever it went and whatever it did. What a remarkable phenomenon! Love asked, 'I wonder how far this can go?' With that, Love set out to have an adventure. This was good, because each soul was about to discover its own irreplaceable value in the universe. There was only one mistake in this adventure. Souls **forgot** that they were essentially Love. They defined themselves by their memories,*

228

accomplishments, and failures rather than by their fundamental nature as Love. They compared and judged. Eventually they became dependent, even addicted, to 'experience' as a way of knowing themselves. Love was confusing, and so they traveled away from Love and sought other ways of explaining life. This was the darkness of separation.

"*Regardless of your experiences, your true being has always been Love. You cannot know yourself as anything else. You must discover that truth again for yourself, and stop running from it. That is the actual meaning—and the occurrence—of repentance. Once you have gained that basic restoration, all your experiences can become valuable and meaningful. At last, you may know that your will is truly free and your choices are potent. What you choose for your life makes a difference in the whole of existence—not just for yourself!*

"*From the beginning, your growth has been the result of your inner nature interacting with the various influences of the environment. There is no such thing as being independent of the universe, since you are part of it. You affect it and it affects you.*

"*In addition to your perceptions of experience, your soul has its own developing, flowing, and flowering path. You ARE the unfolding. As you mature, you begin to recognize that evolution proceeds only by uniting both the inner and outer worlds. Evolution itself becomes the goal of experience. Ultimately the greatest experience, and the one that takes you into your final maturity, is that of responding to the movements of Spirit and knowing them as the breath that gives you life. In this state, you do not have to do anything except relax, surrender, and allow the Spirit to move you. This brings freedom from all attachment and expectations. This is the death of ego. When this happens, reality opens up as a succession of moments, each experienced as 'the present'. True Being knows itself only as 'present moment' or Presence. I use the word 'Presence' rather than present time because true 'now' is not a moment of time. It is more of a medium, a continuous and boundless essence of all existence unfolding in perfect synchronicity. Every experience of this endless Presence brings fulfillment to the soul.*

*"In the fullness of 'now', one discovers unconditional reality. This is the 'real time' of the soul, and the soul's real life. Every other experience is simply a challenge, a distraction, or an opportunity to re-establish one's sense of value in a new situation. If you would like to know the true age of your soul, ask not how much time has passed since your birth or how many adventures your soul has passed through. Ask instead, how familiar are you with 'real time' in comparison with the passing events of life? How easy is it for you to know that all is 'now'? How easy is it for you to BE NOW in the midst of chaos? The soul's age is not measured by one's formal pursuit of spirituality, but rather by one's ability to see Spirit in all things. It is not measured by perfection of behavior, but by a deep confidence of Being that cheerfully submits one's actions to self correction or correction from others. Most of all there is a sense of humor. A very young soul is one who identifies so closely with his behavior that he regards himself as being **equal** to the behavior. If the behavior is bad, HE is bad. If the behavior is good, HE is good. Even the slightest correction to a soul at this level of development can be crushing. Even a subtle compliment is taken for more than mere appreciation. Many rigid moralities have been built around these unyielding assumptions. This is a very restrictive and stressful place in the life of a person or soul. There is very little movement or opportunity for progress until something finally happens to loosen the tight association between behavior and Being.*

"The soul has its own path, which unfolds according to self-discovery as an experience in itself. Just as your ability to manage external events increases with practice, so too your understanding of yourself as 'The Experiencer' grows with confidence in being who you really are. Often the most difficult challenges of Being come to pass just before the dawn of enlightenment. The soul was born in perfection, and experience can neither add nor subtract from that truth. Therefore, experience, well managed, presents a stage upon which the light of your life may shine brightly.

"The soul's growth is entwined with experience, but it is fulfilled through understanding the nature of experience. The soul's growth is uncontrived, innately intelligent, and purposeful. It unfolds in a way that is right for each person's nature and potential. Therefore, it would be foolish to think that you can attain your fulfillment with an external plan or with predictions of what will happen next. You can only be certain of the present moment. When you are genuinely engaged with your experience, the next unfoldment will happen in natural order. This is not irresponsibility or passivity. As life unfolds, you may always select the way you experience it. You are now invited to partake of an even greater mystery – the realization that you attain your fulfillment not by directing it, but by BEING IT. The perfect coordination of your life with God's will is revealed only through complete IMMERSION into the power of Spirit. This is the true initiation of Baptism."

Correlations

Ecclesiastes 3:1 "There is a time for everything, and a season for every activity under Heaven."

Proverbs 3:13-20 "Blessed is the man who finds wisdom, the man who gains understanding, for she is more profitable than silver and yields better returns than gold. She is more precious than rubies. Nothing you desire can compare with her. Long life is in her right hand; in her left hand are riches and honor. Her ways are pleasant ways and all her paths are peace. She is a tree of life to those who embrace her; those who lay hold of her will be blessed."

Matthew 16:26 "What good will it be for a man, if he gains the whole world, and forfeits his own soul?"

3 John 1:2 "Beloved, I wish above all things that you may prosper and be in health, even as your soul prospers."

ℑℎℯ 𝒦ℯ𝓎

There is a story of an Italian peasant woman who came upon a monk sitting along side the road. She had seen him before as he walked from her village to his monastery high on the hill. Since he had paused for a moment she took the opportunity of asking, "Father, I've always wanted to know what you men of God do up there on top of the mountain. It seems to be so close to heaven. What is it like to lead a life of holiness?"

The wise old man responded with humility and a touch of humor. "What do we men of God do up there on the holy mountain? I'll tell you, my dear. We fall down; we get up. We fall down; we get up. We fall down; we get up. This is the way of growth. It matters not whether you live in the valley or stand on the mountain. The only thing you need to learn is when you stand up and walk, you do it with God inside. When you fall down, you do it with God outside."

Now let's consider the monk's remark to the peasant woman. What keeps us standing up and running, pursuing greater things? What holds us down and stops us from making changes in life about which we can be passionate? Only one thing EVER stops us from upward acceleration. We have formed a false belief that all the power of love and life is **outside ourselves.**

In "The Message of a Master", by John McDonald, the author makes a stunning and powerful statement: "The cause of confusion prevailing in your mind, that weakens your thoughts, is the false belief that there is a power or powers outside you greater than the power within you." The Gospel of John makes a very enlightening suggestion that we are already endowed with the power to do amazing things. "He that believes on me, the works that I do, shall he do also; and greater works than these shall he do." Within us is a Power greater than we are alone and yet one with ourselves. This Power allows us to cultivate the hidden soil and seeds of our being and to master the circumstances of our lives.

Though we may sometimes feel lonely, we are never alone. Wherever we go, whatever we do, we are part of the great connection of Spirit and all of life. There is no moment of life in which you do not influence something and receive influence in return by something else. Exchange of influence causes perpetual movement in the universe. The great wheel of life teaches us that change is always happening. It also teaches us that the wheel of our life turns around a constant center that is the True Power. While the rim of the wheel grinds on the highway of life, the hub provides power and energy to propel the forward movement. When we are young and eager for external experience, or when we have suffered the pain of too many bumpy roads, it is easy to place our attention entirely on the rim of the wheel and to believe that the wheel turns because the road is pulling it along. Confrontation with the truth, or a moment of awakening, will reveal that the "road of life" is more likely to give us resistance than propulsion. The power that turns the wheel is not outside of it! As we seek, enjoy, or endure the circumstances of our lives, it behooves us to remember that nothing external is an end in itself. To think that somewhere there is an external event that brings fulfillment is the anatomy of a trap.

The value of undergoing challenge lies in introducing (or re-introducing) us to ourselves as the master of living. The key to fulfillment is to know oneself as the Experiencer rather than the experience.

Inspirations

The Buddha (b.563–d.483BCE) India:

"My actions are my only true belongings. I cannot escape the consequences of my actions. My actions are the ground on which I stand."

Immanuel Kant (b.1724–d.1804) Germany:
"It is not only God's will that we should be happy, but that we should create our own happiness."

James Allen (b.1864–d.1912) America:
"As a progressive and evolving being, man is where he is that he may learn that he may grow; and as he learns the spiritual lesson which any circumstance contains for him, it passes away and gives place to other circumstances."

Emmet Fox (b.1886–d.1951) America:
"It is the Law that any difficulties that can come to you at any time, no matter what they are, must be exactly what you need most at the moment, to enable you to take the next step forward by overcoming them. The only real misfortune, the only real tragedy, comes when we suffer without learning the lesson."

Applications

The applications here are designed to enhance your understanding of what it means to be "The Conscious Experiencer."

1. Deliberately select an experience or incident while you are in the middle of it. It matters not whether it is pleasant or unpleasant. What matters is that you consciously select it and examine the nature of your experience. Now change your

focus. Find another aspect, perception, priority, or feeling to which you may move your attention. Observe how your experience changes.

2. Using innocent perception, notice the influence your environment is having on you. Notice the influence you are having on it. Do you like it? If so, how can you acknowledge or enhance it? If not, how can you contribute to improving it?

3. Consciously notice during your day what is happening. Ask, "Is this the experience I want to be having?" If so, see the brightness that comes from consciously affirming and expressing appreciation. If your answer is "No", then notice the power of that awareness to bring forth alternative possibilities for you to examine. When you know that you are "The Conscious Experiencer", life responds accordingly. Many options will open to you that were not there before.

Meditation

When you are liberated by silence and no longer involved in the management of life, but in the living of it, you will discover a state of awareness in which there is no distraction. Life, itself, becomes a prayer. The silence is prayer, and the world of silence in which you are immersed is a baptism of spirit.

Silence brings enlightenment. Enlightenment brings humility. It is the greatest irony that there is no sense of importance within the glorious, radiant, and loving true self. Only the imaginary self must defend and compare its accomplishment with that of others. That is a vacant reality like one shadow comparing its length with another. In the end, there is no joy in what does not exist. The truest joy, the greatest freedom, is in humility, for in that the heart is rediscovered. This is the source of all good, refreshing the soul as if it were a garden.

Let us contemplate sacred happiness, which is free from the sorrow of judgment and insufficiency. May you feel happiness and all the causes of happiness. May you be free from sorrow and all the causes of sorrow.

As a child I traveled far
Within my dreaming mind
To lands of old, with visions bold,
Lost treasures sure to find.

A mind may travel far and wide
But like the dove in flight,
Returns to where the heart resides,
As day gives way to night.

I too returned from wonderland
In the twilight of my soul
And found a rose within my hand,
Its petals to unfold.

It spoke in songs of silence
To the beat of butterfly wings.
Pleading: behold and experience
What this timeless moment brings.

Now is the hour. This is the place.
There is nowhere else to be.
And the world did end with infinite grace,
With the fragrance of immortality.

Close your eyes now and enter the divine silence of endless space; the divine silence of perfected knowledge; the divine silence of the unseen guide; the divine silence of your Sacred Heart. Be still and know there is only God.

Prayer

Through all my journeys, keep me in the buoyancy of hope.
Transform dark valleys into sunlit paths of inner peace.
Teach me to face everything with love,
To dissolve my worry in Your eternal grace.
Teach me to live in each present moment
As if only love mattered.

Amen

19

The Soul's Purpose

The Message

"There is a purpose to your life. You were born to fulfill that purpose in a way that no one else can. You bring to life talents, gifts, and experiences like no other. Every experience is a key to your purpose, every talent a tool for your purpose, every person in your life a coach for discovering or refining your purpose. Each life has a natural built-in reason for being. Purpose is the creative spirit of life moving through you from the inside out. It is the deep mysterious dimension in each soul, which carries with it a profound intuitive sense of personal identity.

"Your soul's purpose is to be the love that you are! You move toward this ultimate state of being by facilitating the purposes of life as they are presented to you. Purposes are indigenous to life, and all of life carries within it the purposes of its origin. When you can observe and respect this in others, you can find it in yourself. As you honor the power of purpose, that power will honor you. It will bring you into the highest knowledge of yourself that is possible. It works like this... As you serve the purposes of life, you build character. Then, layer by layer, as your character grows, it gives evidence of the deep invisible potential stored within your being. Character is the summation of your personal history and experience as it conforms to a central purpose that you could not have seen in the beginning. That purpose is not visible until it is manifested through service. Purpose refines and directs your contribution to life.

239

"Many people are 'hung up' on the subject of purpose because they are looking for purposes to be handed to them. They are looking for external enhancements of acquired purpose. One person will cling to a purpose that gives him strength, and another person will reject any purpose with which he cannot be well positioned. Others try to own a purpose as if it was their special acquisition of self-worth. There is only one purpose you may own in that way, and it is your soul's purpose to BE THE LOVE THAT YOU ARE. All other purposes are the products of engagement with something. Even the soul's purpose is the result of union with God, but it is your eternal gift to have as your own. Purpose is your engagement with life, and what you make of it.

"The power of purpose belongs to life itself and exists in any living entity. Purpose is waiting to be activated by life like a seed in the ground is awaiting rain. You have a purpose in life because you have the power of purpose within you. You do not know what that purpose is until it is stimulated by some form of involvement with life. If you wait for a purpose to be revealed and confirmed before you reach out and touch life, you will wait forever wondering what your purpose might have been. You also cannot figure out your purpose, for it was not invented by your mind. Purposes emerge from the connections and affiliations you make and the inborn nature of your being. However, you do have a barometer for knowing what kind of purpose is likely to emerge from any given situation. That barometer is your heart. There is also an external guideline and that is the value of your actions to others.

"The energy of life is in everything, either animating or passing through in the case of non-life forms. Life is a powerful force, much greater than electricity. When connections are made, energy is released and purposes are revealed. Many people seek, rehearse, and develop purposes in their minds, hoping that a well-formed purpose can elicit a desired connection. Sometimes this works to form an initial link. Once an association or relationship is acquired, however, the energy indigenous to that union has a life of its own and rarely conforms exactly to prior expectations. Purpose always brings

surprises. The best way to insure a positive outcome is to love and serve with ability, dedication, and flexibility.

"You can cost yourself a great deal of time, effort, expense, and opportunity by being too defensive, controlling, or reluctant in 'planning' your purposes or looking for them to be served on a silver platter. It is much better to plunge into life, knowing that your true purpose of BEING LOVE will carry you into a worthwhile experience and eventually to safe harbor. It will serve you better to let purposes take care of themselves, and for you to place your attention on the kind of affiliations you are making. Do they bring satisfaction to you? Do they serve others? Are you better with them than without them? These questions apply to things and activities as well as people. If you want a new purpose, consider changing the way you make connections or the nature of them.

† "One purpose is not more important than another. What elevates one purpose over another is the dedication you make to it, the value of it to others, and the satisfaction it brings to you. There are two major blocks to seeing your purpose more clearly, and both are very common in today's world.

† "The first is lack of self-esteem. That condition is always a challenge to the discovery of purpose, because purpose is what grants meaning to your life... from the inside out. When you feel unworthy to know your value to others, you will block your purposes. You cannot have deep and enduring satisfaction unless you have self-worth. This is one reason why work, service, and contribution all help in preparing you to know your purpose. †

† "The second block is a loss of the sacred. Purpose is the recognition of the sacred within us. That realization will lead you to a choice of work that is in harmony with sacred presence. It may find expression through family, community, relationships, work, creative activities, and practices of faith.

† "Purpose belongs to life and life is sacred. Logos, the Divine Reason for life, is the inner purpose within each soul...indeed, within the universe. There are certain pathways for that to be revealed. Purpose is like the mountain that connects heaven to earth. Through

pathways up the mountain, man can raise himself to the divine, and through such sincere effort, the divine can reveal itself to man. For many people, this pathway up the mountain is through nature and all things natural. For others, it is through creativity and intuitive exploration. For some, it is through work and human service. For others, it is through spiritual, ethical, or intellectual discipline. For all, it is through some measure of faith and explorations of the heart.

✝"Discovery of purpose is a continuous activity, and revelation of it is an ongoing process. We each live this process every day as we listen to life and shape our destiny. If there were any shortcuts to finding your purpose they would consist of establishing priorities, dedication, and satisfaction; and last but not least, joy.|Wherever there is joy, there is purpose. The most fortunate people on earth are those who have found a calling that is bigger than they are, a reason for living that moves them and fills their lives with constant passion, aliveness, and growth. Your soul's true purpose is to be the love that you are!" ✝

Correlations

✝Ecclesiastes 1:3 "To everything there is a season, and a time to every purpose under the heaven."

✝Romans 8:28 "And we know that all things work together for good to them that love God, to them who are the called according to his purpose."

✝ The Key

When I think about purpose, I am reminded of my college days in New Orleans when, despite my vaguely formed visions of success, the only thing that I knew with certainty was who I was.

There was such comfort and strength in that personal understanding that risk and aspiration were just the winds filling my sail. There was always a mild, yet intriguing, anxiety about not knowing the future. My senses were more alive then than I can ever remember. To this day, I recall the smell of rain in the magnolia trees, and the warm breeze wafting off the Mississippi River. The world was new and fresh to me, and the day at hand was enough. Tomorrow was uncharted territory that I somehow was being drawn toward from the depths of my being. It is the special energy of youth that provides knowledge without evidence, desire without complication. I moved into my life like the wild geese returning home.

Unfortunately, as we begin to actually shape our lives in the world, we often lose this courageous tenderness and begin to associate our reason for being with external goals, objectives, and even justifications. We have often made mistakes and immediately apologized for our actions with these words… "I didn't do it on purpose." This instant-reflex answer reveals a great deal about the way we hold 'purpose' in our minds. To most of us, purpose is a first cousin to intent, or the reason why we do something. We think that to act without reason or intention is to have no purpose. Sometimes we see purpose as a far off goal or ideal that provides an incentive for continuing in our work. To Jeshua, purpose is the inner driving force that connects all of life and defines the relationships, priorities, and passions within it.

Whether you are discovering your purpose or pursuing a known purpose, there is one common truth. To serve your purpose is a choice, and that begins with establishing priorities for your life, each day of your life. Without priorities, there is no sense of meaning in life, no direction, and no emphasis. When Jeshua said that a man could not serve two masters, he was referring to this mandatory requirement for priorities in life. Effective priorities then lead to the use of our gifts, talents, and acquired abilities, for they represent our greatest satisfaction to self and value to others.

When we are truly dedicated and involved in the connections that we are making and serving, there will be passion.

Most religions and spiritual traditions speak of an essence central to our being. Those individuals who have developed a sense of purpose know the core of their being. Conversely, those who know the core of their being also know their purpose. Jeshua said that our true and essential purpose is to be the love that we are. This is the key to purpose and the beginning of wisdom about it.

Through time and experience, our core essence develops character and ability. This allows for the emergence of purposes unique to each individual and to particular situations. Finally, through the activities of our life, we make further connections and these contain purposes as well. In fact, human needs tend to focus our attention on activities. Some of these activities carry so much importance and absorb so much of our time, such as making a living, that we begin to confuse them with purposes. We can correct this tendency in large measure by establishing priorities, and by selecting involvements that compel our dedication. The secret is to discern the purpose of an activity and not to confuse it with the activity itself. Purpose carries with it a compelling sense of dedication that sustains a cycle of action to its completion and beyond.

Purpose has a way of ordering time and energies around itself—perhaps that is its real power. Priorities are shifted and passions are activated. When we are moved by something, many things previously thought to be important fade by comparison. We begin to eliminate what is irrelevant. A new importance emerges and natural simplification occurs. The process continues forever.

A mysterious voice calls us to our gifts and into the relationships of our life. In this calling, we find our purpose, our essence, where we have a profound sense of who we are, from whence we come, and where we are going. This deeper calling is heard from the inside out. The call of purpose resounds to our deepest dimension—our eternal soul. True purpose affirms the love that we are.

Inspirations

Benjamin Disraeli (b.1804 d.1881) England:
> *Speech, June 24, 1870...* "The secret of success is constancy to purpose."

John F. Kennedy (b.1917 d.1963) America:
> "Efforts and courage are not enough without purpose and direction."

Dale Carnegie (b.1888 d.1955) America:
> "Are you bored with life? Then throw yourself into some work you believe in with all your heart, live for it, die for it, and you will find happiness that you had thought could never be yours."

James Allen (b.1864 b.1912) England:
> "Work joyfully and peacefully, knowing that right thoughts and right efforts will inevitably bring about right results."

Johann Wolfgang von Goethe (b.1749 d.1832) Germany:
> "Each indecision brings its own delays and days are lost lamenting over lost days...What you can do or think you can do, begin it. For boldness has magic, power, and genius in it."

Applications

Purpose is not merely an idea that explains and conceptualizes life. It is one of the powers of life. For humanity, purpose is a deep emotional need and an ongoing process of search and discovery. The following guidelines can simplify your search and make it more effective and meaningful. Every great discovery has many incremental steps toward its attainment.

Discover your gifts. This is how you will give to others.

Discover your passion. What moves you? This is your calling, and no one else can hear it for you.

Discover solitude. To hear your calling, you need to listen to your deepest yearnings on a regular basis. Your purpose often arises as that mysterious voice from the deepest place within, calling you to your gifts. Set aside time each day for contemplation, meditation or prayer.

Discover your special pathway to the divine.

Discover what is needed and wanted by others.

Organize your life, and assign priorities.

Look for greater meaning that is leading you to a higher calling.

Follow your heart.

Meditation

Since purpose is the essence of life, the most profound meditation for the development of purpose is to focus on this question: "If I knew these were the last days of my life, how would I spend them? What would be the most important things to experience and accomplish?" The Roman emperor, Marcus Aurelius said, "Let every act and speech and purpose be framed as though this moment you might take your leave of life." How much more clearly does life come into focus after losing a loved one or after surviving a challenge to one's own life? Life is precious. Life is sacred. And we are most worthy to receive the fullness of it. In that knowledge, purpose is revealed.

In this meditation, we will cherish and adore the blessings of life by surrendering to the inevitability of death. As Jeshua has taught us, we must lose our life to truly find it. Locate a quiet place and take a comfortable position. It is recommended that you sit with your back straight in a chair or other position that you can hold without distraction. Begin to breathe deeply and rhythmically. Place your attention on each single breath, knowing that your very life rests upon it. Appreciate the gift of life each breath is bringing. Feel the beat of your heart moving the blood of life through your veins.

Now shift your attention forward until you arrive at the end of your life. Do not look for a time or a circumstance, for that is unknown. Simply be in the quietness and stillness of that inevitable experience.

Life is a cycle. You are born and then one day you die. Physical death is certain. Reflect on that fact. Then recall all the people you have known personally or have lived in your lifetime who now have died. Notice the various ages at which these people took their leave. Some died as children, some in their early adulthood, some in their middle years, and others after a long life. Experience the emotion of these passages from life to death. God gives us the wonderful privilege of seeing with different eyes how different individuals and families respond to the most high sacrament and final rite of passage.

Notice the variety of circumstances in which life ceases. Death is inescapable, but the time and causes are unforeseeable. Therefore, nothing is more certain than life in this present moment. Reflect on what is most essential and meaningful to you. What is your joy? What are your gifts? What is your passion? What do you most want to do? What do you value most? How can you release the potential that life has given you? With whom do you share life? These are the elements of your purpose. Feel with all your senses, the energy of life bringing you the answers to those questions. Hear, feel, sense, smell, and appreciate your life within this present moment. Seize the fullness of this instant and be present with life. In this feeling is the essence of your purpose. Relax into it and breath deeply as you allow both life and death to bring your purpose into greater focus. There is much to be revealed through the art of living one's death.

Take a few deep breaths. When you are ready, open your eyes, and begin to stretch. With gratitude and expectation, invite the power of life to enrich all your activities of living with greater meaning and value.

✝ *Prayer* ✝

O Divine Creator,
Reveal Your presence within me that I may know the
Purpose for which I was created.
Fill me with creativity so that I may bear the
Fruit of Your will.
Grant me the wisdom to produce and share
Whatever is truly of service.
Keep me on the path of true purpose.
Help me to discover the rich opportunity of
Each present moment.
For You are the ground of my being and the
Power of my fulfillment.
You are the joy in my work, and the
Peace that calls me to rest when day is done.
In You, I am made whole again.

Amen

20

Prayer and Meditation

The Message

† When I asked Jeshua to teach me about prayer, he said, *"I will teach you about reunion with God, and prayer will take care of itself."* When I asked him to teach me about meditation, he said, *"I will teach you to receive the Holy Spirit, and meditation will take care of itself."* As always, he taught from the highest level of priority and understanding.

† *"God knows the measure of man, but man in his own consciousness has not yet attained that understanding. Man has been a prodigal son in his state of consciousness, having wandered to strange and distant lands, often diverting his energy and power into wasteful and fruitless activity. Man is the son of God, the expressed image and likeness of his Creator. When I say son, there is no respect of gender, for the measure of man is a spiritual being, which is neither male nor female.*

† *"Humankind is the progeny of Love, Light, and Divine Intelligence. There is much seeking in the world for common knowledge, but I would recommend above all else that you first know yourself and your true nature. You are love dwelling eternally as spirit, exceeding your mind and all its attributes.*

† *"Nothing is impossible. Indeed, all things are possible when you know yourself. If you would go within and contemplate the depth and height of your being, the potentiality would begin to take form. Every law and principle of the universe can be found within the human constitution or consciousness. Even living tissue of the body*

249

can be sustained and multiplied outside the body indefinitely. The reason it does not happen inside the body is because of the mind's interference, misconceptions, and judgments, disconnected from Divinity.

†"You are part of everything, and everything is part of you. To know this, you must first admit to your connection with the earth and then look upward to heaven. Within everyone is the very substance of matter, love and spirit, created to seek and fulfill perfect union. In fact, there is an embedded awareness of this destiny in the root meaning of the word 'man,' for it means 'the one who looks up.'

†"When you recover your ability to say 'I AM' in the fullness of its meaning, you know that you are spirit. You see that you are not your body or your mind ... that your life is something broader, deeper, and higher than all appearances of form. Whenever you conceive a thought and speak a word, it goes forth and finds a way to make itself known in reality. Thought has force and energy. Therefore, when it moves into outward expression, it manifests as form or function. Everything you see began in spirit and thought!

†"Your first act of faith is in claiming the words 'I Am' for your very own. The 'I Am' is the Spirit of God dwelling in you. Your second act of faith is in using the power of those words to call forth your reality. It is your Creator's good pleasure to give you the kingdom. You may have the whole kingdom and all therein—all the wisdom and knowledge and power that constitute the kingdom of God, for it is within you ...within the 'I Am'. As you know yourself, you will discover the possibilities inherent within you. They will then begin to show outwardly.†

"This is the first and most important value of prayer: to establish a living connection with your Creator, the Perfect One who knows you by your true name. All other virtues and blessings of prayer come from that. The 'I Am that I Am' is a spring of Living Water that rises from the secret places within you. In its presence, there is no hurt, no disease, no insufficiency, no meanness, no arrogance, and no pretense. In knowing yourself as 'I Am,' you know yourself to be whole and sufficient. This brings unshakable faith that will move all things *toward you. You will not search for things, and yet all that you need will find you. In this state, you will not be dependent on things, conditions, or personalities. You will be self-complete, resting only in the power of God.*

"If you had the faith of a grain of mustard seed, you could change the world. For the whole earth is subject to your call and command, and all of nature waits upon your word, with eagerness to obey. When you who have faith in your heart, you shall ask, and it shall be done.

"Every prayer I have ever taught was to give this knowledge, and reinforce this truth. You cannot truly understand the power of prayer until you have some correct estimation of your own measure and your place in creation; and understand the power given to your consciousness. Every prayer is a step toward greater awakening.

"I taught my Apostles not so much a prayer as how to pray. The great prayer that has become my legacy was actually a blueprint for all prayer. It is a pathway for unfolding the essence and power of prayer in your heart. The purpose of prayer is connection with God. Therefore, the first words must be to establish that connection and to honor the power of the name of God … I Am that I Am. From the name of God comes your own power, for you were created in the image of God. From the power of the name, all things are given to you, and you may command all things through taking the name for yourself as an heir to the Divine.

"It is translated that I said, 'Thy will be done on earth as it is in Heaven.' That is close in words, but much of the teaching is lost. It really means that the Father loves the Child, and has given all things into his or her hand. Therefore, as you are joined in the same true knowledge of self, all things and power are received. You need not ask for anything, for all has been given. All temporal seeking is vanity, or uselessness.

"Every line of this eternal prayer is a brief summation of long and tireless teaching of some important point about personal reunion with God. Often, the greater lesson is lost because of brevity, or because the context for expanded awareness is not revealed. For

251

instance, when it is written, ⌐'Lead me not into temptation, but deliver me from evil' … there is a great misunderstanding. I never used the word 'evil', nor included it in my lessons. Evil, as you think of it today, was not in my mind or vocabulary, and I would not have portrayed right and wrong as a black and white polarity. In Aramaic, the language of my culture, the word that translated as 'evil' actually meant 'uselessness'. ⌐The Devil, or lord of demons, was a reference to the power of uselessness, distraction, and wastefulness; a condition of living which inevitably leads to disease, depletion, and disorientation of a soul.⌐

⊥ "Your Heavenly Father would never lead you into temptation. At the same time, there is always temptation to become distracted into useless diversions. If you are not confident in your relationship to God, these distractions may be indiscernible from purposeful activity. That points to the real meaning of the words, 'Father, allow me to feel and to know your true presence within my spirit, that I may not seek for it in worldly goals and become distracted with vain and useless pursuits. In Your presence, I am focused and dedicated to my soul's true purpose. Be with me always and abandon me not in my days of proving.' This is not a petition for help. It is an assertion of desire for higher degrees of consciousness. God is Love and your proving is that of being a spiritual being created in His image, and endowed with His authority over life.

"Your relationship to God is by the law of grace, and that is the law of freedom. This means you have a choice in all things, including how you see yourself. You were created in the light, and therein began your freedom of choice. Your basic and original choice, your enduring choice, was not between light and dark. That would have been too easy, because darkness is totally an illusion. By examining the nature of light, the real choice can be exposed. All the ancient seers knew what science has confirmed that light is omnipresent. It is a tremendous energy, and yet without direction, it scatters. The only thing necessary for light to be turned into creation is for it to be focused and directed. Since light is omnipresent, it has no opposites. Therefore, darkness did not exist until such time as that *illusion was necessary. There is, however, a real choice WITHIN light. It can either be dispersed in a chaotic random array, or be focused and ordered into creation and purposeful manifestation. The legend of Lucifer is the personified memory of this dilemma: the real choice for a soul is not between light and imaginary darkness, but rather between purposeful light (God) and scattered light (Lucifer) which is the basis of all vanity. Light seeks to be freed through man to discharge itself one way or another Ï through chaos or through directed patterns of creation. Your soul is a lens for channeling light into greater unity and creative applications. When you choose this path, you move toward fulfillment and reunion with your Creator. When light is scattered and without direction or purpose, life becomes confusing and depleted. Then, the shadows begin to give form and structure to perception. This is how your trials began.*

"When a person's light has been scattered and made useless, shadows become the only definition within it. Then one begins to explore the darkness, and look for meaning and power within it. Shadows become a relief from the glare of scattered light, and darkness seems to be a viable option to it. Under those conditions it is easy to believe that darkness was equal to light from the beginning and exists as an opposite polarity. Your trial and your proving is how long it takes you to discover that in organizing the shadows, you have organized nothing. Darkness is only an imagined reality caused by separation from God.

"By returning to the light and entering upon it with a fixed attention and dedication to unfold the purpose of your soul, then enlightenment and victory are attained. When you walk in the light and love the light, you see a world that is beautiful and glorious. You are free of the illusion of darkness and see the truth of your own being. All nature bows down and serves those who seek the Truth. All things move toward you and act for you, and you are conscious of eternal support. No longer will you be fooled by useless behavior, and superficial appearances. You will see through passing events and circumstances with a vision that goes beyond all senses, as I concluded with my prayer: 'For Thine is the kingdom, and the power, and the *glory forever.' All of this is attainable through the power of prayer. Prayer, when truly practiced, is the pathway of reunion with God.*

"Meditation is a powerful complement to prayer, for it takes you to a secret place where you may cleanse your mind, prepare your heart, and relax your body for the purpose of listening. It is the silent practice of waiting upon God. But what you are waiting upon in truth is the Holy Spirit. Meditation connects you with the Holy Spirit as prayer connects you with the Creator. There is little mention of meditation in The Bible, because until my life, there was little understood or revealed about The Holy Spirit as a knowable Power in the life of man. Before that, Spirit was seen as the breath of life, the voice of inspiration, and the energy that moves the stars. The actions of Spirit were recognizable, but not fully accessible to human consciousness.

"Within each soul is a deep longing, a desire that worldly attainment cannot satisfy. That yearning is to be in complete reunion with the spiritual presence of God dwelling in the temple of your soul. Devout men and women throughout the ages have responded to this higher calling. They nurtured themselves through a contemplative life and perfected their understanding in service to others. As a soul matures, external gratification and achievement are less satisfying than they once were. The soul begins to hunger for higher revelations of consciousness that can only come through knowledge of an Indwelling Power. This connection has been there all along, waiting with eternal longing and infinite patience to reveal the liberating truth. Such revelations are beyond the intellect of man, and therefore must come through the intuitional intellect as a manifestation of Spirit to Soul. This revelation of a higher consciousness accessible to man is what Paul was referring to in his letter to the Colossians as 'the mystery that has been hidden from ages and from generations, but now is made manifest.'

"In your eagerness and impatience, you have turned over every stone and leaf to find the light of truth, but you have not known how to wait upon the Spirit. Therefore, the voice within has not been given the grace to speak. Teachers can be valuable in conveying higher

*principles, and in taking you to the threshold of enlightenment, but they cannot cross it for you. This was true even with me as a teacher. Had I remained with the Apostles, I doubt if they would ever have moved beyond their attachment to my words and the mannerisms of my personality. There is **no** external initiation capable of bringing about internal illumination. Always, each person must wait upon God for the higher revelations that are lasting and real.*

*"Your inner sanctuary is sealed from the outside world, a sacred place, which no one else may enter. Each soul must go there and directly receive the counsel of Holy Spirit. That which the Holy Spirit would say to you, and do through you, is a great secret even to you until the moment when it is brought to life. Learn to be still and let Spirit move within you to search far below your conscious mind and root out things in your nature of which you were unaware. As it removes all that is **not you**, it will reveal the power of 'I Am', and you will be transformed. It will bring light to all the dark places, and fullness where there was lack.*

"Do not be anxious or in a hurry for the full manifestation. It may come in the twinkling of an eye, or as a rushing storm. On the other hand, it may grow steadily as the grasses of the meadow. Remember always that your desire, as great as it is, is actually God's desire in you. 'You have not chosen me, but I have chosen you and ordained you that you should go and bring forth fruit.' It is His great pleasure to reveal your true potential by revealing the secret of His Presence.

"You mistook His desire for your own, then felt lonely. Make no mistake. The yearning you feel is because the Holy Spirit is already moving through you. The desire enlivening your heart is the same eternal energy that moves the stars and galaxies in their orbits; the same Power that keeps the earth in balance, and the birds in flight. So do not strive, worry, or be anxious for the Presence of God. This is what I mean when I say that you must learn to wait on God. You cannot force the inner revelation, for it will come of its own power. It will come from on high, in its own time as the descent of the Holy Spirit. Therefore, prepare yourself in silence, in cleanliness, in

listening, vigilance, and patience. The Spirit will come and teach you all things.

"There are many procedures of meditation, and many teachers to help you with it. All meditation is designed to help you experience intentional surrender. The important consideration is: 'To what am I surrendering?' If you would fulfill your soul's highest purpose, that surrender will be to the secret place within, where in reverent silence, your connection with God can be known. When you understand and practice meditation this way, it is the perfect companion to prayer. Through these combined practices, you will eventually arrive at complete reunion with your Creator, and be able to say, as did I, that 'I and my Father are one'."

Correlations

Psalms 49:3 "My mouth shall speak of wisdom; and the meditation of my heart shall be of understanding."

Psalms 119:15 "I will meditate in thy precepts, and have respect unto thy ways."

1 Thessalonians 5:16-19 "Rejoice always, pray without ceasing; give thanks in all circumstances."

1 Timothy 4:15 "Meditate upon these things; give thyself wholly to them; that thy profiting may appear to all."

Matthew 6:5-6 "And when you pray, do not be as the hypocrites are: for they love to pray standing in the synagogues and in the corners of the streets, that they may be seen of men. Verily I say unto you, 'They have their reward. But you, when you pray, enter into your closet, and when you have shut the door, pray to thy Father which is in secret; and your Father which sees in secret shall reward you openly.'"

The Key

Prayer and meditation are the keys to your higher reality, and the doorways to your larger self. There is a world inside you that no one, including yourself, has ever seen. It is waiting to be discovered and begging to be revealed. There is a world beyond you waiting to be entered. It is a world beyond the limits of your dream horizons. Your soul is more ancient than your mind and recalls its origin with instinctual certainty. You feel this immensity in prayer and meditation, and remember that your body is in your soul and not your soul in your body.

Prayer is the humility of your soul seeking to know its nobility and the nobility of your spirit seeking to express its humility before the great unknown. When you pray, you connect with God and the ancient treasure of your being. Meditation is your surrender to the guidance of Spirit.

What mystics call the void is not a void. It is full of a different kind of energy that has created everything. There is a power that creates and organizes this energy, and turns the chaos of quantum soup into galaxies, stars, organic life, and human beings with thoughts, emotions and desires. Jeshua said that this primal energy was composed of Adamantine particles, One Spirit, and Love, which together are the power of creation and unity. Everything is part of the One Essence, and since there are no limiting boundaries to that, every atom is potentially the center of the universe. When we look at this from every angle, it seems as though creation resulted from God exploring God's self through every new movement, form, and experience. Through every insect, flower, or blade of grass, through every molecule of water and lightening bolt, God is exploring the Great Self. There is no time and space for God, because the perspective of Divinity is omnipresent and all knowing. Is there any doubt that God can know when even a sparrow falls? Is there any wonder that profound revelations can come through the power of prayer and meditation?

Although we have a more fixed perspective, we too are capable of going beyond our material boundaries. Yet, we often fail to value this ability. When mystics and saints describe their wonderful journeys into transcendent realms, they are describing quantum reality Ï a transitional dimension that connects the known with the unknown. Everything that we experience as material reality is born in an invisible realm beyond space and time, which is not an empty void, but the womb of creation. Therefore, despite the fact that we establish boundaries for our normal earthly existence, we are always connected with realms beyond.

The proven results of prayer confirm that there is a reachable place beyond material reality. For more than twenty years, researchers have conducted experiments to examine the effects of prayer and to find out under controlled conditions if there is indeed any visible evidence for claimed results. For example, seriously ill patients in hospitals were placed into two groups Ï those who were "prayed-for", and those who were not. Both groups were given the best medical care, and neither was informed of their spiritual assistance. At the end of the study, there was clear evidence that the "prayed-for" group recovered more quickly and more fully than the other group. In 1998, a highly trained research team at Duke University came to the same conclusion using rigorous control methods, where all manner of variables were taken into consideration. One hundred fifty patients who had undergone invasive cardiac procedures were the focus of this study, but none of them were informed about the prayers. Seven religious groups from around the world were included in the prayer team to diversify the power of belief that might be projected through the prayers being offered. There was no personal contact between those giving and those receiving the prayers. This study revealed that surgical patients recovered 50 to 100 percent better or faster if someone prayed for them.

These are astonishing results, and especially revealing for those who have little or no religious beliefs! Yet, skeptics also played a part in shaping our understanding of these results. Without the traditional language of religion, new metaphors and new descriptions of what was happening had to be developed. There is now much written about how prayer is a journey into consciousness—how one travels to a place different from ordinary thought. In this place, the patient is not isolated from the whole 'self' of the universe and not a stranger to any other inhabitant. The one who prays and the one who receives are united in a dimension of consciousness where boundaries of the body no longer exist. Somehow, two people have joined across the space-time boundary. Many former skeptics would now describe prayer as a quantum event carried out in a dimension of relative connectivity. Almost a century ago, Einstein and other pioneers of quantum physics broke through the barrier of material reality to discover that all of matter and energy are relative to the constant of light. Is it also possible that all of mental, spiritual, and emotional reality is relative to our connection with God, and that through this Holy connection we are able to join with anything or anyone in existence? Perhaps light in every form from particle light to Divine light is the constant in our patterns of relativity.

These same findings would also apply to meditation if we use them to connect with the center of our being. Through solitude and contemplation, we see beneath the surface of reality. Just simple moments of silence often give us a larger perspective and renew our energy from a deeper well. We know not with the mind, but with the heart. Our intuitive faculty recognizes a power beyond the natural and rational and accepts the unknown on faith.

Inspirations

Samuel Taylor Coleridge (b.1772 d.1834) England:
"He prayeth well, who loveth well, Both man and bird and beast."

Mahatma Gandhi (b.1869 d.1914) India:
"In the attitude of silence the soul finds the path in a clearer light, and what is elusive and deceptive resolves itself into crystal clearness."

James Allen (b.1864 d.1912) America:
"The more tranquil a man becomes, the greater is his success, his influence, his power for good. Calmness of mind is one of the beautiful jewels of wisdom."

James Montgomery (b.1771 d.1854) Scotland:
"Prayer is the soul's sincere desire,
Uttered or unexpressed—
The motion of a hidden fire
That trembles in the breast."

Lao-Tse (b.604 BC) China:
Tao te Ching,
"The tao that can be told is not the eternal Tao.
The name that can be named is not the eternal Name.
The unnameable is the eternally real.
Naming is the origin of all particular things.
Free from desire, you realize the mystery.
Caught in desire, you see only the manifestations."

Applications

The essential application for this chapter is to practice its content. This means developing a conscious recognition of the value of prayer and meditation in your daily life. Make it a regular practice, but not routine without thought. The length of time you spend in prayer and meditation is not as important as the value you give to it in the unfolding of your day.

Through prayer and meditation, you cultivate inner strength and true piety, and your ability to confront the unknown increases. Many wonderful character traits can be traced to that kind of strength. In fact, it might be said that the ability to confront the unknown is the yardstick of greatness.

As you gain inner strength, you begin to sense your connection with God and the Holy Spirit within the invisible worlds. You learn that a prayerful presence alters everything. You begin to accept that your blessings do not come from what you can control, but from what is controlled on your behalf by the greater powers of love.

In the days to come, realize that love is the power behind all blessings. All healing, nurturing, and prosperity is but an outward sign of love ... giving of it, and the willingness to receive. When you pray, there is no power in your words except that you are giving consent for the love of God to fill your life. Love is an invisible river of living supply. Each life is like a tributary of that river, but you are given sole authority over your own love. Your love will never be subtracted from or added to except by your consent. Prayer is the way you give that consent. Therefore, as you seek blessings for yourself and others, remember that you are asking God to receive your own love and multiply it in the dispensation of blessings. You are asking for God's love that your own life may be cleansed and lifted to a higher state of well being.

In your daily life, put all that you are into the least that you do. Listen to your hopes, desires, and vulnerability. Honor the call of your soul. Listen to the hopes, desires, and needs of others. Honor their place in your life. Love yourself, and as you do, love others. Every utterance of love is a prayer, and the giving of love IS prayer.

$\mathcal{M}editation$

Meditation is not so much an objective or even a procedure as it is a process of attuning yourself to the presence of Holy Spirit and the Spirit of Nature, both of which fill and sustain your being. Meditation is a lifelong practice that develops at a rate consistent with the time and effort you devote to it. It begins wherever you are in life and becomes a pathway for raising your consciousness many levels beyond your present state of awareness. This applies to anyone, regardless of one's present state of enlightenment, for the pathway of Spirit is both relative and endless. With meditation, there is always a place to begin and always places to go. The profound gifts of the Holy Spirit—awareness, compassion and direct experience Īare always available to us, whatever our language, our beliefs, or our understanding. The council of Spirit transcends our limitations, and reveals that which we could not otherwise comprehend.

The important thing to know about meditation is that it involves listening, connecting with Spirit, and surrendering from the attachments of self. Keep your meditations simple. Their purpose is not to induce any particular state of mind, but to bring clarity to whatever experience you are having in the moment. Do not force your meditations. An attitude of openness, interest, exploration and curiosity will help you to let go of judgments, expectations, and other distractions that keep you from being fully present. Also, do not think that you must meditate alone. I have given you guided meditations because of the value of companionship in Spirit. There is no element in which we are more connected. Each of us can benefit greatly from having friends who genuinely support our spiritual journey. We meditate because we want to sense our life more deeply, to be more connected, to be more in touch, and to feel at home in our own lives.

All meditations have four aspects in common:

1. Relaxation
2. Breathing
3. Concentration
4. Attentive surrender

To begin your meditation, sit comfortably with your back straight, but relaxed. Pass your attention over every part of your body and check for any points of stress or stiffness. If necessary, stretch, shake, or massage the area. Sometimes it is enough to acknowledge the discomfort. Ask your body if it is ready to surrender to a period of relaxation and to enter a state of perfect unity with your spirit, mind, and emotions.

Begin to notice your breath. It is not as important to breathe deeply or in any particular way as it is to rest your attention on the rhythm of your breathing and on the air that you inhale and exhale. Be natural in this, not forced. Do not visualize your breath or control it. Just experience it. Breath is both a reality and symbol for your exchange with life. When you can be aware of it fully, moment to moment, as it really is, then your awareness of life will begin to take on that same clarity.

Focusing on your breath is also your first step toward concentration. This is a great tool. If you become distracted, just notice your bothersome thoughts without becoming annoyed, and return to concentrating on your breath as soon as possible. Focus on your breathing but maintain an open awareness. Thoughts and sensations may pass through your mind, but do not attach to them, reject them, or draw conclusions about them. Just let them pass. As your mind becomes peaceful, focus more deeply on the totality of breathing, notice how the organs and cells of your body engage in respiration as well. Consider that every human being and every animal is also breathing the same air. Experience that connection. Trees and plants are involved in creating the air you breathe. Experience that connection. Focus deeply on your breathing and allow that to be your passage into total concentration.

Concentration is the third main pillar of meditation. In quietness, you develop a stability of mind. This allows for gathering and focusing energy that has become scattered by the various activities of life. It recovers depleted energy into harmony and vitality. This state of concentration is alert but unattached. It is tranquil, relaxed, open, yielding, and accepting. It is awake, present, and deeply connected with what is going on, while allowing everything to be whatever it is.

The fourth main pillar of meditation is attentive surrender. That means being aware without interference and allowing reality to be what it is. It matters not whether you have heightened or reduced perceptions, except that you are mindful of them. This is not about imagining, desiring, or avoiding your experience. Attentive surrender is the ability to see nakedly and directly what is happening in the moment. It is through attentive surrender that you are able to receive council from the Holy Spirit, and become more informed about your body and your life. Attentive surrender allows you to see the truth of your life. Only in attentive surrender are you able to release completely attachments that no longer serve you, forgive completely, and receive completely the blessings of life coming in. Attentive surrender is awareness of what is.

To these four main pillars of meditation, you may add a theme or direction for your experience. This is not necessary, but it often helps to capture the energy of a situation or environment and direct it to the highest spiritual understanding.

This chapter's meditation is to observe, or perhaps really learn for the first time, the **process** of meditation. As you progress into a meditative state, consciously establish and observe the four main pillars of meditation. Allow yourself to relax, breath consciously, concentrate your energy and attention until it has surrendered to a state of tranquil unity, and be mindful and accepting of whatever is in your life. In this state, I give you these words on which to focus:

"Whosoever shall seek to save his life shall lose it; and whosoever shall lose his life shall preserve it" (Luke 17:33). This is the breath of immortality which transforms our lower worldly identity into the higher transcendent self, thereupon being capable of receiving instructions and renewal from on High.

Prayer

Lord of Life, I give you my heart.
Beyond all considerations of this world,
I submit my life to the miracle of Spirit.
You placed within me Your Ancient Harmony,
That I may receive the harvest of life,
And know the fullness of it.
You gave me the memory of Your Ancient Creation,
That I may be joined with the spirit of nature and know
The secrets of the woodlands,
And the pathways of the stars.
Grant me compassion to know how others feel.
Grant me opportunities to mend
That which I may have harmed.
Lead me to acceptance and understanding.
Awaken me to the inner truth of my own Being.
Above all else, let me be one with You.

Amen

21

The Miracle of Life

The Message

"Eternity echoes the voice of God. I am Truth. I am Love. I am Life. I have given myself to every creation, every form, and every creature. Where truth, life, and love are present, I AM. Wherever I am, there is cohesion."

These words were spoken with a composed majesty. I was stunned and speechless, but before the opportunity passed, I managed to collect the few words needed to ask what I would ask of no other. "What is life?"

"Life exists on many levels, from spiritual to physical, and Love creates all life through its desire for experience. It is the nature of love to attract, communicate, and to form agreeable pathways for exchange. It is also the nature of love to know itself AS love, and to secure its integrity with a sanctuary known only to itself. Long before there were any forms or activities that you would recognize as life, these attributes of love were well in place and generating the future of all existence. The attracting power of love causes aggregation and coherence. Its communicative power causes exchange; and the recognition of inner integrity is the basis of BEING.

"Long before life became organic, there was animation. Animation, which is the first manifestation of life, is more than movement. It is motion, ever changing the patterns and connections of unity. And, life is more than animation. Animation can change or cease abruptly. Life is the constant that never ends. Therefore, you

must look beyond the physical manifestations of life to behold the true miracle of it. Life is the presence of God, whether it is in physical form or spiritual essence. In life, there is unconditional being, spontaneous renewal, and instinctive conveyance of love.

"From God there extend three powers that support all of existence: Love, Spirit, and a mass-creating particle. This spontaneously emerging particle is irreducible, and indivisible because nothing preceded it. Yet, every form of matter comes from it. Its nature is adamant, because it ignites all formations. Therefore, an appropriate name for it is adamantine.

"You may wonder how the endless variety of this universe could be the product of only three forces, even if multiplied to the highest power! It is the character of the adamantine particle that accounts for the diversity and complexity of existence. The spontaneous nature of adamantine particles not only crucial to life, it is **essential** *to the creation of discrete complex forms and endless variety. By their nature, adamantine particles can emerge to create anomalies at any level of simplicity or complexity. It is from such randomness, multiplied many times over, that diversity is developed. Layer upon layer, new aggregates and molecular forms develop into the wondrous arrangements of this universe. Love is the life-generating cause of it. Spirit provides the unity. Adamantine particles are the substances and sparks of creation! Life begins with atomic cohesion, progressing to small molecules that become increasingly complex compounds with novel properties, until the most extraordinary thing happens; organic life, as you know it, emerges!*

"A critical change of awareness accompanies the transition from pre-life into life. Certain molecules that have a special affinity for each other unite, and a desire arises for containment and self-recognition. A semi-permeable membrane called a vesicle develops around this union and protects it. Now there is an internal environment as well as an external one, allowing for the first conditions of integrity.

"You might say that all of life begins in a womb. Two different environments – an inside and an outside - are always necessary for the

creation of life. This remains true at every level of life, becoming even more evident in complex organisms.

"The chemical basis for this crucial transition to life was very simple and common. It occurred through the medium of water. Since its beginning, life on earth has been in water. Bacteria move in water, and all metabolic exchanges take place in a watery environment. Cellular membranes are attuned to the electrical polarity of water. Certain molecules are hydrophilic (attracted to water) and others are hydrophobic (repelled by water). A third kind of molecule is composed of fatty substances known as lipids. The binary language of water (its polarity) generates a variety of structures as it repels, attracts, or combines lipids.

"The cell membrane is the basic component of organic life, and is the only element common to every living organism. Cell membranes serve to compartmentalize assemblages of protoplasm and separate them from the vagaries of an external environment. In its barrier capacity, the membrane enables the cell to maintain control over biological functions and perceptions. Cell membranes, so thin that they can only be observed using the electron microscope, are more than containers for protein development. A cell senses the environment and converts that awareness into 'information', which then can influence the activity of genetic patterns and environmental exchange. The behavior of the cell is controlled by the combined actions of coupled receptor proteins that provide awareness of the environment, and effector proteins that convert 'perception' into 'physical instruction'. By strict definition, a receptor-effector unit represents the origins of physical perception. A cell is a protein perception entity that provides the foundation of biological consciousness.

"From a biochemical perspective, the cell membrane is a liquid crystal semiconductor with gates and pathways. In fact, the cell membrane is an organic prototype of the silicon chip. Cells read their environment, assess the information, and then select appropriate behavioral programs to maintain their survival. Though there are hundreds of behavioral functions expressed by a cell, all behaviors can be classified as either growth or protection responses. Cells move

toward growth signals and away from life-threatening stimuli. Since a cell cannot move forward and backward at the same time, a cell cannot be in growth and protection at the same time. At that basic level, growth and protection are mutually exclusive behaviors. This is true for human response systems as well. Perhaps you can see in this alternating function a sensitive correlation between consciousness and health.

*"Science has traditionally considered life to be a closed system; to thrive only in a very narrow range of environmental support. This consideration will soon be revised. Even organic life is not restricted to this range. As greater understanding of life develops, it will be discovered to exist in extremes of temperature and environmental stress not yet considered possible. You will also come to understand that the same definition of life that allows it to be observed in extreme physical conditions also allows it to be found in non-solid electromagnetic fields that can trans-migrate throughout the universe. More importantly, it will be discovered that these extremes are a vital part of life's **open** system.*

"In closed systems, energy and space are generated through polarity and united by the constant of light. This has been well explored. Much is yet to be learned about energy in open systems, because open systems are based on rhythm rather than polarity. In open systems, time is the key factor required for unlocking energetic reserves. Progress in this direction is slow, because at the edges of any closed system, there is a fear of dissolution—in this case, of all time and space. The irony is that only by moving into an open system can time truly be accessed ... and infinity be understood.

"One of the most dramatic contrasts between open and closed systems is revealed through the nature of time. In open systems time is simply pure motion. True time is the actual essence of motion, which is unlimited. Open systems rely on a special type of regulation that only time can provide. Time is the rhythm of exchange that allows motion to regulate itself from imbalance into balance without needing to have closure. This is why you are so deeply affected by music. Both

the rate of exchange and the nature of energetic encoding are recognized as time and rhythm.

In closed systems, time and space function interdependently to form coordinated patterns and directions, and these convert motion into electro-magnetic energy. Every closed system is a kind of energy-space-time grid that repels anything outside itself. This is essentially what creates boundaries around atoms, molecules, and larger objects. These countless systems create an illusion that space is just the distance between points within a coordinated system. In closed systems, energy is perishable, and subject to entropy, because it depends upon coordinates of time and space to produce and maintain it. These coordinates must persist in a particular arrangement if energy is to also persist. Therefore, you have experienced time as a record of progressions necessary to continuity. This is the past, present, and future 'reality' with which you are familiar. When these progressions begin to falter, time appears to be in short supply. Fortunately, only closed systems are in limited supply of time and space. In open systems, existence is awash with time!

"The processes of life are always in dialogue. The most basic dialogue is the recognition of inner and outer realities. Every cell maintains vigilant attention to organization and replication while exchanging with an outside environment. From the most rudimentary vesicle to the most advanced living entity, life is sustained with alternating functions of open and closed systems. It works like this: internal equilibrium establishes the basis for self-awareness and replication. Exchange and mobility (which are inherently imbalanced) provide a basis for adaptation and inclusion within greater reality. From this perspective, imbalance is healthy and assures continued involvement with the environment.

"This two-phase rhythm of life is also the basis for your perceptions of subjective and objective reality. Inner equilibrium brings a perception of wholeness, wellness, and peace. Imbalance within physical existence ceaselessly propels change. Both phases are essential. Life is the activation of love into forms that possess a

presence of being, yet can change and continually reshape according to the dictates of truth and reality.

"A very good example of how life utilizes both open and closed systems can be seen in the development of immunity in children. From birth to about the age of seven, a child is developing the most basic biological organization that allows him to define his physical and emotional needs and to filter out destructive elements that would diminish his health. He is also reaching out for new experiences, connections, and exchanges. Indeed, for the rest of his life, this rhythm will be vital, and will apply to all things including community. Socially, there is a certain balance required between personal integrity and supportive exchange with others, and sharing and receiving the bounties of life.

"The alternating phases of opened and closed functions in life are innately fluid and adaptive. You would seriously misconceive them if you viewed their differences as a form of polarity. Polarity is the basic organizing power and function of non-life forms and forces. A crucial aspect of the transition to pro-life forms and forces is the development of fluid systems for comparative choices. This allows for the evolution of purpose, ability, and thought as well as forms with complex organization.

"Once you have a grasp of this concept it is easy to spot the systems of your life that need attention. Often a person will have more difficulty with one side of the equation than the other. Some people nestle their whole lives behind the closed walls of protective systems and stagnate for lack of fresh ideas and stimulation. Others are so open that their energies dissipate for lack of dedication and integration. One particular area may be stronger than the rest. Sometimes one open system will serve to balance many closed systems, or one closed system will balance many open ones. It can be perilous when too much has been invested in one area alone. Deep health comes from a fluid movement where the wholeness of life may knit seamlessly together.

"Whenever opened and closed systems are harmoniously attuned there will be health and happiness. This produces a whole,

*and therein life. Life is its own Divine System. If you could stretch your imagination to see Love, Spirit, and Adamantine particles in such harmony that the whole is greater than the sum of all parts, **that is Life!** You cannot comprehend life because it fills you, surrounds you, and embraces you. You see it everywhere, and yet there is no perspective from which you may detach and view it with complete objectivity.*

*"However, you are blessed with consciousness, and consciousness is a perfect mirror of life. Consciousness facilitates all of life, including non-material extensions of it, and **is** the highest form of life. As you understand consciousness, you know life. Therefore, by examining the nature of consciousness, a universal definition of life can be grasped. These same attributes define both life and consciousness:*

1. *Being: Self-defining awareness*
2. *Love: Attraction and support*
3. *Communication: Exchange with the external environment*
4. *Reality: Able to form agreeable and effective pathways for mutual existence*
5. *Creativity: Seeks to perpetuate itself through growth, regeneration, and replication*
6. *Self-awareness: Recognizes the intrinsic difference between external and internal systems*
7. *Integrity: Adapts to maintain its unity with others and reality, and yet remains constant to its own nature*

"Wherever you find these qualities, you find life. Wherever you cause these qualities, you contribute to life. It matters not whether you are focusing on organic life, human life, cosmic life, or consciousness; wherever you find life you will find nourishment in one form or another. The web of life is connected through all dimensions.

"Much of the power of prayer will be exposed when it becomes clear that it is facilitated by invisible extensions of life reaching to the Divine. In much the same way, telepathy occurs through the medium

of intangible life. Just because you can walk through space without resistance, does not mean there is not life and presence within it. What you commonly think of as space is merely another type of connective element that does not resist denser objects. As humankind grows into a greater understanding of open systems, better forms of food, medicine, and energy will be discovered and there will be less competition for survival than is currently the case. Competition always intensifies as the ecological system narrows. As the system expands, competition subsides. Through expanding the networks of life and your consciousness about it, abundance increases for all."

One more question was welling up from the depths of my heart. "Does health restore life or does life restore health? From what you have said, I now have a strong feeling that you first restored life to those you healed, and healing was a natural consequence."

"That is correct, and you and others may do the same to the degree that you understand life. When you support, enhance, and magnify life, healing will follow. Life is the source of health and happiness. Life is not only in you, but all around you in abundant supply.

"The true reserves of energy are maintained, magnified, and distributed because of unity, and the Whole sustains all its parts. Anyone can heal who remembers his or her union with God. A healer is merely a facilitator who brings forth a greater abundance of life and the presence of the Holy Spirit. Love and faith accomplish this, although consciousness plays an important part because it supplies the information and understanding to administer to life more effectively. Otherwise, all procedures are only temporary measures. Skilled treatment can arrest disease and trigger awareness in the body that healing is now being supported and requested. Ultimately, all cures come from a greater Cause

"The miracle of life is that the whole remembers and supports all of life within it. The parts and the systems do not have to recreate themselves or repair themselves. The whole remembers and loves. To

redeem any part of your life you only need to remember the whole and honor it. The whole will remember you and honor you."

Correlations

Job 33:4 "The Spirit of God has made me, and the breath of the Almighty has given me life."

Proverbs 4:23 "Keep thy heart with all diligence; for out of it are the issues of life."

Proverbs 16:22 "Understanding is a wellspring of life unto him that hath it."

John 1:4 "In him was life; and the life was the light of men."

Romans 8:38 "For I am persuaded, that neither death, nor life, nor angels, nor principalities, nor powers, nor things present, nor things to come, will be able to separate us from the love of God."

Acts 2:28 "You have made known to me the ways of life; you shall make me full of joy with your countenance."

The Key

Life is in its own sacred essence that extends well beyond the containers we use for accessing it and claiming it to be our own. The key to a fuller, richer life rests in knowing that life is the vital force that exists beyond all other contexts. It is life that restores health, and not health that restores life. The ultimate realization is that life is available beyond all physical form and is not lost just because physical forms may perish.

Jeshua described the universe as being composed of three basic elements. The first is Love, the second is Spirit, and the third is a substance that is **finer than anything** — yet identified by science! It is finer than the atom or any of its component parts. As the ultimate simple particle, **it is the irreducible building block of the universe!** Comprehending this particle is currently a major objective in particle physics. It is variously referred to by several names, including the "Higgs boson", and some have even called it the "God Particle". There is an ironic truth in that sarcasm. This particle precedes all particles with predictable behavior, which accounts for its difficulty in being studied. Apparently, it **creates mass**, whereas other particles are the **result of mass,** thus being more predictable.

These particles represent a continuous flow of high frequency potential, which manifests into discrete forms and arrangements under the command of love. Unfortunately, humankind is so dominated by sensory perception and structural containment, that we are virtually unconscious of this powerful moving force. This ever present and never-ending river of life eludes our normal perception.

He called these particles "Adamantine". Their significance for us to know is not limited to particle physics, galactic travel, or etheric realms. It is critical to our understanding of life as we live it. Through heightened awareness of this life force, you will begin to understand why the plant you love is the one that blooms. Where love is present, there is a free exchange of adamantine particles, which accounts for the dynamic interaction of living entities. These sub-atomic particles are the building blocks for all complex forms in the universe, and because they are under the command of love, they are especially fluid in organic life. Therefore, is there any wonder that immediate improvements occur when a plant or a pet is introduced into an otherwise sterile environment?

Most often our vacations are directed toward some form of return to nature, whether to the mountains, the beaches, the high seas, or even the skies. We have a great yearning to connect with all of life, and our modern life of specialized indoor activity does not support that. It appears not to matter whether our connection with nature is conscious or intuitive. Exchanges still occur according to patterns of synchronicity within the environment. It is a marvel to see how well the fisherman "senses" where the fish are biting and the woodsman "feels" his path.

The sharing of adamantine particles is the breath of life. There is an ongoing exchange of these particles throughout existence. They not only comprise organic life, but also the planet, the wind, and every substance that is. Everything breathes for the whole of its duration. Inhaling and exhaling, these particles bring vital balance and connections to life. To one who is attuned, an illness is clearly revealed through irregularities in the breath of life. In the presence of love, a natural rebalance occurs. This is how the 'laying on of hands' can help to restore health to another. Such is the power of healing touch or even a simple hug.

Continuous exchange creates a web of life, and we are connected with every part of it. There is no rupture in the continuity of life. As we learn to recognize our connections and to accept our responsibility for them, we will be led to new possibilities for exchange and growth. The following reports are examples of such possible discovery and exploration. I do not present these as proof of anything or evidence that I have personally verified, but they are indeed striking examples of how our consciousness is engaging with pathways of connection never before thought possible.

1. A fascinating story appeared on the front page of the Hindustan Times, Sunday, June 29, 2003. According to this story, Hira Ratan Manek (aka Hirachand) has not eaten in eight years. Instead, he lives on sunlight. Outrageous as this may sound, the 64-year-old mechanical engineer has been tried and tested by the US space agency, NASA! In June 2002, NASA verified his claims when he spent 130 days with its scientists drinking only water. They have even named such subsistence — water and solar energy — the "HRM (Hira Ratan Manek) phenomenon". Now NASA wants him to show them how he does it. They hope to use the technique to solve food storage and preservation problems on space expeditions.

Hirachand, who lives in Kozhikode, belongs to a Gujarati family that moved to Kerala 120 years ago. In 1992, Hirachand began to develop a strong distaste for food. In 1995, after returning from a trip to the Himalayas, he stopped eating altogether. Now, he has a special taste for solar energy. His wife Vimla reports, "Every evening he looks at the sun for one hour without batting an eyelid. It is his main food. Occasionally, he takes coffee, tea, buttermilk or some other liquid."

He says that eating through the eyes is best done in the evening when the sun's ultra-violet rays are least harmful. He explains this process as completely scientific and not miraculous. In addition to the nutrients derived from this "solar ingestion", there are added benefits. Is sunlight endowed with consciousness? Hirachand believes that most people have accessed only five percent of their intelligence, and that the other 95 percent can be activated through sunlight.

2. It would never occur to a plant or animal physiologist to test plants for consciousness. Plants are living things with <u>cellulose</u> cell walls, lacking nervous or sensory organs. Common experience would rule out the possibility of plants having feelings or perceptions similar to human feeling or perception. Plants do not have brains or any advanced intelligence. Or do they?

A best-selling book called *The Secret Life of Plants* presents scientific research from around the world. It explored the nature of plant intelligence. One chapter is dedicated to the work of a retired New York City policeman, Cleve Backster, who is one of the world's experts on polygraphs. In 1962, as a lark, he hooked up his plants to a polygraph so he could monitor their responses to being watered. There was such a pronounced change on the polygraph that he then approached his Dracaena with a lighted match and acted as if he were going to burn it. Not only did the plant go *wild* on the graph, but every other plant in the place did too! With excitement, he continued to experiment. He discovered that the plants responded to his thoughts even when he was miles away. One day, on the New Jersey Turnpike, he decided to send them a "thought message", that he was on his way home. When he arrived, he found that the plants had responded excitedly on the graph at the exact time he was communicating to them. Proximity was not a factor in their ability to sense his intentions!

Since that time, Cleve Backster has conducted hundreds of experiments showing that plants respond to our emotions and intentions, as do eggs, yogurt, scrapings from the roof of a person's mouth, and many other forms of living substance. All of his "subjects" responded to his thoughts and emotional states, even at remote distances.

3. Related to this are reports from patients recuperating after organ transplants. Many have experienced a "ghost effect" of feelings and inclinations not before present. When recipients report the appearance of different abilities, preferences, emotions, and even memories, we may wonder if more than an organ has been transplanted. While some medical experts explain these acquired tendencies as post-surgery stress or reactions to anti-organ rejection drugs, others explain them as cellular memories and emotions.

Dr. Candace Pert, a pharmacologist and professor at Georgetown University, believes the mind extends throughout the body by way of chemical chains and cellular pathways. Her ideas could explain such strange transplant experiences. In her book, *Molecules of Emotion*, she explains how the mind and body communicate with each other through chemicals known as peptides. Peptides are found in muscle tissue, the brain, the stomach, and all other major organs of the body. She demonstrates in a convincing way how memory can be accessed anywhere through the peptide/receptor network. For example, memories associated with sugar may be linked to the pancreas, and such associations could be transplanted from one person to another along with the organ.

In reading these reports, many of you will be energized and inspired to look for life beyond common perimeters, perhaps because you feel more comfortable with open systems. Some of you, who are more comfortable with closed systems, will be challenged to think of life outside boundaries of predictable and/or controlled behavior. Before either side begins to congratulate itself on extremes of preference, remember that **both** open and closed systems are essential to life, health, and happiness. Without a sanctuary of personal reality to call your own; where you may find peace, integrity, and equilibrium; where you may select what does and does not support your needs and values; your very survival will be in peril. Without free and open exchange with life outside "containers", your personal life will focus on issues of mortality and limitation. Eventually you will be depleted from excessive competition with other closed systems and dissipate from lack of supply. In every area of your life from health to relationships to careers, there must be balance if you are to experience a glowing state of happiness. Balance within wholeness can also redeem any failure. The wholeness of life heals, and this is the pathway to miracles.

When we contemplate unity, it is easier to bring all the systems of our life into balance. Were it not for all of life, the smallest part of life would not be possible. The smallest part of life can, and does, influence the whole. All of life is connected through its common elements and extended matrix. Whether you are referring to organic life of Earth or life of the cosmos, it always occurs in a context with other life, in unison with other life forms. Life is a property of whole systems, not of any individual organism. Life is assured because it is the summation of three eternal elements: Love, Spirit, and the Adamantine Particles — the essence of creation — the presence of the Creator.

Inspirations

James Montgomery (b.1771 d.1854) Scotland:

"Beyond this vale of tears
There is a life above,
Unmeasured by the flight of years;
And all that life is love."

Henry Wadsworth Longfellow (b.1807 d.1882) America:
"Life is real! Life is earnest!
And the grave is not its goal;
Dust thou art, to dust returnest,
Was not spoken of the soul."

Ralph Waldo Emerson (b.1803 d.1882) America:
"Will you not open your hearts to know
What rainbows teach and sunsets show!"

Bhagavad Gita ($1^{st}-2^{nd}$ century) India:
"I am the taste of water.
I am the light of the Sun and Moon.
I am the original fragrance of the earth.
I am the heat in fire.
I am the life of all that lives.
Of lights, I am the radiant Sun.
Among stars, I am the Moon.
Of bodies of water, I am the ocean.
Of immovable things, I am the Himalayas.
Of trees, I am the banyon tree.
Of weapons, I am the thunderbolt.
Among beasts, I am the lion.
Of purifiers, I am the wind.
Of fishes, I am the shark.
Of flowing rivers, I am the Ganges.
Of seasons, I am flower-bearing spring.
Of secret things, I am silence.
Know that all opulent, beautiful and glorious creations
Spring from but a spark of my splendor."

Applications

Any of the following activities will revitalize your connection with the greater supply of life. Choose according to your personal availability, vitality, and preferences. Watch a sunrise, a sunset, or a full moon and feel the nourishment of energy that bathes and connects with your whole being. Go for a walk or swim in a natural body of water and allow your body to be moved along by the flow of life reaching for you as part of itself. Sit in a garden and notice how life is recognizing and entreating you to be one with it.

As you experience this, observe how the open and closed systems integrate harmoniously and how the greater whole of life weaves them together. While in this ambiance of wholeness, review your life and allow areas of strength to come to mind. What made this so successful for you?

Now, allow areas of weakness or difficulty to come to mind. Ask yourself these three questions:

What have I not done to support others or to connect with the environment more effectively?

What have I not done to support and be true to myself?

How can I supply or correct what has been omitted?

Meditation

All too often, we think of nature as something outside ourselves — woodlands, rivers, wildlife, and mountains. We take vacations to go back to nature, but it is impossible to achieve that union without knowing how to go back to the great indoors, to the nature inside ourselves. How often do we take walks in the park and forget to look at the landscape within and follow its pathways? Through separation, we fail to see that our psychology and physiology are also material expressions of natural law, and that we are direct participants in the design of life. Our problem is that we have engaged in separation and judgment for so long that our own attitudes and habits are running interference on our health and happiness. We are not set apart from nature as something distinct and different, but intimately included within it.

The laws of God orchestrate healing and wellness. As an expression of nature, our hearts, minds, and bodies move in cycles, much as seasonal regeneration allows glorious springtime to emerge from the barrenness of winter. Without interference, natural regeneration simply occurs.

The healing value of nature's wholeness has been acknowledged by every culture. The desire for wholeness is far more than a personal yearning. It is the desire for life to join more fully with itself, to find, to take in, and to maintain even more of life. Such desires are essential to our participation in life. In this regard, it is perfectly natural to want more and more of life and to expect these longings to be fulfilled. No goal is more compelling than the desire to feel the full depth of our own wholeness and healthiness, because it rejuvenates all other aspects of life.

This meditation will give you the opportunity to remember your deepest and most complete self. You will be led to connect with the most expansive aspect of selfhood where everything is already connected, and to experience life from that place where you are most whole. Once you are there, savor the inseparability of yourself and nature. When you regain this integrity; this memory of who you really are; this inner wholeness; life begins to feel complete rather than piecemeal, as though you have come home. Health is maintained by this abiding confidence in natural law. Whether by prayer or by practice, we are more enlightened to seek that which we truly need.

To truly stay connected to life and the flowing nature of existence, you must learn to release your attachment to praise and blame. Neither is a reflection of who you truly are. Release and non-attachment are the ways to self-discovery. As Jeshua taught, *"You must lose your attachment to self in order to truly find yourself."* In a similar way, Buddha taught that praise and blame, gain and loss, and pleasure and sorrow come and go like the wind, but the spirit remains forever.

It is difficult to remember that all things pass when we are feeling blame, loss, or sorrow. We are reluctant to accept it when we are in a high moment of achievement. Clinging to frozen moments, whether good or bad, only stunts our growth and openness to life. We become like a tree that never fully opens to the sky. Dwelling on our difficulty prevents it from passing away, and attachment to victory puts everything else in its shadow.

Consider the mighty trees that have survived the storms of many seasons because they neither resist nor hold onto the wind. The wind by its nature moves on, and the tree by its grace has no hands with which to hold it. Consider the wind: have you ever seen it? Yet, you see those things that are moved by it. Consider the rushing river: how the banks are resilient to the flowing water. Neither one change in nature, and yet never is the same water touching the same riverbank. There is an eternal dialog between change and changeless-ness which, when perceived, reveals our deepest connection to life. This dialogue forms the rhythm of our truest nature.

In this meditation, you are going to stand like a tree, move like the breeze, and flow like a stream.

Stand beside a fully-grown tree. Breathe in its wisdom.

Raise your hands to heaven and look up to its branches. Watch the breeze rustle the leaves and notice how the branches stay open to the movement.

Stand firm, like the tree, and feel both praise and blame rush through as the wind passes through the branches. Breathe deeply, and feel gain and loss circle you and pass on. Open your heart. Breathe slowly, and feel pleasure and sorrow pass through your leaves. Stand still, holding on to none of it.

Kneel beside a stream if you are able, or imagine one flowing at the base of your tree. Place your hand in the stream and see it elude your capture. Yet your hand is bathed and refreshed. Put your hand in again. Did you touch the same water twice? But your hand is bathed and refreshed again. Although there is change, there is also constancy.

Now in quietness, look within. Remember a past moment of health and wholeness. Recall a time when you felt totally radiant, expressing a quality of internal energy. Notice that your intelligence is bright and lively, your thinking expansive and clear, and your emotions are stable and easily expressed. In this recollection, you are the picture of health. You can feel your health in every cell of your being. You are one with yourself, integrated in all aspects of life. This is the joyful feeling of well being, where body, mind, and emotions work effortlessly together as the expression of health. To remember this is the sweetest medicine, for it teaches your body to recall what glowing health feels like. It brings to mind what natural wisdom is like, and allows your heart to rejoice in the glory of being.

Engage with life. Within you is the whole of a universe. Wholeness means a unified life … intrinsic and extrinsic order and balance. Internal harmony is perhaps the most salient feature of all living systems, expressing the intelligent growth and regulation of all aspects of nature. All of life is arranged to uphold and express nature's intelligence in a vast unity of balance and cohesion.

In the words of William Blake, open yourself…

"To see a world in a Grain of Sand,
And a Heaven in a Wild Flower,
Hold Infinity in the palm of your hand,
And eternity in an hour."

Prayer

Teach me, O God
The majestic lesson of Your seasons.
Teach me that everything is Reborn from winter,
In its own time according to its own purpose.
Teach me the freshness and joy of springtime.
Teach me the expansion of summer,
Ripe with gratitude.
Teach me the silence of autumn,
Fulfilled and content.
Teach me the surrender of winter,
That accepts and unites.
In these cycles I feel the rhythm of eternity.
Most of all I give thanks for this moment in time,
And for the Fountain of life
That will surely supply my tomorrows.

Amen

22

RESTORING THE TEMPLE

The Message

Miracles of healing are legendary to the life and mission of Jeshua. It is also clear that his intention in healing was not to serve as a physician in the ordinary sense or even to administer blessings as random acts of kindness. He was instructing his followers and all mankind about a subject far more important to him: the spiritual nature of all humanity and the Kingdom of Heaven to which we belong. Healing was simply the best demonstration of that great message. In no uncertain terms, he said in various ways, "The Kingdom of God is within you." (Luke17:21) That idea is difficult enough to grasp today with our more abstract language and intellect. Just imagine the challenge of communicating such a thought to people whose average life span was 45 years, with all of those being a struggle for survival against hunger, disease, and political oppression. Consider the high mortality rate that was a daily contention. How else could people be convinced that the very fabric of their life and body was miraculous, except through such demonstrations? Nothing could have proven the promise of immortality more dramatically than to raise the dead and restore sight to the blind. Such miracles gave irrefutable evidence of higher causes over physical conditions! It also exposed the fact that all the elements and laws of the universe can be found within the human constitution, that there is literally a temple of cosmic presence in each human being.

"In my Father's house are many mansions. I came to prepare a place for you, and that place is within your very own being. Each human being is a temple to the Creator's presence. When I came to Earth these temples, or mansions, were broken, fallen, or challenged with inadequate or wrong understanding. It was my love, my choice, and my duty to enter the temple of human form and to restore it from the inside out that you would have a place to live, in which your spirit could flourish and fulfill its destiny. As an architect, I redrew the plan for human design through my life, death, and resurrection. The place that I prepared for you is a restored temple within the blueprint of human potential. Now it is up to each soul to choose whether or when to accept that restoration.

*"**Man's doorway to that perfection is the Sacred Heart. Seek it first and all else shall be given to you.** When your relationship to the heart is sentient and alive, it is the most natural place to be. In that center of priceless wisdom, you will find dimensions of specific intelligence, which are ever guiding your life into pathways of right action. Seven dimensions of intelligence resonate outwardly from the center of your heart. You may at first regard them as principles for living, but as you master them more fully, you will see them as extensions of your own BEING. They are **unity, love, life, respect, honesty, justice, and kindness.** Through these dimensions or aspects of consciousness, the heart can restore wholeness in an infinity of ways, to achieve an infinity of results, from an infinity of starting points.*

"It is imperative that man acknowledge the heart's higher intelligence, for the mind alone cannot tell him who he is, and genetic intelligence is a lethal weapon when combined with the technological potentials in the world today. By comparison to the mind, the heart is a function of intelligence based on the ultimate in simplicity and synchronicity. Its matrix is a synergistic center of awareness, which perceives a unified relationship with all that is. Only the heart's simplicity can comprehend both infinity and form, connecting Heaven with Earth in a meaningful way.

"Ultimately there is one infinite and connected intelligence. Perhaps you could refer to it as the great cosmic mind, although the term 'consciousness' would more accurately describe its nature. Consciousness is activated and personified by the Holy Spirit in whom all souls are born. You are born of spirit by the Holy Spirit into an infinite potential. You are part of infinity, not part of the resulting forms. Your position in the order of things allows you to have a viewpoint of infinity and to look upon the vastness of physical creation while remaining in your true spiritual nature. The heart is your eternal bond with the Creator.

"This is the 'I Am' center of your being. It is the hub of your own spiritual wheel of life. Only from this center can you perceive your place in the unity of creation and comprehend love as an extension of your being. **Unity and love together create frequencies of energy unique to the 'I Am' of your being. These are immortal and unchangeable energetic 'bodies' that form the identity of your Soul.** *A soul is not an essence that you possess, but the spiritual signature of who you are, written in the language of unity and love. This is with you always regardless of whether you choose to fulfill it or deny it.*

"The love that you are has a history also, and that began when you first noticed that you were capable of action and influence. There was a moment when you rejoiced in celebration of BEING, and in that moment your unique rhythm and personal melody was begun and your consciousness of life was born. Life is love in action, and the consciousness of life is like no other dimension of awareness. **Life itself is your third body of consciousness.**

"Life empowered your purpose and with that you set out to have an experience. Your first lessons were those of respect—respect for God, for universal and natural law, and other beings. **The respect that you learned, and are learning, constitutes your fourth body of consciousness.** *This is unique to each being.*

"The demands for respect created lessons of that nature. It also created barriers that could only be resolved through an appreciation of honesty. Therefore, you learned to express your intentions with

honesty and to discern honesty in life and others. From this, you accumulated perceptions of truth unique to your nature. Truth is a difficult subject for a soul, because truth is universal and yet perceived uniquely by each individual. This body of consciousness seeks to distill universal constants from personal experience. This is where you must decide and be accountable for your beliefs, understandings, and opinions about life. You might say **honesty is your fifth and philosophical body.** Many agreements and disagreements are formed in this body, and often there is not a perfect match with others.

"Thus, you became aware that coexistence can bring stress and that your considerations about what is true needed to be examined in the realm of cause and effect. Conflicts begin to arise, creating the need for adjustment and for justice. You observed and participated in these adjustments. You saw cause and effect around you and passing through you. A great deal of memory, data, and feelings accumulate around these experiences. **This resulted in the creation of your sixth body—justice—that plays out in the stories of your life.**

"As you experience yourself in the throws of life, receiving the consequences of all deeds—yours and others—you have, for the first time, a need to develop the **seventh body of consciousness. This is where you begin to comprehend the value of mercy and kindness.**

"All of these dimensions/aspects/bodies of consciousness are known by the Sacred Heart and accessible through it. I have told you about this in other contexts, and taught you to consult your Sacred Heart as an access to higher intelligence. I am now taking you to a higher level of understanding and revealing to you that these dimensions of consciousness are parts of your being, like arms and legs of your body. They are the rooms within the mansions of your soul, the pillars of your temple.

"This may seem quite incredible to you from your present perspective, but the fact is, you did not begin your existence as a physical entity. You began as a divine spark, a child of 'I Am That I Am'. Then you had a long history as a soul, with many thoughts, feelings, experiences, and decisions. Finally, your life force was breathed into physical form as the completing stage of your creation.

In the history of your soul, which is ancient and beyond time, there is too much experience and awareness to inventory every thought and action without considering its place in the whole context of your BEING. You would be 'churning the milk' of your past thoughts, actions, hopes, explorations, disappointments, successes, failures, pleasures, pains, and errors forever. You cannot work your way to salvation through a wheel of life or any worldly process of accountability. It would be endless and inescapable. Were it not for the law of grace you could not transcend the process of creating experience. You would miss the larger picture and be caught forever in the events of life.

"By grace, you are given the freedom to know and return to a state of wholeness and remember your original incentives and aspirations for entering the realm of experience. Each dimension of consciousness is propelled by a certain aspiration. Whenever your heart remembers the true aspiration, you are delivered from delusion and set back on the path toward fulfillment. Your life is elevated above the dramas of the world and your authority is reclaimed over the experiences you are having, even though you may choose to continue. You also have the authority in your heart to know when you are complete. Living by the sacred aspirations is a simple path since they are uncomplicated in their processes. Regardless of the time involved, these keys to the kingdom will take you home.

"**The first aspiration is innocence. This is the key to the door of unity.** Innocence is the sweet fragrance of the soul, forever young and reborn eternally in the presence of the Holy Spirit. This is our yearning to be the innocent child of God. Often it must be restored through atonement (at-one-ment). Daily it may be practiced through innocent perception. In the presence of innocence, there is no separation or judgment, and all is One.

"**The second aspiration is compassion. This is the key to the door of love.** Compassion means to 'feel with.' One who is in a state of true and complete compassion simply 'feels with' life and shares his own energetic life force with others for the restoration of wholeness. The same restoration comes back to oneself.

"The third aspiration is abundance. This is the key to life. Its foundation is gratitude. Unlike the prosperity of material acquisition, gratitude does not take its power from attitudes of scarcity, hoarding, and greed. The unconditional state of abundance expands through sharing, caring, and giving. Life was created for abundance and to ever expand in that way. By simply removing all systems and beliefs that gain power through creation of scarcities, much pain and suffering would vanish from the world.

"The fourth aspiration is wisdom. This is the key to the conscious domain of respect. Wisdom teaches you to respect the laws of God, the laws of life, and the agreed upon laws of mutual conduct. Wisdom teaches you to respect others and yourself. Through wisdom, you can reach a higher place that stands above the betrayals and disappointments of coexistence. It allows you to convert your experience to higher understanding. In the Book of Proverbs (8:1-2), King Solomon exclaims: 'Does not wisdom call out? Does not understanding raise her voice? On the heights along the way, where the paths meet, she takes her stand.'*

"The fifth aspiration is peace. This is the key to the domain of honesty. Chaos does not foster honesty, but honesty can resolve chaos. You will never meet a truthful, violent man. Honesty is also not available through debates over reality, nor is peace attained through worldly order. Peace is cultivated by bringing order to yourself. Only then is truth revealed.

"The sixth aspiration is forgiveness. This is the only and ultimate key to the domain of justice. Justice has all the power to enforce the laws of cause and effect. Were it not for the law of grace, there would be no escaping the consequences of limited foresight or the absence of good will. The law of grace is invoked through the aspiration of forgiveness. Forgiveness does not mean indulgence or tolerance of destructive behavior. The true nature of forgiveness is a contrite and humble heart that understands the fleeting nature of experience. The heart is mindful of error and seeks to correct it but makes no lasting attachment to grievances.

"The seventh aspiration is joy. Joy is the key to kindness. Joy is the soul's celebration of being the love that it is—a blessing to the world, yet not of the world! Unlike happiness, joy is not the result of conditions or other needs for positive reward. Joy is the soul's exaltation of life that transcends all circumstances. It strives to express its appreciation of life through kindness to self and others.

"It is my pleasure and joy to give you these keys to the kingdom. As you use them for the betterment of your life and that of others, remember your origin as a child of God. Remember the 'I Am' presence that is the spark of your life. Allow your soul to expand without boundaries or limiting structures, and your body to conform to the ways of your spirit."

Correlations

Luke 17:21 "The Kingdom of God does not come with your careful observation, nor will people say, 'here it is', or 'there it is', because the kingdom of God is within you."

John 14:2 "In my Father's house are many mansions: if it were not so I would have told you. I go to prepare a place for you.

John 2:19-21 "Jesus answered and said unto them, 'Destroy this temple, and in three days I will raise it up.' Then said the Jews, 'Forty and six years was this temple in building, and will you rear it up in three days?' But he spoke of the temple of his body."

Acts 5:20 "Go, stand and speak in the temple to the people all the words of this life."

I Corinthians 3:16 "Know you not that you are the temple of God, and that the Spirit of God dwells in you?"

I Corinthians 9:13 "Do you not know that they which minister about holy things live of the things of the temple?"

The Key

We live in a multi-dimensional universe, within a multi-dimensional body, where the greatest measure of it is space. To visualize this, just imagine the nucleus of each atom in your body enlarged to the size of a baseball. All the atoms would be about 2,000 miles apart from each other. By contrast, if you extended a solid steel rod from San Francisco to New York and removed all the space between its atoms, the rod would then be about an eighth of an inch long. Matter as we know it is mostly empty space. It seems solid because the energy fields of sub-atomic particles create impenetrable barriers to outside influences.

These repelling grid lines give us the impression that matter is solid and that solidity is what determines the wholeness and boundaries of physical objects. Modern science, as well as ancient wisdom, informs us that such casual assumptions are simply not true. Just as different rings of energy surround an atom, providing each with a different frequency and resistance to penetration, larger configurations of matter are also designed with multi-dimensional boundaries of containment and influence. Most of the forces that hold configurations in place are invisible. The most obvious example of that is our solar system with its central sun and orbiting planets, each with different densities, environments and electromagnetic fields. The planets are obvious, but without understanding, could you "see" the dynamics holding them in orbit? Is there any reason to believe that a complex organism such as the human body would be an exception to having diversified energy fields with invisible forces holding the configurations in place?

Jeshua taught us to look beyond the illusions of physical form. Once, we could only take this on faith. Now we have confirmation from science and the hands-on experience of healing practitioners that there are indeed subtle energetic bodies within and beyond our physical body. Each of these subtle "bodies" has a different purpose, nature, and frequency unique to its function, and most of them are invisible to normal perception. They are mostly detectable by consciousness and revelation. An analogy of how this works would be the relationship between the common radio and radio waves. Different frequencies of radio waves mingle indiscernibly until a radio receiver tunes into them and reports the separate data streams. Consider telephone messages humming together along a single optical fiber. As long as they keep their separate frequencies, they can coexist as unique entities in the same space and be available for separate interpretation. With this model in mind, perhaps we could call the frequencies of energetic potential within us to be "bodies" of consciousness.

Throughout the ages, many seers and healers have sensed and attempted to describe the "extra bodies" that coexist within the realm of human life and personal identity. Many have been very insightful, and at times effective, in treating the imbalances and ailments of the whole person through such perceptions. On an intuitive level, more was sensed than seen. More could be known intuitively than any conscious models or descriptions of this phenomenon could reveal or describe.

It seems that, of all our *specialized knowledge*, the science of consciousness has been the slowest to develop. To compound this problem, the first theories advanced were egocentric, just as theorists before Copernicus explained the complex movement of our solar system by assuming that planet Earth was the hub of this enormous wheel. In a similar way, pre-quantum physicists were convinced that the absolutes of existence could be located within the laws of solid matter—the substance to which we could relate physically and directly. Now we know that physical matter is merely a derivative product of a much grander pattern of integration. Likewise, in our typical egocentric way of thinking and explaining existence, we have often envisioned that the soul was created to replicate, perfect, and perpetuate the body in the etheric and spiritual realms.

It is time we reversed the egocentric pattern of thinking and considered the relationship of body and soul from a new perspective, which is also the oldest wisdom. As Jeshua has instructed, our bodies are merely the momentary servants of a much grander reality of BEING. The soul is created in the image of God, and our bodies are instruments for gathering experience, developing consciousness, and exercising faith for **the soul's fulfillment.**

An astonishing point to consider about Jeshua's healing miracles is that none of them focused on the body as a primary objective. In many instances, the body was never touched, or at least there is no mention of it. Always the emphasis was on faith and spirit! Often there was a mention of the Kingdom of Heaven. The faith he taught was about the Loving Divine Presence that lived within us, and sustained and supported our lives from invisible and intangible realms beyond normal human perception. To him, the body was like a grain of sand in an oyster, from which a pearl would eventually grow if nurtured properly. If the oyster was killed, what happened to the grain of sand was irrelevant, and if the oyster was healthy, the destiny of the grain of sand was assured. The oyster was the soul and the shell was the Kingdom of Heaven in which it lived. That analogy is overly simplistic, but it helps move us to the real point of his instruction: that our bodies are the tiniest part of a much larger self. That larger self, with its own dimensions of reality, is not created in the image of the human body, but rather, in the image of God!

In recent years, we have learned a great deal about the extra dimensions of our being from those who left their bodies in near-death experiences and then returned to tell about their extra-dimensional adventures. These reports come from ordinary people in all cultures, religions, and age groups. Their stories are amazingly consistent. The experience begins with some physical trauma that induces the soul's exodus. Death is felt, but also great peace. The soul floats outside its bodies, often staying close by, but sometimes flying toward a tunnel of light where it communicates with beings of light, or with deceased loved ones. Then, miraculously ... it comes back!

A Dutch research team has studied this in depth. The team is lead by Pim van Lommel, M.D., a cardiologist at Rijnstate Hospital in Arnhem, Netherlands. Their findings were reported in the December 15, 2001 issue of *"The Lancet"*. The researchers studied 344 patients who were revived after their hearts stopped beating. All of the patients had been clinically dead. As soon as the patients were well enough to talk, they agreed to an interview with van Lommel's team. Nearly one in five patients reported a near-death experience. Two years later, and then eight years after that, the researchers interviewed these patients again. Forty-one of sixty-two patients not only stuck to their stories, but also reported it as a profound experience that changed their entire perception of life.

Harry Oldfield's book, *The Invisible Universe,* exposes some dramatic discoveries about energy fields surrounding the human body, and indeed, all life forms. Through a process that he calls Polycontrast Interference Photography, he has captured the changing patterns of light energy emanating from all living things, including the human body, plants, animals, and even crystals. By his own assertion, he was a "Newtonian" biologist 25 years ago, interested only in the concrete evidence of hard scientific fact. While pursuing his traditional studies, he stumbled upon a way to adapt an older technology commonly associated with satellite pictures of hot and cool land and sea masses. He perfected this application after many years of research into Kirlian photography. This was developed further into a polycontrast interference device, which can distinguish between many different grades or qualities of light. This later development rests on a computer program that allocates a number to each grade of light and then color-codes each number. The result is an image that can be displayed on a computer screen and fluctuates with the actual changes in the life energy of the subject under examination.

In his book there are many staggering photographs of biological specimens, including a caterpillar and maple leaf, before and after their disconnection with the energy of life. Included in his photographs are even ghost effects where traces remain of former life entities no longer living in a particular environment. Most importantly, from a practical viewpoint, his photographic technique reveals fluctuations in the energy around a human body that may be used to detect physical or mental illness. For example, there are definite energy patterns associated with actual or impending heart disease. Oldfield's technology is now used in three hospitals in Britain and several clinics in Europe. The profiles of depression, schizophrenia, and cancer are quite characteristic. In this type of photography, cancer shows up as a chaotic, riotous explosion of light fibers. The most disturbing image was that of a 15-year-old cocaine addict. The light around his head was fractured and forming a drain while seemingly detached entities clung, suction-like, to the lower limbs. On a more positive note, there are photographs documenting the practice of spiritual healing and the laying-on of hands. These clearly show the phenomenon of empathetic resonance, with the lights of two beings joined. There are others showing brilliant imprints of babies forming in the womb.

A great deal of confusion exists regarding the terms *spirit* and *soul*. We know from Jeshua that the spirit is within all things and is the ultimate Source of everything. By the grace of God, and as an eternal gift, the "I Am" presence of each individual has been given a place to live within Holy Spirit, if we so choose. We are invited to build our mansion within the safe haven of spirit and to dwell with our Creator forever. The process through which this union unfolds has been a subject for endless debate. Perhaps the answer is not fully within the grasp of our consciousness, yet we can sense and utilize the progressions toward unity that extend outward from our being as the Divine reaches for us. We cannot always see these progressions clearly since they tend to take on our identity as they extend through our personal life. They surrender to all manner of open possibility as they reach toward the infinite. Many theoretical designs, configurations, and mystic formulas have been devised to provide explanations for progressions of reality between human and divine consciousness and to serve as systems of containment for this connection. None of them are sufficient, if useful at all, since it is the very nature of the Divine to surprise us with unforeseen potential.

Nevertheless, from this union the soul is born and receives unto itself the life force of the universe. The soul unites with spirit in mutual consummation of life. The Divine "I Am" gives unto each individual expression of consciousness a presence that is capable of building its own life. To fulfill this mission, the soul is equipped with formidable intelligence and self-adjustable mechanisms to bring harmony and balance to any situation. Jeshua described the hub and seven principle dimensions of our wheel of consciousness that connect the center of one's personal being with Divine Presence. To summarize his message, they are:

The "I Am" center of being (the hub): This is the spark of God within. It is our point of Infinite potential, stillness, simultaneity and absolute silence. It can be experienced as our Sacred Heart, the place of synchronicity with our Creator's Will. This is the eternal being, invisible to itself.

Unity is a state of consciousness where judgment is eliminated and opposing factions no longer exist. When achieving this awareness, the soul realizes there is but *one spirit.* It is relieved from the obsession to judge and to separate from whatever is misunderstood. This is the body of wholeness, touched by the grace of Holy Spirit. It is received through the aspiration of innocence.

Love is the highest power in the Universe and the source of all creation. Within this dimension, one can experience love as the ultimate source of power, and surrender from the conflicts of polarity. This is the body of creativity. It is attained by the aspiration of compassion.

Life is love in action, and that is the combination of unity and love in perfect harmony. Through this unity, *Life Force* generates creation. This is the body that receives and is grateful. It is fulfilled by the aspiration of abundance.

Respect is the awareness that honors and directs the *Life Force* into harmonious and productive purpose. This is the body of purpose. It is governed by the aspiration of wisdom.

Honesty is the ability to see oneself as love and life as it is. Honesty allows one to see beyond all projection and judgment and to practice innocent perception as a child of God. This is governed by the aspiration of peace.

Justice is an equalizing awareness that allows one to maintain balance in life. In some philosophies, this is called the karmic body; it is the place where resolution of cause and effect plays out. True resolution is attained through the aspiration of forgiveness.

Kindness is the application of compassion to the acceptance of life. This is where you hold your experiences of pleasure and pain and learn to recognize the pleasure caused by kindness or pain caused by cruelty. Our physical body is the teacher that allows us to overcome the illusion of false or destructive reality and finally learn to know the unconditional feeling of joy.

Each level of consciousness is an energetic body, not necessarily definable by boundaries or configurations. Nevertheless, each one is a discernible frequency of energy, awareness, memory, and future potential capable of health, expansion, and enduring presence in whatever state of existence it may be. Knowing the true relationship between body and soul **is the key to the Kingdom of Heaven** and to restoring the temple of one's life.

Inspirations

Thomas Moore (b.1779 d.1852) Ireland:
"Earth has no sorrow that Heaven cannot heal."

Orison Swett Marden (b.1906 d.1975) America:
"Wisdom is knowledge which has become a part of one's being."

Kahlil Gibran (b.1883 d.1931) Persia:
"Your daily life is your temple and your religion. Whenever you enter into it take with you your all. Take the plough and the forge and the mallet and the lute, the things you have fashioned in necessity or for delight. For in reverie you cannot rise above your achievements nor fall lower than your failures. And take with you all men; for in adoration you cannot fly higher than their hopes nor humble yourself lower than their despair."

James Allen (b.1864 d.1912) America:
"Before a person can accomplish anything of an enduring nature in the world, he must first of all acquire some measure of success in the management of his own mind. If a person cannot govern the forces within himself, he cannot hold a firm hand upon the outer activities that form his visible life."

Applications

Wholeness is its own power. Yet within it, essential parts contribute to the rich patterns of your experience. Outward from the center of your being — the true "I Am"— there are seven expanding dimensions of consciousness that contain the totality of your experience, beliefs, goals and capabilities. In a manner of speaking, they represent seven aspects of your spiritual body, endowed by God and developed through your engagement with life. Together, in unison, these dimensions of higher consciousness connect at the center of your being—a place that Jeshua calls the Sacred Heart.

As you gather experience and make decisions about life, it is doubtful that you see all of these dimensions of consciousness with clear-cut boundaries. More than likely, you see a mixture of them at work in any particular situation. It would be a mistake to become analytical about these particular states of consciousness or to separate the different energies and principles into cubbyholes of limited scope. Each represents a specialized interpretation of experience; yet, they are integrated and dependent on each other.

Wholeness is an enigma that reveals itself only if we accept and support its many parts. Whenever we develop a belief in separate members, wholeness gives us a game!

All beings possess a natural and radiant wholeness that always prevails, even if we only see and feel broken parts and pieces. Sometimes we mistake the illusion of isolated segments of reality for reality itself, and fail to look **beyond** the illusion. Indeed, we even deny the possibility of wholeness, because we have learned to see the whole as an assembly of parts instead of an indivisible union. When fragments are in disarray, our faith is often not strong enough to reveal the cohesion of life. This is where the power of the Holy Spirit is truly our counsel and salvation. At times, there are no threads capable of mending our torn lives, and yet they miraculously heal when the wholeness beneath the tear is acknowledged and restored. A state of newness emerges, which is not the result of patching or fixing.

Wholeness gives us an interesting dilemma. When we immerse ourselves in it, we lose a sense of the parts; and when we focus on the parts, we lose a sense of the whole. Yet, there is an answer to this riddle, and it lies in the feeling, instinctive nature at the center of the whole. For every part created, the central unifying power of the whole has **an aspiration**.

Our center is the Sacred Heart. It seeks fulfillment through the seven aspirations that originally impelled the seven dimensions of consciousness. By directing our attention upon our heart's aspirations, we have a much better way of reaching all the dimensions of consciousness without extracting them from the whole or treating them as separate dimensions. The pathways and principles to accomplish this have been revealed throughout the teachings of Jeshua.

Jeshua brought into consciousness and practice a revolutionary new idea ... of a temple that could not be destroyed once it was fully established. He honored the idea of a sacred place, or temple; but for him, the fundamental prototype of every temple was the Sacred Heart Ï a place central to every human soul, mind, and body where one's connection to God is everlasting. With this profound invitation for humanity's return to its original connection with the Creator, a new covenant was established. That new covenant was for the rebuilding of the most ancient of all temples Ï the one within Ï where in true sanctuary, man would be in a complete state of love with God and love of others as himself.

You can make progress toward restoring this temple every day of your life, in whatever you do, by remembering the seven aspirations that dissolve the conflicts of life. They are:

INNOCENCE ... COMPASSION ... ABUNDANCE ... WISDOM... PEACE ... FORGIVNESS ...JOY

Meditation

Your life is your temple, and within that great temple are many specialized temples. To varying degrees, these may be broken temples. Columns are standing tall in some temples, and shattered in others. Some passageways are open and some have collapsed. Some temples are full of song, and others are haunted with the memory of dreams that were lost or abandoned. Some temples you cannot bear to enter because you cannot forgive.

The purpose of this meditation is to draw all parts of your life into a single, unified whole. It is all right and appropriate to keep whatever feelings are currently associated with the parts and passages of your life. You cannot recreate a meaningful whole with dishonest feelings about the former events. Some of the parts will be full of joy and excitement, and some may be full of anger or grief. Other parts you would rather not look at again. I assure you that they do not go away simply because you do not accept them. The place to start is with the way things really are.

Be seated in a comfortable chair, close your eyes, and breathe easily without effort or forced attention. Relax your body and release the tension of the day. To help this along, start with your toes. Wiggle them and move your feet until they are free of tension. Move up to your ankles, and gently rotate them until you can begin to feel the relaxation move up through your legs. Continue upward into your lower body. Consider each body part as special, and acknowledge its membership in the whole. Take this opportunity to show each part of your body its membership in the whole and express your gratitude for what it does. If there is any pain, discomfort, sickness, or dysfunction, notice the feeling in that organ or body part and acknowledge that feeling as part of the whole no matter what it is. No part suffers alone. Continue moving up through your body to the top of your head and your scalp. Squint your eyes and release them. Repeat this several times to relax your scalp and the muscles of your face.

Now sink into relaxation and focus on your breath. This is the breath of your life.

Imagine that you are sitting inside an enormous, clear bubble and the walls of the bubble reflect back to you the events of your life. Find a place on the walls of the bubble for every part of your life Ï for every joy, hope, duty, triumph, disappointment, boring endurance, and exciting adventure. Find a place for every exquisite feeling, every sickness, every loss, and every moment of happiness.

With every breath, inhale into your consciousness whatever memory is available for you to examine. There is no order of importance, because everything has a place in the whole of your life. Not everything is available at one time, and this meditation is something you can repeat throughout your life. Therefore, patience and acceptance are crucial attitudes as you proceed into this examination of your temple.

The most important thing is to accept each memory, incident, or event that comes forth as YOUR experience. See and feel what was really happening for YOU! Look at every sensation, every opinion, and every conclusion you made about this incident at the time it happened. Now look to see if there were also feelings, opinions, beliefs or decisions, which were NOT yours, which had an influence on the way you responded. Exhale with gusto, and release everything that was not yours. See the energy of others dissolve into particles that blow away. Carefully place the part of the memory that was truly yours back on the inner wall of your bubble. Know that it will be there for all time, but it may now take on a different order of importance or a different meaning as your own true experience.

Repeat this as many times as your interest and energy can be vitally engaged with the process. When you begin to feel a sense of completion and restoration, that is enough for one day. Before you end, survey the inner wall of the bubble and notice if any new alignments have happened. Perhaps it is now lighter and more sparkling, or more resilient and flexible. What makes the walls of your temple hard, brittle, and breakable are elements that are not truly your own. These elements are the contributions of others that you have held onto out of vanity, misunderstanding, confusion, or lack of forgiveness.

As you restore the pillars of your temple, you will notice the progress first by a greater sense of innocence and a willingness to see and accept your experiences exactly as they were without judgment or false coloring. As your acceptance increases, forgiveness will become easier, and you will find it possible to retain the memory of events and people, while forgiving the hurt and disappointments connected with them. That will be the hardest part of your progress. After that, you will find more and more peace as you clean and restore the pieces of your temple. Wisdom will come as you begin to take the restored pieces and find new meaning and new patterns of integration. It will be as if you have taken on a new life. Your heart will begin to fill with the miracle of a restored temple and you will behold the amazing abundance of all you have lived and experienced. Joy will fill every part of your being. From this place of fulfillment, compassion will take on a new meaning as you look around at the world and all those with whom you share life. There will be love, tolerance, true understanding, and reverence for the presence of Christ in your life, pouring through you to others. These are the feelings and benchmarks that you will recognize as you restore the temple of your life.

*P*rayer

O My Creator,
I invite You to enter the temple of my life.
From the sacred basin of Your love,
Sprinkle living waters upon the altar of my heart.
Awaken me to Your presence, and
Open my eyes to the Heaven of Your Truth.
Take me to where love creates a seamless whole,
And perfection is all there is.

Amen

23

THE END OF STORY:
THE BEGINNING OF LIFE…

The Message

"In the beginning, life was given as a gift unto itself. It existed long before there was a story to tell about it and life will endure long after the last story has ended. Life does not depend upon stories for its authenticity and authority, although it does seek to experience and fulfill its nature. For that reason, life connects with stories. Stories are the containers of experience.

"Human beings are natural storytellers. They enjoy their stories, learn from them, and explore the future with unbounded freedom through that creative medium. Whether they are told, lived out, or just held in one's mind for the meaning they bring, stories provide a context for sharing, learning, and including others in the pageants of life. Stories are as ancient as language, and storytelling is a unique facet of human sentience. Stories are a marvelous creative tool for sculpting awareness and developing character as long as one knows they are stories. The only problem is that stories are often misused and confused with other important functions and principles of life. For example: in the absence of a purpose, a goal, or a mission in life, a person will look to his story or acquired stories for instructions about what to do next. Stories begin to direct his life and steal authority from him. Often social leaders will manipulate communities and nations with stories that embrace the history or aspiration of large numbers of *people. You are not your history, and you are not the obliged servant of your history's perpetuation. You are also not your story!*

"Time is a wondrous and powerful dynamic of our universe that is yet to be seen accurately. Time is a dynamic of energy, coordination and attraction, and not just the basis of history and future potential. Through the addiction to stories, however, time is feared, maligned, and considered a source of aberration. When you view time as the consecutive record of events (whether physical or social), you create history…his-story, her-story, its-story! For lack of higher understanding, people make sense out of time with the stories they tell. This creates the desire to see the future as a continuation or correction of the past, and nothing new ever happens. When a story ends, there is often pain and sorrow. This is falsely blamed on time. The real hurt is caused because you believed in the story more than you believed in life. You took an identity from the story that you believed in more than yourself. Then the story ended. You felt betrayed or lost. When I said long ago that a man must lose his life to find it, I was referring to the delusion of story-generated identities. If you would truly possess the fullness of life, you must shift your attention from the identity you hold in stories to the truth of who you really are.

*"Complete dependency on stories will cost a person his personal liberty and destroy creativity. He will long for the past, and even more so to be 'in present time' as if that were a strange and special place to be. I promise you, there **is nothing but present time!** It's just that you can't perceive it when you are completely engaged in the perpetuation of your history. What you long for is to be free of your stories, while yet retaining the positive connections and experiences that built them. There is a way to do that, but first you must understand the limited nature of stories and the greater power of life.*

*"Stories express the adventure of life, but they can become prisons when **they begin consuming your life for the sustaining of a story!** Some stories are so widely believed they seem like reality. Many souls endure their stories with thoughtless submission, and others,*

sensing a trap, react rebelliously. The drama between teenagers and parents provide many examples of this. Teenage conflict is nothing more than a young person pushing back on a parental story at a moment in time when he has gained enough self-awareness to envision a different destiny.

"At our best, we make choices about life each day as we go along. Some choices are of long duration and consume much of our life. However, we still need to acknowledge frequently that the choice was, and is, ultimately ours. Otherwise, one may become entrapped by habitual expectations that reduce consciousness. All compulsory behavior, every unnatural habit, and dependency has its roots within some story hidden just beneath the surface of consciousness. Many valuable therapies have been developed to help a person bring submerged stories up to conscious view thereby releasing dysfunctional content. Many times this kind of healing has changed a person's view on life and restored a willingness to live. Even so, this is not the ultimate answer for personal liberation. There are simply too many stories to examine and resolve. Too much involvement in reviewing past events can reinforce an already strong belief that one's history is actually the key to one's future. This is just a new dependency and a new story.

"To be truly liberated from your history, you must first be restored to the knowledge that you were created to live beyond and above ALL stories. Your life is special unto itself. You are a creator of stories and Love is the redeemer of stories. Every story—one way or another— is potentially a love story. It may not be about fulfilled love, but still it is about love: desired love, denied love, lost love, broken love, oppressed love, tender love, tough love, forbidden love (jealousy), refused love (hate), forgotten love, sacrifice, service, or compassion. Your challenge is to find the power of love within whatever story you live.

"By discovering the presence of love weaving through all stories, regardless of how unlikely its presence, you are led to true enlightenment and personal fulfillment. The touch of genius in writing, telling, or living any story is to find love in forms, expressions, *and places that have not been observed before. Because Love is the master creator of the universe, there is love in every authentic creation.*

*"You have a choice in every story you live or write. Will you focus on its drama, or will you focus on the power that gives it greater meaning? When I speak of being reborn into a new life by the power of the Holy Spirit, I am not offering you a better story for your old one! When I speak of being lifted from the turmoil of earthly life into a higher life, I am not referring to a better script on a higher stage. The alternative I am presenting you is not between two classes of stories. The choice is between life in its true and higher nature ... and life in its captured state. The best description I can give you of the difference between Heaven and Hell is that Heaven is the **end of capture by stories**. A soul is restored to his love in the presence of others being their love. In that blessed state, one is free to simply BE or to create new stories from the heart. This can be accomplished on the earth **now**. By contrast, being in Hell is being captured by the stories of your life, which are now 'creating you' and driving you to become the inevitable conclusion of that story. There are many degrees of this capture. Some degrees are subtle, and some are almost unbearable. This also is happening **now**.*

*"The law of entropy governs all stories left to their own unfolding. Therefore, stories **capture life to seize energy**. All stories that follow their own inertia to the bitter end, do just that —end bitterly! Stories can bring endless experience and opportunities for growth, but unless love enters and creates a perspective outside the story, there is no fulfillment or escape. Many souls are caught in the clutches of story simply to discover the outcome, or perhaps in hopes that it will be the one story in all existence that can write its own happy ending. There is a great trap in being blindly committed to a story out of false pride or misguided loyalty.*

"All happy endings are created by souls that step outside their story, realizing that their loyalty is not to the story itself, but to themselves, to their loved ones, and to the spirit of love pouring through the story. Stories are not sacred! Souls are! It is a great crime to perpetuate any story to the detriment of souls suffering within it or

because of it. When you realize this, you will step above the dramas of earth and into the Kingdom of Heaven.

"In my life on earth, I was always in service to God and those who needed me, but I was often viewed as rebellious. This is because I was vigilant about disengaging from stories. Although stories have their value, there is a much better way of relating to life; by having purposes and goals that lift one to a higher level, and then applying oneself to achieve them. Purposes, goals, and missions parallel the elements of story, but connect with one's Source and play out on a higher level of consciousness. My purpose is to serve the will of God completely and to fulfill the oneness of that relationship. My goal, or intention, two thousand years ago was to redeem the earth from its darkness and conflict. My mission was, and is, to teach love and be a living model of how to love God with all one's heart and others as oneself. To these ideals, I gave my whole being. I passed through many stories and created a few, but at no point was I dependent on the consent of a story to accomplish my purpose, goal, or mission. By being firm in this, I demonstrated that when one's life is for a purpose, it transcends all stories.

"The ultimate maneuver of my life was to accept my role in a story, with the intention of transcending it. As the Messiah, I was expected to fulfill the prophecies of Jewish sacred and political history. I did fulfill the promise in every way, but I did not adhere to human expectations of how that story would unfold or what the ultimate result would be. I was condemned for claiming to be the Messiah when I did not play my part according to the common interpretation of what that was believed to be. My purpose, goal, and mission required that I bring about the fulfillment from a different perspective. For that, I was crucified. Through my death and resurrection, the goal was accomplished. I am fulfilling my purpose every day and the mission continues.

"Not only was it necessary to fulfill my mission from a perspective unforeseen by human consciousness, it was also vitally necessary to demonstrate the power of ENDING A POWERFUL STORY! The story to which I was born was an ancient river of

prophecy, history, and religious tradition with many tributaries flowing into it. This river could have rushed on forever, seeking a Messiah and finding no one worthy! God makes promises. People build stories around them. Often these stories become more valuable for motivational energy than the promises they represent. This has happened many times with nations, societies, and religions that were founded on golden principles. The profit from 'marketing' a great idea or way of life, or in manipulating large numbers of people with it, leads to great temptation. When that happens, it is necessary for the story to be ended so that life can re-emerge in newer and more benevolent ways. Ideally, this happens through natural and graceful transitions. Unfortunately, such is not always the case. The need for change is sometimes so major and so long overdue that nothing short of sacrifice is able to bring it about. Examples of this would be the American Revolution and other human revolutions that came about to support growing needs for liberty and justice. Such a sacrifice was unavoidable with my own life.

"All of history changed two thousand years ago. Whatever you believe about my life, or conclude about its importance; whatever you believe or conclude about my crucifixion and resurrection; one thing can be seen objectively in the world. There was a wholesale ending of stories in the first century after my life on earth. It was my intention to end the large political stories so that life could be reborn in a new state of consciousness and choice. By ending these stories, a greater spirit could be released upon the earth.

"In those days, time was measured by stories. They were interchangeable and thought to be the same. Therefore, when I said that the end of time was at hand, I was referring to the monumental end of story that was about to occur. I taught my family, friends, and followers how to prepare for the transition through discerning the difference between life and stories. I also talked about a more distant end of time that would be greater than anyone could imagine. That time is NOW! This is not the end of geophysical time or biological time. It is another end of story on such a massive scale that one can only survive the forthcoming changes by honoring life, love, personal

integrity, and community above all stories. The whole earth – land, sea, animals, plants and atmosphere– aches for the end of its troubled stories. Most of all, the hearts of men and women ache for them to end. Each will play its part in seeing that it does.

"In some cases, change will happen because of innovation — unexpected and accelerated areas of progress and discovery. This will create a great shift in values as new opportunities arise for redefining reality. Ideals will leave the powers that have previously supported them and reappear in new parts of the world, in new contexts. Planetary changes will contribute to shifting populations. Massive relocation of people will transform economic systems and the way people relate to each other. Belief systems will be fully reexamined. There will be so much transformation in the next century that what you now consider reality will only be found in history books. Whether this is peaceful or bloody depends on how attached people are to their stories and how faithful they are to life and the living.

"Stories serve only to be containers of experience, to support the evolution of consciousness, and give passage to the soul's enlightenment. As truth emerges, the container is cast away.

"Examine your life. Are you living purposely with goals and missions that are relevant to your being and those you love? If not, discover your purposes, goals, and missions and step out into the stream of life. New stories will naturally shape around you that fit the true nature of your being.

"I will always be with you, sharing your hopes and anxieties. I will be in your heart to guide you in your choices. But remember ... I am a servant to love, and often a rebel to story. Therefore, I will never hold any story above the truth or love needing to emerge from it. Nor will I conform to the promises of any story over and beyond the opportunity of elevating you or all of humanity to a higher level. I am delighted to surprise you with revelations of truth and love that lift you to freedom. Through the guidance of the Holy Spirit, it could be no other way."

Correlations

Psalms 90:12 "So teach us to number our days, that we may apply our hearts unto wisdom."
Ecclesiastes 3:11-13 "He has made everything beautiful in its time. He has also set eternity in the hearts of men; yet they cannot fathom what God has done from beginning to end. Know that there is nothing better for men than to be happy and do good while they live. That everyone may eat and drink, and find satisfaction in all his toil—this is the gift of God."
2 Corinthians 6:2 "I tell you, now is the time of God's favor."
Romans 13:11 "And do this, understanding the present time. The hour has come for you to wake up from your slumber, for your salvation is nearer now than when we first believed."

The Key

Some stories we never want to end. Others are such agony we would pay almost anything to exit from them. When I was a girl, my mother would say, "All things pass, both good and the bad." There was a touch of sadness, though, in her expression, or at least in the way I heard it. Jeshua's teaching about the end of story was similar to my mother's remark, but with an affirmative promise. He was referring to the end of our need to define our lives by the stories we live. It was an assurance that life continues beyond the limitation of all stories.

In his message, I found the greatest comfort for past unhappiness and the greatest reason not to judge anyone. Every facet of life is greater than any story ever told. Even the greatest epics are not great because of the narrative, but because of the love that triumphed through it. It is interesting also to realize that many achievements made within a story are not regarded as success by the soul, and many of the dark challenges of a situation may actually be victories for the soul. There is obviously a parallel between the life of the soul and the stories of earth. Yet, these dimensions of reality are not always connected in a direct or obvious way. At least not when we focus only on the earthly parade of events. Until we redefine success in higher terms than the plots of our life, we will never understand that connection. How much better would it be for our growth and enlightenment if success endured far beyond the saga, and any errors exposed then resulted in character growth rather than blame upon the story?

There is possibly no greater anesthesia to consciousness than to believe that by playing out a story we are fully living life. In many different ways, many times, Jeshua has said *"Leave behind your story and follow me."* Stories are like glue to the soul. We cling to accomplishments and acquisitions that a story has provided. We also endure dark passages in hopes that our continuing efforts will somehow repair the past damage brought to others or ourselves. Stories contain many traps, and the ego thrives on all of them. It finds the achievements of a story easy food for its manufactured esteem, and the miseries of a story satisfy the guilt-laden insufficiency of ego.

When Jeshua spoke of the parallel nature between the elements of story and the development of purposes, goals, and missions, I believe that he was giving us a key to translate our stories up to a higher level that our souls can command. Neither our potential nor our worth is defined by the history of events. We define our lives and fulfill our existence with the purposes, goals, and missions we honor and support.

He gave me another metaphor to contemplate as a model for how to engage in a story for the experience it can bring without becoming lost within it. That was the image of a wheel of life. He asked me to draw a wagon wheel in which the various structural parts were clearly visible—the axle, hub, spokes and rim. Then he instructed me to label its parts with elements of my life. As I studied the wheel, I concluded that the rim of the wheel carries the motion, absorbs the stress, and grinds upon the road of life. Therefore, I labeled this "the drama and experience of worldly existence". The hub of the wheel is the central unit that grips the axle and disperses that energy through the spokes into the rim. So, I saw this being equivalent to the heart, or center of being. The axle, I called "Love". In continuing the metaphor, I decided that the spokes represented different aspects of responsibility, character, ability, and opportunities to connect with others. To that, I added my purposes, goals and missions in life.

When I had finished, he asked, *"From what part of the wheel are all other parts of your life visible and manageable?"* The obvious answer was "the hub". Looking outward from the hub I could survey my entire world, but from the rim, I could, at best, see the road and perhaps one spoke of the wheel. How limited our perspective is when we are embedded in the stories at the rim of our lives! It is very difficult to see the bigger picture or even to relax and let the wheel roll on.

With such a simple diagram, I had seen in an instant the importance of living from the heart. Like our center of being, the hub of a wheel has very little motion compared to the rapid turning of the rim. Yet, it generates all the motion and steers every direction! At last, I saw the answer. The secret to having a story without being it is to know the central purposes of one's life and to restore the temple within. It is the duty of any soul to first find its own authenticity, from whence living may be facilitated. When I extend outwardly from my center, the world assembles itself around me as if to say that it sees all things that I Am!

That image of the wheel has changed my life. Now I view my life as an expression of possibilities extending from the present moment in **all directions**, past and future. Even my past has more meaning! Much more important to me are the passions, patterns, inclinations, and capabilities of my heart. I strive to connect my past and my future through the character of my heart and the creative possibilities of my soul. By seeing the inner truth of each present moment, it is easier to envision a future and to review the past and resolve any stuck points within it. Only through this clear viewpoint of present time are all points of my life genuinely connected with power and truth. The **key** to safely living within the stories of our life is to remain always in our personal authenticity. We then step into the stream of life and allow the patterns of life to shape around us as we truly are. What survives all stories is the true nature of life and spirit.

I haven't a clue how my story will end, but isn't that the adventure? Often I see it clearly. Sometimes it vanishes behind a fog. When you know your prevailing direction, the unknown does not stop you. When a person sets out on a journey and night covers the road, he doesn't conclude that the road has vanished. If he is cheerful and expectant at heart, though the night is black and the road cannot be seen, he will look upward and see a thousand stars.

Inspirations

William Shakespeare (b.1564 d.1616) England:
"All the world's a stage,
And all the men and women merely players.
They have their exits and their entrances;
And one man in his time plays many parts..."

Plutarch (b.46 d.120) Greece:
"Pythagoras, when he was asked what time was, answered that it was the soul of this world."

Fachpur-Sikri (17th century) India:
Inscription on the Great Mosque: "The world is a bridge. Pass over it. Do not build your dwelling there."
The Buddha (b.503 d.483 BCE) India:

"There is only one moment when it is essential to awaken. That moment is now."

T.S. Eliot (b.1888 d.1965) America:
"With the drawing of this Love and the voice of this calling,
We shall not cease from exploration
And the end of all our exploring
Will be to arrive where we started
And know the place for the first time."

Applications

Before presenting the applications for this chapter, it needs to be said that a story and a relationship are not the same thing. Some relationships are wholly contained within a story, such as business/client relationships that were created through one's work. Most relationships, however, pass through many stories. The fact that a story needs to be refined or ended does not mean that the relationships within it must be held in contempt or terminated. Learning to allow relationships to transcend stories is as important as allowing oneself to rise above them. In mastering this, you will also begin to recognize that many times, what you thought was a relationship problem was really a story problem. On the other hand, there may actually be relationship problems masked by a "good story". In making these applications, it is vital that you know the difference between a relationship and a story. Let's take the example of a mother and child. In addition to the vital symbiosis of that relationship, there are countless intricacies of feelings and patterns of interaction. Then there are the life stages from birth until the child's departure in young adulthood. As life unfolds, so does the relationship. The bond and love is unique with each child. In addition to that, there are stories through which the relationship passes. These stories could range from maturational crises, such as adjusting to daycare after Mom goes back to work, or to situational stories such as relocating to another city. There may be pleasant stories such as baseball years, or stressful stories such as health problems or divorce. The teenage years are full of too many stories to list. Yet, when the relationship is strong, the stories are viewed as just that ... stories. They come and provide their experience and lessons, and then they pass.

Once I witnessed a poignant state of unhappiness between two women who had formed their friendship on the basis of mutual vulnerability. One of the friends had become healthier and more successful in life. Their affection for each other had not diminished, but the one who was still vulnerable had a sense of being left behind. Emotionally, she would try to hold the other back. So, there was hurt and misunderstanding. In counseling these two, the loss was healed when they saw the difference between stories they had shared for a while and the enduring marvelous friendship they would keep forever.

A brief mention should also be made that stories are not the same thing as bona fide, objective history. In many ways, history redeems us from our stories, because it provides a broader context and firmer foundation for us to examine the fluctuations of momentary events. Many times, we can put our stories into clearer perspective by comparing them with the larger movements of our collective history.

Now, look at the stories of your life. How do you feel about them? Are they serving you and others, bringing more good than the cost of maintaining them? Are there stories you have worked so hard to create, maintain, or resolve that you have neglected the relationships within them? Are there exciting stories you are living to the fullest? Are there difficulties you have blamed on relationships or external conditions, when really it is just a story that needs to be revised? Are there good stories covering up difficult conditions or unhealthy relationships?

A story is healthy when you can see yourself retaining free will, so that you can pursue it, rewrite it, redirect it, or end it without causing undue hurt to yourself or others. Another sign of health is when you can look at a story independently of the external conditions and relationships that are involved. A story is unhealthy when so much of one's love, life, and consciousness is invested in it that all would be lost if the story ended. These stories often contain many misunderstandings, blame, and fear.

As you look at your life, you may find a mixture of healthy and unhealthy stories. Notice the difference. Notice how, with the healthier ones, there was a sense of life moving into the story and then continuing beyond it. There will be a sense of honor and a sense of humor. Notice how, with the unhealthy stories, there is a continuous drain upon your energy or perhaps an empty hole where the story once was. There is a heaviness of spirit whenever you think about it.

The good news is that any story can contribute to the soul's growth when you align it to higher principles. The following questions will help to liberate you from the capturing power of your stories:

1) How did your life and energy feel before the story began?
2) What events or purposes carried you into the story?
3) Where is your authentic place within the story?
4) How do you feel about your purposes in present time?
5) Are you being true to your purposes, disregarding the opinions of others or pressures to agree with them?

Now look ahead, and envision your energy and love surviving the story. How will you feel on the other side? What will you carry away as the valuable experience?

If you can answer all these questions easily, you are operating freely within your stories, even though there may be commitments and restrictions around certain activities. If you cannot easily answer these questions about a particular story, you may want to consider leaving that situation or seeking professional guidance in dealing with it.

One of the great mistakes we make is by thinking that when we end our involvement with a particular story, that story is finished with us. That state of true completion only happens when we have risen above our need to use stories for defining our lives. Accomplishing that requires a higher level of work. That is the work of recovering your authentic self, discovering your purposes in life, and restoring your temple. In fact, it is the entire work of this book.

Meditation

In this meditation, you will listen to the Holy Spirit. Allow its presence to relax your mind and guide your heart with Divine counsel. Select a quiet place where you find it easy to be who you really are, without need for identities or role-playing. Be seated in a comfortable position and prepare for the meditative state. Begin by reading the following passage slowly, savoring each sentence. When emotions arise, allow them to release before reading further. Respond appropriately, and then move it into a contemplative and peaceful state after each display of emotion, knowing there is a greater wisdom guiding your life. When you reach a high point of release or realization, accept the blessing, relax, and let that be your completion for the day.

Some of you may need to process this meditation for many days before you reach an end. Others may read the message all the way through without any interruptive responses. That could mean that you are already deeply in touch with the truth of this message. More than likely, it means that certain inner defenses are not permitting you to be sensitive at that moment. Either way, simply listen with your heart, earnestly absorb the message, and be with it in peace. Return to the meditation each day for three days and see what stirs in your consciousness after repeated absorption of these words from the Holy Spirit:

"I am here to comfort you in your life, but I also want you to know that I am interested in YOU and not your dramas. Your strife and struggles, betrayals and injustices are only important that they may increase your strength, faith, and compassion. In the face of eternity they are small.

"What I want to know is whether you are ready to take responsibility for your life, for the events and circumstances that fill your days, for the consequences of your thoughts, words, and actions? Are you resolving problems, or are you being one?

"Are you sincerely and actively cleansing your life, and purifying your heart, mind, and soul?

"I am not interested in your story, but I deeply care about your orientation in life. Are you coming from love, or are you traveling into resentment and darkness? Are you seeking clarity and understanding, or are you hiding in the shadows of conformity, ignoring what is lurking behind veiled perceptions?

"What you have done to others and what others have done to you pales by comparison to the greater question: Are you truly appreciative for the good that has you're your way? Are you truly repentant for the trouble you have caused, forsaking the ways of hate, and seeking love and forgiveness? Are blame, rage, and vengeance pulsing through your veins? Do you think you can wish or intend harm on another without it coming back on you and yours?

"I am not interested in your personality type, or what your race, education, or social status happens to be. I am truly interested in how you are developing your talents and to what ends you are applying them.

"I also want to know if you can stand at the door of your life and hold sacred space. Are you living in your temple? Are you honest with yourself, abandoning your masks of deception, and living an enlightened reality?

"I rejoice for you when things are going your way. But, I am more concerned with how you handle adversity. Do you react when you are challenged, or do you respond to confrontation as an opportunity of becoming stronger? Do you trust Me and surrender to My guidance? Can you face obstacles and difficulties with an inner peace and assurance that all things work for good?

"Can you love and be loved? Can you respect and be respected? Can you trust and be trusted? Can you forgive and be forgiven? Are you kind to yourself and others? Can you do unto others as you would have done unto yourself?"

Prayer

Gracious Creator

Be with me as I learn the great lessons of life.
Teach me to cherish my experiences
For the grace and intelligence they bring to my heart,
For the sharing they give me with others,
For the richness they bring to my life,
For the certainty they demonstrate of Your love.
Give me the courage to release my attachments to story
Like a cup returning its water to a flowing river,
And in that moment
To know the true meaning of reunion.

Amen

24

THE WAY

The Message

"*You are on a great adventure, and you have traveled far. Love has ventured into remote places so that each soul, through unique experiences, could know itself as an individual and eventually arrive at its fulfillment within the Heart of God. The Creator, in his great wisdom and boundless love, propelled himself AS LOVE into countless dimensions and particles of love, which are his children. As love, you were created in the image of your Source, and each point of consciousness seeks to know itself as I AM. With all journeys, there are surprises and mystery, forgetfulness and awakening, discovery and learning, abandonment and forsaking. As the adventure unfolded and personalities began to emerge with radically different qualities, it seemed that each was not only separate from the others, but from its Source as well. Birthing has been a painful experience for many souls, because the illusion of separation was believed to be real and the comparison of divergent pathways was often used to discriminate, deny, alienate, abuse, and reject. Such diversity has also provided a magnificent symphony of interrelated possibilities.*

"*Motion is the power and the instrument that has made this expedition possible. Motion is an awesome force that is not limited to the actions of physical matter. Motion also propels your thoughts, feelings, and personal essence from past, to present, to future in an instant of fluid awareness.*

"Change, as it is normally viewed, is the outer mask or result of motion. It is a local symptom of larger patterns of motion passing through or announcing their arrival. For example, life propels itself through movements of creation, growth, expansion, and decay. These show up in the cycles and seasons of your life. Often they affect such broad areas of integration that resulting changes are equally subtle. At other times, change is frivolous, a meaningless alteration of circumstances, which provides diversion at best and distraction at worst. Either way, the soul's experience of change typically has been that of 'being an effect' of it, or occasionally grabbing control of it for personal advantage.

"I urge you now to rise above your limited perception of change, and to view it from a newer and higher perspective. For the first time, you are called to develop a positive masterful relationship with motion, the power behind change. This is essential to your fulfillment, because there is a paradox in your being: you are an eternal being, resting in stillness, and yet growing through experience in an ever-changing universe. Change will never end, but you, the eternal soul, are about to achieve a new level of consciousness defined by your BEING, where you will see change for the illusion that it is. In doing so, you will learn the essential value of motion to your freedom as a being.

"You were born of the Great I AM, to know yourself forever as an individual. The challenge here is to escape the limiting definitions of your story, and to know yourself as love.

"You are also the child of Spirit, and so you are given to know yourself in stillness. When you master stillness, you discover your own true nature. When all the actions of love have come and gone, what remains is the love that you are, residing in perfect stillness. When all the actions of others have come and gone, regardless of whether their deeds were fruitless or fruitful, the love that they were remains in the stillness left behind. To perceive and to know this beyond all circumstances is unconditional love.

"Motion is all around you. It carries you from yesterday to tomorrow and into all your adventures. It is the creative energy

moving through you, and propelling all your thoughts, desires, hopes, and dreams into reality. Life is love in action, and motion is the river of life flowing on forever. This will always be, and you are ready to elevate your perception of it.

"Unity is the presence of God in nature and ongoing creation. The scope of this Presence is beyond human comprehension. Nevertheless, you contribute to unity by being who you are and by mastering what you are given to understand. Man is always shortsighted when it comes to unity. Each person sees himself as an individual with everything else as a supporting backdrop for his story. How different the picture is when every being is viewed as an individual, with unimaginable capacity to impact the lives of others because of the unity that binds.

"Many humans attempt to engineer or affect unity in pursuit of control and dominance. This is a recurring societal problem that will not be solved until the majority of individuals shift their focus to the task at hand of mastering individuality, stillness and motion. The irony is that unity does not have to be mastered, only appreciated. In the presence of right action, unity is a spontaneous eruption of encompassing power, which binds without capturing, and supports without limiting.

"These four foundation powers—individuality, stillness, motion, and unity--generate all existence. Each power is driven and sustained by love. The three elements that man has been given to master are individuality, stillness, and motion. Unity, the fourth, is the province of God. I have already taught you about individuality and stillness. Mastering motion is the subject of this final key, because motion is the force, which can empower you to move into a higher dimension, or carry you even further from home if you remain in the illusions of change. Mastering motion can bring you great fortune, and failing to do so can strip you from all you have. What happens in your future will not be the result of blind fate or the will of God; for in the Heart of God, nothing but good is ever intended for you. What happens will be the result of your own readiness, attentiveness, empowerment, and love.

"The subject of motion is as difficult to teach as it is to grasp. Pure motion is energy, thought, and feeling driving all perceivable phenomena. That primal force filled your consciousness long before you had words or concepts with which to contain or even examine it. Pure motion is instantaneous, having no boundaries in time or space, and no constant but itself. Therefore, describing motion is like stepping twice into a flowing river, and thinking that you are touching the same water! If we took the easier route and focused only on the phenomenon of change, the power of this message would be lost.

"Change is not the subject of this key, but motion...the power behind it. I will, however, begin by addressing the difference between the changes of God, which are rooted in unity, and the less predictable changes of man, which are rooted in the need for experience and diversity.

"Within the intricate web of life, there is an unbroken network of energetic connections tying all dimensions of reality together. Unity embraces all relationships, from sub-atomic particles to galaxies. It creates a tapestry so sensitively woven that any true change will deeply impact everything else with great consequences. Therefore, the kind of change that reforms a whole environment or ecosystem can only occur in God's timing. If the timing is right, a butterfly emerging from its cocoon can set off a worldwide change. If the timing is not right, even attempts at war and global maneuvers to seize political advantage have no lasting effect.

"The changes of God are pure motion powered with the performance of unity. They are like the seasons, imbued with such power that even the tides could not hold them back, for indeed the tides are part of that same unity. When spring arrives, everything responds to its warmth. After a child is born, everything changes in the life of its parents. Not a shred will be left untouched. So, it is with death. It is always sad to lose a loved one, but the closure of that event can be felt for months before and after it happens, as God adjusts the patterns of unity to facilitate the movement of a soul and the changes occurring for everyone. When God makes changes in your life or health, they are not symptomatic adjustments, but a deep reformation

of wholeness at a foundational level. The changes of God are not limited to nature and to cosmic events. They are also deeply moving within human consciousness, where they may be seen as heightened awareness, discovery, creativity, sustainable improvements in human community, and epiphanies of excellence.

"Only from the perspective of God, does motion equate perfectly with change, and in so doing alter the fabric of unity. For mankind, there may be close correlations between motion and change, but often they lead to very different results. There are those who sail with the winds of opportunity, and there are those who consume all their energy resisting or trying to prevent changes that are beyond their control. Many languish in depressing circumstances because possibilities for improvement seem out of reach. There are those who are so willful in their efforts to earn, push, and intend their own position in life, that they miss a thousand real opportunities along the way. Fortunately, there are also those who bring their lives into attunement with the grand order of things and watch for invitations to move into new patterns of unfoldment. These immensely valuable souls expedite the true and sustainable changes of life.

"Motion is what performs ... regardless of the panorama of events that surround it. If a person acted only on motion he would be phenomenally successful, wealthy, and fulfilled, because this is true empowerment. Instead, man often spends his precious resources of time and energy on changes that have no foundation in any moving forces. Why does that happen? The answer is simple ... most people do not have a right relationship with change and do not know how to direct and master motion. Instead of responding to motion, they most often initiate change out of restlessness or fear. They do not like what has been set in motion and are dodging the effects of it. To compound that, others are attempting to force upon them some responsibility for their own unwanted effects. Therefore, they are dodging that. In between resisting one thing and another, there is stagnancy, or loss of motion. They are compensating for that. This is why so many are driven to fruitless, restless change while missing opportunities for actual growth and improvement.

"Observe the inner workings of a mechanical clock. Wheels move other wheels. The consciousness that created a clock was very attuned to the way motion produces change. Now ask yourself, 'How am I moving on the wheels of life? Am I traveling with the motion or against it? Am I moving in such a way that I can gracefully transition from a smaller wheel to a larger one and consciously direct the motion? Or am I like a gnat hopping from one wheel to the next as if he had found some Ferris Wheels on which to play?'

"Fortunately, life is more fluid, complex, and subtle than the wheels of a clock. There is quantum richness in every movement and possibility, but the operative words for humankind are 'readiness' and 'attentiveness'. This is because human choices are more about participation and involvement—whether to flow with or against the motions of vital energy. To attract possibilities for change, it is important that you release your fixed assumptions about how life must be. Motion is in everything and always available to you according to your authority over what you would use it to change. There are many things you are not free to change, including the lives of other people. Instead of accepting these prohibitions for what they are, you have built them into beliefs about limited freedom to change yourself and that which is offered to you.

"Many people are so vested in their efforts to cause or resist changes beyond their control that they miss the richness of opportunity opening up with every turn of events. Unfortunately, man wants to direct his efforts toward changes he thinks he can 'own'. Therefore, he focuses his attention on controllable effects to the exclusion of greater movements that could bring true success."

This caused me to pause and consider. Human beings often seem powerless to bring about profound and lasting changes in life. We distract ourselves or pump ourselves by moving things around, shifting possibilities, rearranging power structures, and external appearances. Then in moments of reflection we see that we have not really changed anything. Is change just an illusion, or is it just that we humans are impotent to cause meaningful enduring change?

"Neither is true. The changes you make within your heart, mind, and soul are not only significant and lasting, but they have an indirect effect on everything around you. The changes of God are real, and show up in the evolutionary patterns of the earth and nature.

"Man's futility with change is due to the fact that most of his efforts toward change stem from discontent and intolerance, and often are focused on altering or removing that which he cannot forgive. This is just hatred under the guise of progress. That motivation for change is against the laws of God (Love). Therefore, whatever comes from it will have no lasting value. Instead, consider all that draws you by love, and change it by assisting it to become stronger, to thrive, and to carry a more visible presence in the world. Seek inner change and allow that energy to release your attention from conflict and loss, thus moving you into the greater miracle of transcendence. Transcendence happens when you leave to God what you cannot change, and move on to a higher reality.

"If man took more pride in bringing peace to the world, and were less pompous about the changes he thinks he is engineering, there would actually be more progress. He would be getting out of God's way to make the truer and more profound changes that are needed.

"To know how and what to change, you must first know what is yours and what has been given to your care to influence or determine. These things you may change in an instant of reconsideration: your mind, your heart, your attitude, your values, your willingness, and how you spend your days and nights. There are other things that you may influence progressively, such as your effects in the world, good or bad, your companions, your knowledge, your goals, purposes, and missions in life, your stewardship of resources, your health, your wealth, and your freedom. There are other areas to which you may only contribute. In those, you may never be able to bring about a complete change, because the will of others is implicated as strongly as your own. If change occurs, it is because Divine will, and the collective will of nature and humanity, are supporting you in achieving that goal. This would include your relationship to the larger environment, your community, and the threads of reality that God has woven into the tapestry of life at any given moment.

"Having a right relationship with change is more important than the immediate results of it. You might think that bad change is simply the opposite of good change, but that is not true in all respects. The **motion within change** is the secret to its ultimate value. Even within negative change, motion may be seized and turned toward a greater good. Any change that you can master is better than any change that masters you, even if it temporarily brings positive reward! The decisive difference between good and bad change is not so much in the immediate or even long-range effects that it brings, but whether it fosters in you a masterful relationship to the movements of life.

"If you do not understand the nature of motion and change, there will always be log-jams in your life, and more than that, when the river rises, you will not know how to sail upon it. Knowing how to deal with motion and change is critical to freeing your life from its predicaments. Most people are stuck in unwanted conditions because they have no understanding of how to accept and direct the needed changes.

"The greater revelations of truth come as motion passes over and through the stillness of your soul. If you will only dismiss the illusions of change and rise above the false changes engendered by restlessness and discontent, you will hear the true voice of Spirit. Motion is within you as well as outside you. Mastering change begins with discovering your eternal changeless self, because perfect motion is already being at the point of your destination. Perfect motion causes instant elevation.

"There are four human attributes, which lead to this mastery. They are **attentiveness, readiness, empowerment, and love.**

"**Attentiveness** means to be fully present, centered in your heart, and aware of everything around you. It means to be watchful and alert, caring and diligent in your attention to life. It means to be in a state of knowing about your orientation to life, your values, desires, purposes and goals. Attentiveness means having a direction and being focused on it.

"*Readiness* means to be mindful of your resources, and ready to use your abilities. You are in possession of your experience and willing to put it to further service. It may also require more education or other skills than those you already possess. Readiness may require nurturing, or improving health, just as you would make an automobile ready before a journey. Readiness is dynamic anticipation. It studies and seeks to recognize the larger movements of change. To cultivate readiness, release all worry, apathy, and any state of mind that would undermine your alertness or prevent you from responding to a new invitation.

"*Empowerment* is when your wheel of life engages with a larger wheel of greater scope and movement. True changes will come now because you have earned the pleasure of God's good grace through your attentiveness, your readiness, and by surrendering to motions of change that are greater than anything you could have personally engineered. To receive empowerment, set aside your self-importance and be willing to receive a bounty of good fortune that you did not cause, that is given to you and many others as well. When the river rises, put your boat on the water and follow the current. The Creator's motions are so profound and broadly sweeping that much, if not everything, of what you were resisting will be swept away. The motions of God are like rivers that carry you to new places, to fertile valleys that have not been tilled, where new friends abound and old friends are welcome, where forgiveness is easy and opportunities are plentiful.

"*Unconditional love* is essential to mastering motion and to stepping outside the conditional nature of change with all its potential for distortion. This means that you are able to perceive love in the stillness of an eternal moment above all the conditions of change and individual differences. Knowing yourself and others as love gives you the power of recovery and continuance, a source of equilibrium in an ever-changing flow of experience.

"Study the four attributes, cultivate them in your character, and practice them in every part of your life. Because of the fluidity of life and its ever changing currents, all of these attributes are relevant *at all times, but there are moments when focusing on one will serve you better than the others. These attributes also apply to each of the powers of creation—individuality, stillness, motion, and unity—and allow you to have greater understanding or mastery of each one.*

"Motion is an essential part of creation, for the river of life flows on forever. Yet, the heart of man was also born in stillness, knowing itself as I Am. You are encompassed by unity and yet the motions of thought and life move through you. All of these are equally part of you. As you learn this, you will turn from your search for external causes, and look more directly for the Source. You will find that time is not your enemy, but merely a servant of motion over which you will gain mastery. In this, you will find your greatest freedom ... to be in past, present, and future with equal grace and perfect integrity, and with endless opportunities for growth and expression.

"The sixth day, the creation of the children of God, has been the day of adventure. It was the great expansion of living, learning, experiencing, challenging, denying, fighting, hurting, polarizing, and moving at great speeds in opposite directions, so that each might lay claim on a place in which to be. This is now done. You are at the end of seeking to know yourself by external conditions. The irony is that you were always in the place of your own true being.

"There is a new horizon emerging for mankind, not just a new millennium for the world, but a new era of human consciousness. There is a great reunion about to happen upon the earth. First it will happen within the individual, and then within units of two, three, and more until all of mankind is encompassed by the reunion. This is the great marriage of heart and soul, mind and body, self with self, and collectively to all in the oneness of God. Because of the illusion of separation, you have come to believe that your lower self is on the earth and your higher self is to be found only in Heaven. Through adventures and experiences, you have stretched beyond the limits of your memory. Forgetfulness has built an imprisoning distortion of who you really are. Truthfully, all the parts of you have always been engaged. You never left your Creator, your brothers and sisters, or

yourself. What you left was the stillness of your true essence filled with the motions of thought, feeling, and life. You moved into the experience of change and became enthralled with its effects. It defined you; indeed, it captured you … for a moment. Now you are ready to master motion that you may at last be free from the illusion of change.

"The secret is to see beyond limiting illusion. You are not trapped inside a prescribed form that has a particular height, weight, gender, and age. You can directly experience your true nature and see that it lives everywhere at once across space and time. As you do that, you will have the ultimate realization of arriving in the place of your destiny and discovering that you were there all along. When you can move through the past and future, and be within them both as if they were now; when your journeys of the heart are as real as your journeys of the body; then you will begin the most difficult, the most powerful expansion of all. You begin to exceed all the limits you have ever known and discover the meaning of compassion.

*"Your quest is to discover that flesh and bone do not bind you; you are actually the embodiment of love; and you are reduced by nothing unless you give it consent to bind you. Each soul is an unlimited presence of freedom and endless possibility. Your whole body, in every dimension, is nothing more than your soul in manifest form. Break the chains of your judgment and your limiting beliefs, and you break the chains of your body as well. The path that I have given you does not take you toward something or away from something. It is both a practical and mystical path of moving through the infinity of your own **true being**. This is your path of freedom. This is 'The Way.'"*

Correlations

Deuteronomy 28:12 "The LORD shall open unto thee his good treasure, the heaven to give the rain unto thy land in his season, and to bless all the work of thine hand."

Psalms 1:3 "And he shall be like a tree planted by the rivers of water, that brings forth fruit in his season; his leaf also shall not wither; and whatsoever he does shall prosper."

Galatians 6:9 "And let us not be weary in well doing: for in due season we shall reap, if we faint not."

Matthew 6:27 "Who of you by worrying can add a single hour to his life."

Matthew 25:13 "Therefore keep watch, because you do not know the day or the hour."

Matthew 28:20 "I am with you always, even unto the end of the world."

John 5:35 "He was a burning and a shining light: and you were willing for a season to rejoice in his light."

The Key

This chapter began as a surprise and soon became my greatest writing challenge of this nearly three-year project. I had expected I would be completing this work with a chapter entitled, "You Are My Beloved." Jeshua gave that to me in the original table of contents, and such a culmination would have been very much in keeping with the final chapter of *Love Without End...Jesus Speaks.* It is interesting, and probably deeply appropriate, that this chapter began with a profound change that moved me to the core of my being. I was just waking up one morning when I saw light coming through my window before I raised the blind, and heard footsteps softly crushing the carpet. He was there. Fully embodied, and present to all my senses as in the original visitation. He silenced my startled response with a gesture indicating that I needed to listen totally and quickly before the moment passed. He spoke these words and then facilitated an action that was to change my perception of everything.

"Everything will change now, for I will teach you about motion. Set aside everything you have ever thought about change or motion and everything you have anticipated about the next chapter. There will be a new understanding and a new chapter. It will be the final topic and key to the book."

I must have looked confused or disappointed as I said, "But…"

With only a pause he continued, *"You were not ready for this until now, and I could not have predicted your readiness or that of others who will read this. I am pleased to give you more than was expected. This key is the way to true freedom through the infinity of your own being. It is far better to discover for yourself that you are The Beloved of God than to be told that you are, even by me."*

As he said that, I began to feel a motion happening within me. The changes within revealed that everything I had taken to be solid and real were just perceptions and now those perceptions were moving into different configurations. There was a new Heaven and a new Earth emerging within myself. I was shaken to my foundation to see that everything I had credited or blamed for the condition of my life had been created only to support my own beliefs and attitudes. The life of my body was a reflection of my soul, but more than that, everything in the larger scope of my life was bound by the thoughts, feelings, ideals and consciousness of my being, at least insofar as it affected me. The motion pouring through me was like a river that carried me to a safe island in the midst of its currents. My heart yearned to be centered in the greater possibility of what could be, and for the first time, I saw no reason to restrain it. For the first time I saw an answer to my own burning question, "How possible is it for Heaven to be on Earth?" That all depends on how fully we immerse our souls in the larger flow of life they so desire. How willing are we to step outside our stories and restore the temple within? Are we willing to completely reorganize our values and change our directions if that is required? Interestingly, I had no sense of this being a sacrifice, because mostly I was releasing burdens!

The movement within accelerated, and I felt the walls of an ancient fortress crumble as a shining temple began to emerge that was full of every wondrous thing. In the blinking of an eye, I could be in the past, the present, and the future, and select whatever was appropriate to my own being and nature. Variety and choices, moving on a conveyor belt of freedom, had replaced my former life of seeking to know myself through reflection of external events. I was no longer hostage to the mystery of unseen future experience in forced compliance with the charade. Everything had changed. My heart was alive and I was free, as I flew on the winds of Spirit.

I was so immersed in my new reality, that I barely heard him say, *"I will leave you now to savor your experience and make choices about what is happening to you. In a few days I will return and we will continue our work."*

That was the most extraordinary morning I can recall, although by afternoon, I was feeling pressures from the reality I thought I had left behind. My head began to hurt, and by nightfall, I was distressed, confused, and feverish. I was sobbing to think that I had been so close to Paradise and let it slip through my fingers, not to mention that all the preparatory work I had already invested in a chapter that would not be written. My husband, Larry, was out of town, and I felt completely alone. After a comforting telephone call that evening to him, I reasoned that a good night's sleep would make everything better.

The next morning, I awoke to an even greater illness. I had a terrible congestion in my lungs, physical weakness, and my head ached like a pounding drum. The one thing I could not bear to think about was my bliss of the morning before. Whenever I did, I would become sick to my stomach and shrink more deeply into suffering. How could I possibly write about the joys of an experience that was now causing me such misery? I could only hope and pray that Jeshua's further teachings would be a salve to the throbbing wounds I had sustained from the first words.

Then, I remembered … his last words … I would have to make choices about what was happening to me. Something within me recognized a truth about change, and I understood what was going on. I had created, or agreed to, the reality I wanted to leave behind. In creating or agreeing to it, I had vested that reality with power over me, and it was just doing its job. It was warning me that its boundaries were being threatened! At that moment of realization, my headache stopped completely, and over the next three days I would return to a highly expanded and improved state of "normal."

This was my first "on the job" discovery that motion and change can be very different phenomena. Motion is what moves us, not only physically, but also mentally, emotionally, and spiritually. Change is the reconfiguration of reality that occurs as a result of motion. I also learned that the universe has a dynamic perfection—a living, moving system that can maintain a constant balance despite a momentary loss of equilibrium. This is how we walk, by first losing our balance and then recovering it. We could not even stand if we were unable subtly to shift our weight around an internal center of gravity. There was a landmark discovery in the history of art around this principle. Ancient Greek sculpture of the human form had been as formal, rigid, and symmetrical as Egyptian statuary until a sculptor named Polyclitus developed a theory now called 'contraposto' (which means a counter-balanced pose). Through this, he revealed, in his sculpture, the natural internal movements of a human body shifting its weight diagonally from left to right. The *Canon* of Polyclitus, written in the late fifth century BCE, was the most renowned ancient treatise on art. The aim of the *Canon*, was not simply to instruct in the sculpturing of human form, but also to achieve *to kallos*, "the beautiful" and *to eu* "the perfect or the good" in it. The secret of achieving *to kallos* and *to eu* lay in the mastery of *symmetria*, the perfect "commensurability" of all parts of the statue to one another and to the whole. It is almost miraculous how this simple advancement of understanding brought cold, hard marble to life. The ancient Greek legend of Pygmalion (which in modern times was reinterpreted as "My Fair Lady") was likely created around the miraculous life that Polyclitus was able to bring into his sculpture simply by portraying **internal motion!** His theory traces back even further to that of Pythagoras regarding something called dynamic symmetry. Static symmetry is a configuration where two halves are balanced in a state of equilibrium. Dynamic symmetry is where the whole of a composition is integrated so that all parts of the design convey energy to all the others, yet there is stability within the movement. Mathematically, Pythagoras applied this to all of life.

There is a never-ending hunger and ache in the hearts of men and women to experience life as dynamic symmetry, and to enjoy everlasting change that always returns to its center with ease and grace. The desire is to experience changes that expose the truth of our being instead of altering it. Fortunes are made to buy this feeling, and many overspend to acquire this feeling. Without knowing what the feeling represents, one will simply lose balance and then return to the process of becoming lost in more distorting changes.

Fortunately, my teacher would return and offer me greater strength in making the transitions of reality upon which I had embarked. The secret to mastering external change is to first build strength through internal motion of the mind, heart, and soul. Until you can do this, external change will threaten your sense of self. This is why many people hang onto their place in stories. They are also afraid of losing those they love if the stories were to change. I now understand why some of the most intractable people, with the strongest opinions, are that way—because they fear losing themselves if their story should change. Others are afraid that their reputations would be damaged by change. The tragedy is, we are blocking the internal movements that inspire the mind, illumine the soul, and fulfill the heart because we are afraid of the pain connected with change!

Scientists tell us that we are living in a universe that is not solid. Even the most solid atom is comprised of a nucleus and orbitals that are themselves pure energy. Solidity, as we suppose it to be, is the product of particles of pure energy. There are no truly solid elements in the physical world. The distance between the nuclei of any two atoms is proportionately more distant from each other than the distance between two galaxies. The space in between them is alive with spirit. Thus, we are comprised of 99 per cent pure consciousness that can be changed in the blink of an eye.

So, why doesn't change happen that easily? It is because of another force, mighty and tenacious, that is yet to be fully recognized … the power of our agreements about what is! These agreements are so powerful that we could miss the sunlight at noon if we believed it to be midnight! These agreements are so powerful that they can retrieve us from a flight of freedom and creative inspiration and slap us right back into a straight-jacket of subservient living … all because we gave them permission to do so! These agreements are so powerful that they can make us feel like less than nothing whenever we attempt to change them … all because we have given them the right to say who we are!

We attempt to change what we believe is so, and it attempts to change us! There must be an answer … and there is. That is through understanding that motion is the master of change. We move through the internal worlds of thought, mind, heart, and spirit, and then emerge to make whatever changes have yielded to the motion. The fluid concurrence between motion and change could be like the patterns of dynamic symmetry, moving, shifting, and changing but returning always to a center of internal equilibrium. When we strengthen ourselves with internal movement, and apply ourselves with whatever adjustments of reality are ready to yield, we are beginning to master that process and follow the rhythm.

Even then, when change is uncomfortable, you may strengthen your resolve by considering the external value of change to yourself and others. In other words, what is right to change? It is right if it:

Supports life and the living.
Brings order out of chaos.
Increases your responsibility and consciousness.
Builds community and greater well being for all.
Is sustainable in terms of growth already emerging.
Moves external conditions closer to true essence.
Creates greater cooperation and understanding between
        God and man.
Is inspiring, revitalizing, and unifying.
Restores or preserves freedom.

Change is usually wrong if it:

Brings harm or chaos.
Sets in motion consequences for which you cannot be
        conscious or responsible.
Manipulates others into receiving your own unwanted
        effects.
Violates the inner sanctity of your true essence.
Is merely a ploy for seizing power.
Is a stolen opportunity, actually belonging to another.

The messages in this book and especially this chapter are meant to move you deeply. At first, you may unconsciously prevent this from happening because you are uncomfortable with the changes that might ensue. Then as you grasp the deeper meaning, you may rush from your inspiration immediately to attempt changes, and find yourself thwarted. As you experience these phenomena, listen carefully to what is really happening and allow it to teach you about your situation and how to move through it. Remember, whatever reality you are in is one to which you agreed, in some way, or it could not bind you. You agreed through your actions, your words, your feelings, or even through your misconceptions or deceptions. Nevertheless, you agreed. There are no agreements that cannot be changed, but the process may require thoughtfulness, skill, and persistence, and as Jeshua would say— attentiveness and readiness. Then, when the changes are ready to be recognized and empowered by unity, the winds of spirit will fill your sails, and you will move to a new reality.

My experience in writing this chapter is a perfect example of that process. Jeshua returned a few days later as he promised and gave me the words for his message. However, he asked that I listen verbally and transcribe them later. That way, I would have a better opportunity to really listen to him, not only with my ears but also my heart and soul, and assimilate his words into understanding. I followed his instruction, never expecting the difficulty I would encounter. I had felt the clarity on a level of consciousness that was greater than words. Then I sat down to write. There was not a word or a concept capable of expressing what I had heard without diminishing its meaning. For days, I agonized over the inadequacy of language. Out of pure frustration, I wrote volumes more than he said in hopes of finding the golden cord of thought that would capture the meaning and extract the message now buried under intellectual ramblings incapable of expressing it.

Then one evening I was having dinner with Larry, when he said, "I'm here to listen. Just tell me what you are going through." I began to speak from my heart, at first in broken words and sentences that hardly made sense even to me. He continued to listen, and I could see that he was willing to be moved. By the time we got up from the table, I had found the golden cord. It was revealed by the flow of thought between us. My thoughts were now clear. Still there was one more hurdle before I could write. That would not happen until the next morning.

I was refreshed and excited to have a new beginning, but with the first word, I was stopped in my tracks. I started to balk in frustration, but somehow the clarity I had attained the night before allowed me to catch my error. I was trying to convey a new thought by taking a new perspective within an old reality. It was the age-old mistake of putting new wine in old wine bottles. What I needed was to adopt the innocence of a child and allow the motion pouring through me to select the words of a new reality. I began to write and words flowed beyond my understanding as they revealed perceptions about a new Heaven and a new Earth.

Some of you may have found this chapter difficult to grasp at first. Others may have glided through it as if you have heard it many times. Either way, I suggest that you re-read it with the eyes of a child. It is probably the easiest message of the book to understand if you approach it with innocence, because it is the closest reflection of how you, the soul, really perceive life.

When you were a baby, what made your body "young" was not the biology of cellular structure, but the unseen intelligence that had come together in a new expression of universal consciousness. In this moment, you are still imbued with the same consciousness of your birth. You carry within yourself right now the same spirit and intelligence that ignited your spark of life. That life force has not aged, and cannot age. It cannot become sick or emotionally depressed. It is eternally youthful and abides in perpetual health. It knows only joy and oneness with God and the universe. That vital force is you! Unbind your soul from its limiting thoughts, beliefs, and judgments, and your heart from its tortured illusions. Spread your wings and experience the flight. The way to true freedom is through the infinity of your own being.

Inspirations

St. Basavanna (b.106 d.67 BCE) India:
"Things standing shall fall. But the moving shall always stay."

William Wordsworth (b.1770 d.1850) England:

"Wisdom and spirit of the universe! You that are the Eternity of thought! That gives to forms and images a breath and everlasting motion!"

Euripides (b.485–d.406 BCE) Greece:
"There is in the worst of fortune the best of chances for a happy change."

Marcus Aurelius (b.121 d.180) Rome:
"Observe always that everything is the result of a change, and get used to thinking that there is nothing Nature loves so well as to change existing forms and to make new ones like them. The universe is **change**; our life is what our thoughts make it."

The Dhammapada (b.500 200 BCE) India:
"To become enlightened you must cross the river of time. All material things pass away, but enlightenment lasts for all eternity."

Applications

Consider the fundamental elements of all existence:

Individuality
Unity
Motion
Stillness.

They fill your life, but do you see them? Are you making a special effort to explore and understand the power of each element? Notice how these elements play through all of your relationships. How do you share them, and how can you use them to build greater love and understanding with your friends and family?

Consider the four human attributes that facilitate responsible movement and change:

Attentiveness
Readiness
Empowerment
Love

Notice how these propellants of movement are part of every transition and meaningful change that you make. Study the ways that they show up in your character and your progress through life. How could you refine the process and consciously master it to make your transitions from one reality to another even more effective and graceful? How could you assist others in their struggles to change?

The four elements of existence and the four attributes for moving with it are part of every experience. Don't underestimate the value of being conscious even in the smallest actions. Indeed, the smallest actions are usually the ones most attached to our habitual patterns. To catch your pattern in a simple daily routine can be as subtly powerful as redirecting the course of a dream!

There was a small incident in my life that illustrates this point. I have a lovely little angel night-light in my hallway. Its sparkling Tiffany glass wings add a special brightness to that part of my home. Therefore, I keep it on night and day. One day the bulb burned out and I was too busy to replace it. Night after night I stumbled through the dark hallway and promised myself each time that I would change the bulb the next day. However, when daylight came, I no longer stumbled, so I forgot my promise. After a week or more went by, I began to develop a new pattern of caution as I moved through the darkened hall memorizing all the furniture and doors that I needed to avoid. Then I stopped suddenly, not by a stumble, but by a profound and moving thought. This is how we keep forgetting to light our own candle after the stresses of life experience with physical distraction. I groped to find the angel and took her off the shelf. This would not happen again, and to make sure, I carried her back with me to my bedside where I would be reminded to change her light in the morning. Perhaps a real angel had just done that with me.

In this small incident, there were all the attributes that facilitate change. Until I was attentive and ready, there was no empowerment. Once the empowerment came there was the fulfillment of love that gave me a higher recognition of the moment. More than the angel became enlightened that morning. These discoveries can happen for you in the least and largest of patterns as you begin to grasp the internal motions that are essential for producing change.

Meditation

This meditation is designed to move you spiritually into the heart of life, where your place within all existence may be felt. Settle into a relaxed position and allow your eyes to gently close as you float into the silence within.

Relax your mind, and allow your attention to fall like a feather into the deep center of your body and being. Listen only to the beat of your heart and your breath. There is a tiny spark of light within your heart. As you fan it with your breath, it will grow a little brighter. Watch it dance and flicker as it transforms your thoughts into gentle streams of motion flowing through your body and cleansing it of all worldly care. The light is magnetic and calls you to it. You walk through the light, as if it were a doorway into the midst of a green meadow with fragrant grasses, wild flowers, and stately trees. There is a small reflecting pool filled by the springs that feed this high mountain glen. As you look across the green meadow and down the slope, you realize that you have shifted to a higher dimension. You have tuned into an intersection of time and space where the finite and the infinite may meet, where spirit may be seen in complete harmony with the natural world.

You breathe deeply as you feel the warm sun and cool breezes enliven your whole being. Again, you inhale deeply, as a light wind washes over you. It feels as if magnificent wings are fanning your body. Spirit greets you. It descends like a giant dove, with amazing power and awesome wings. Upon its wings, it lifts you body and soul, out of the meadow and carries you to the heavens. Soaring higher and higher, you rise upon the winds until you come to the peak of a distant mountain that had been hidden by clouds. The valley has now vanished from sight.

Through the high clouds, you ascend into an illumined world. The great bird gently places you on a sheltered edge of a high precipice. As you look over the edge, all of existence is laid out before you. You inhale deeply of the clean, fresh air, as strong winds blow around you. With each breath, your soul is filled, and in soft whispers, the wind begins to speak. As if it were singing, it tells you this truth: Without motion there could be no life. You would hear and sense nothing. You could not exist, nor could any part of nature. The motion that surrounds and fills you is the physical presence of Spirit. It touches your very soul, and you leave traces of yourself within it. Everywhere you go Spirit moves you. In knowing this, you will become more sensitive to all of life and all your surroundings. You will learn which environments to enter and which to ignore, which will enhance your life and which will not, what to take and what to leave behind. You will learn to change the quality of your life by listening and engaging with the inner movements of your being.

This message grows strong within your heart as you stand upon the perilous ledge and embrace eternity. Suddenly you feel yourself leap from the high place of splendor and glide on the motions of inner knowing. Each new breath fills you with elation, and you soar like a bird that has left its nest. The earth now calls you back, and the currents of wind catch you and allow a gentle descent. The meadow of your homeland reaches up to greet you. The trees and grasses shimmer with new life. You lift your eyes up to the sky and your being is filled with wonder from the flight of spirit to wonderful new dimensions of thought and feeling.

The stillness of your being and the motion of life have communed for the revelation of a new and greater truth. Gratitude fills your heart for all that has been seen, and for that which will unfold from this new and greater understanding. Slowly open your eyes and behold with thanksgiving the greater knowledge that has now been entrusted to your consciousness.

Prayer

Eternal Creator,

Move me, teach me, and lift me to the high places of my soul.
Take my prayer and expand my being into the living ether of
Your Own Great Soul,
That our hearts may be joined in sweet communion.

In that moment let me see that it is Your will that wills through me.
It is Your desire that desires through me.
It is by Your grace that my sorrows, which are Yours,
Are turned into joys, which are also Yours.
You have known the thirst of my soul before it was born,
And gave of Yourself for its quenching.
May I live my life in growing circles that stretch across all things,
Knowing that I will never complete the last circle
Until I rest in You.

Amen

Synopsis

1. Love is the divine, mystical, and holy power that creates and sustains life for the simple joy of doing so. In its purest form, love is where creation creates itself. The key to love rests in knowing your own connection to that Power. Love is who you are.

2. BEING is fundamental. The light of our being is something to be recovered, not created. It has always been…and will always BE the power underwriting all our experiences. To judge or to celebrate an experience as if it were the reason for our existence is to miss the point of who we really are. We are restored to our true Being through liberation from all attachment.

3. The key to CONSCIOUSNESS lies in acceptance of it as the light of our souls. It is not an external dimension to which we aspire, but rather a way of knowing about life from a higher perspective. Faith is the candle, and courage the force, that carries this light into dark passages of experience, as we gain insight into that which was previously unseen.

4. Compassion is the key to our higher life.

5. Seek the Kingdom of God—feel it, embrace it, express it, gratify it, and celebrate it with all your heart, and what ever desire that passion holds shall be given to you. This is the key to desire's fulfillment.

6. The key to innocent perception lies in a spirit of discovery. Release your expectations, fixations, and judgments. Explore life with the freshness and wonder of a child.

7. PEACE is not found in the world but in oneself.

8. Balance is the key to our Sacred Center. It is to be found in complete relaxation and surrender to spiritual guidance.

9. Belief is the key to our future, and we will always believe in something. To gain mastery over belief one must honestly answer two questions, "In what do I believe, and on what foundation do I base my certainty?"

10. The power of thought and thoughtfulness is the key to creativity.

11. 'The Way' that Jeshua taught is the way of releasing false will and restoring the innate responsibility of our essential self. Discover the love that you are by following the threads of your own experience to their greatest possibility.

12. This moment of NOW is the key to truth. If truth is observed as the passing of events through time, it is elusive. If approached through faith and consciousness, with the simplicity of pure being, truth can be seen as the quality of NOW that permeates all of life, and there is nothing but truth.

13. We always have a choice between reactive and pro-active behavior. The key to pro-active living is found in knowing that miracles are completely compatible with cause and effect. This knowledge sustains hope.

14. Experience is necessary to make us strong and expand our reality. Forgiveness is the key to making experience bearable and liberating us to the higher qualities of life.

15. Our great inner world is the key to attraction. To uncover this magnetic potential and discover boundless energy, we must release our beliefs, ideas, and practices based on scarcity, resistance, and enforced labor.

16. A charitable heart is the key to abundance.

17. Giving and receiving nourishment is the key to community. All of life is shared…one way or another.

18. The key to fulfilling experience is to know oneself as the Experiencer rather than the experience.

19. Our true and essential purpose is to be the love that we are. This is the key to all other purposes.

20. Prayer and meditation are the keys to our higher reality, our larger self.

21. Life is in its own sacred essence that extends well beyond the containers we use for holding it and knowing it. The key to a fuller richer life rests in understanding that life is the vital force that delivers us from limiting circumstances. It is life that restores health, and not health that restores life.

22. Knowing the greater dimensions of the soul, which far exceed the body, is the key to the Kingdom of Heaven and to restoring the temple of one's life.

23. The key to living safely within the stories of our life is to remain always in our personal authenticity.

24. The way to true freedom is through the infinity of your own BEING.

Attributions

Compiling a book of inspiration, which has a theme and yet is widely varied, is much like creating a painting. Perhaps that is where the delivery of this message most closely relates to the talents and abilities that I developed over the past forty years. The only difference between creating a painting and a book of inspiration is that the painting is a reflection of nature and the book is a reflection of the rich accumulations within our cultural and spiritual heritage.

A landscape of accumulated truth and inspiration is the platform on which all inspirational books stand. Just as many artists can paint the same scene, consisting of the same rocks, trees, hills, and clouds, with each work of art being absolutely original, so too can numerous inspirational writers reflect on the same heritage, ideas, and truth, and emerge with completely unique perspectives. This is because inspirational treatises are created, compiled, or integrated first from the inner perspective of personal insight, along with all manner of compelling urges from the world of Spirit. In this, they most resemble art and least resemble historical, scientific, or scholarly treatments, which originate (and often end) with external facts, research, and objective reports.

I am very grateful for the platform on which this book stands, most especially to the new contributions of Jeshua. There are many writers, thinkers, and researchers whom I was also able to credit within the body of the text. Our inheritance, however, is so ancient, and so much of it has been carried through popular stories and teachings in the public domain, it would be impossible to name all those who inspired its creation. To those unknown, I express my deep appreciation for contributions to our quality of community, love, and consciousness. One could compare our anonymous accumulations of wisdom to the size of a mighty elephant, and the tiny rider on his back would be the few writers and thinkers who are known. This is particularly relevant to the sections of meditation and prayer. The art of meditation has been developed over thousands of years, and the components of meditation are so universal as to make any variations almost irrelevant. The original teachers are lost in the sands of time. The same is true with prayer. Many traditional prayers, mostly by unknown authors, gave song to my heart and movement to my pen. What emerged was a new creation with echoes of the ancient past. In this way, this book is a map of our spiritual aspirations, engaging with our inheritance from many cultures and many rivers of thought. Perhaps its greatest gift is the promise that we can look forward to an integrated future in which our shared understanding of truth is more potent than the often violent differences that have marked our historical religious dogma.

Glenda Green, M.A., D.D.

Glenda Green is one of the world's leading teachers of contemporary spirituality. Although her guidance and inspiration stem from a living spiritual relationship with Jeshua, her teachings are not directed toward the cultivation of religious doctrine. Instead, they revolve around universal truths that are uplifting and enlightening to all people of all beliefs. From poetry to science, her teachings move the reader to deep waters of understanding. Within her body of work are some of the most complete, extensive treatments of pure science ever found in spiritual literature. World-renowned scientists have conferred with Glenda about these astounding revelations.

She is the author of best-selling *Love Without End, Jesus Speak,* and artist of the internationally acclaimed portrait of Christ, *"The Lamb and The Lion."* In addition to her writing and teaching, she is also acknowledged by the nation's leading scholars, critics, and museum officials as one of the world's foremost portrait painters and spiritual artists. Her paintings are housed in major public art collections, including the Smithsonian Institution.

She has taught on the faculties of Tulane University and the University of Oklahoma. She is an exceptional public speaker in high demand. "Her warm, witty and confident manner evokes our inner certainty of a higher awareness. Glenda has a clean energetic style, and masterful comprehension of the most critical spiritual issues. Her writing and teaching offer genuine opportunities to acquire a truer, more complete, understanding of the universe and our own place in it."

Biographical references include, *North American Women Artists of the Twentieth Century: A Biographical Dictionary; Who's Who in American Art; Who's Who of American Women; Dictionary of International Biography.*

Spiritis Book Store

Books by Glenda Green:

"The Keys of Jeshua".........................(softbound) $19.88 + $6 S/H
"Love Without End: Jesus Speaks"..........(softbound) $19.88 + $6 S/H
"Anointed With Oil"...........................(softbound) $12.95 + $4 S/H

Tapes: *"Conversations With Jesus"*
Each tape is a full 90 minutes of power-packed information from the original conversations between Jeshua and Glenda Green. This was her original public release. Experience the impact of Divinity in direct communion with a thoughtful and well-educated woman of our generation. Even though *Love Without End: Jesus Speaks* is a close transcription of these tapes, the recorded lectures provide an invaluable expression of human warmth, candor, and vulnerability that cannot be conveyed through the written word. They communicate to the heart with authenticity and immediacy. Truly a course in life!

> 14 Tape album..........................$120 + $8 S/H
> 14 CD album...........................$140 + $6 S/H

Prayers and Meditations from "The Keys of Jeshua"

An audio recording of 12 prayers and meditations from "The Keys of Jeshua" in the author's voice. It begins with a powerful introduction to meditation and prayer, and is enriched throughout with deeply heart-centered music. Two tapes or CDs per set.

> 2 Tape album....................$19.95 + $5 S/H
> 2 CD album......................$24.95 + $5 S/H

Sacred Oils: We have a complete set of rare essential oil blends created by Glenda Green under the direction of Jeshua, which correspond to the seven spiritual aspirations: Innocence, Compassion, Abundance, Wisdom, Peace, Forgiveness, and Joy. We also have Christ Scent, the original aroma that Glenda experienced with his appearances, and Ohm, which is a wonderful fragrance to prepare oneself for prayer and meditation. Each fragrance is available in 1/3 oz and 1/6 oz sizes.

> 1/3 oz essential oil....................,.....$25.00+ $5 S/H
> 1/6 oz essential oil..............,......$15.00+ $5 S/H
> Complete sets available at 15% discount

We offer many other inspirational items including prints, canvas transfers, and giclees of "The Lamb and The Lion," and other spiritual paintings by Glenda Green. For a complete package of informational brochures on all products and services, send $2.50 to our address below. Or visit our website at **www.lovewithoutend.com**

Ordering information: Make checks or money orders payable to: **Spiritis, P.O. Box 239, Sedona AZ 86339. Or call us at 1-888-453-6324.** You may also make purchases on our website. We reserve the right to raise shipping costs whenever postal rates increase.

Bookstores may purchase directly from us, or through most major distributors. Wholesale catalogs are available, and orders may be placed with Spiritis Publishing at **1-888-453-6324**, or e-mail: *info@lovewithoutend.com*

If you would like to be added to our mailing list, please send your name and address to Spiritis, P.O. Box 239, Sedona, AZ 86339 or e-mail it to *info@lovewithoutend.com*

For information on forming study groups, or to find out more about activities, seminars, workshops, and speaking tours you may write to: Spiritis, P.O. Box 239, Sedona AZ 86339, *info@lovewithoutend.com*

Please visit our web site at *www.lovewithoutend.com*